EDUCATION AND ECONOMIC PRODUCTIVITY

EDUCATION AND ECONOMIC PRODUCTIVITY

Edited by
EDWIN DEAN

BALLINGER PUBLISHING COMPANY
Cambridge, Massachusetts
A Subsidiary of Harper & Row, Publishers, Inc.

International Standard Book Number: 0–88410–943–7

Library of Congress Catalog Card Number: 84–3046

Printed in the United States of America

Library of Congress Cataloging in Publication Data

Main entry under title:

Education and economic productivity.

Bibliography: p.
Includes index.
1. Economic development—Effect of education on.
I. Dean, Edwin.
HD75.7.E38 1984   338.9   84–3046
ISBN 0–88410–943–7

45,696

Contents

List of Figures

List of Tables

Preface

A nation's ability to compete successfully in world markets and to improve the living standards of its citizens depends on its economic productivity. The contribution of education to productivity growth is the subject of this book.

The first four papers in this volume—those by Robert Haveman and Barbara Wolfe, W. Lee Hansen, Dale W. Jorgenson, and Mark Plant and Finis Welch—were commissioned by the National Institute of Education (NIE), the research arm of the U.S. Department of Education. All four papers were presented at an NIE conference on Education, Productivity, and the National Economy in Leesburg, Virginia in November 1982. Brief summaries were also presented at the December 1982 meetings of the American Economic Association.

The concluding papers in this volume, by Jacob Mincer and Richard Murnane, two of the discussants at the NIE and AEA meetings, provide comments on the first four papers and reflect further on education's role in productivity growth. (Information about the contributors to this volume and about other participants in the NIE and AEA meetings is given in appendices.)

The introduction supplies background information for the articles in this volume and suggests priorities for future research on the role of education in productivity growth.

The work undertaken in preparation of this volume was performed in my private capacity. No official support or endorsement by the National Institute of Education, my employer when this work was undertaken, or by the Bureau of Labor Statistics, my present employer, is intended or should be inferred.

Edwin R. Dean

Alexandria, Virginia
December 1983

Introduction

Edwin Dean

This book examines how education contributes to the growth of economic productivity. Its authors provide measures of this contribution, examine the research procedures presently used to provide such measures, and explore policy problems that have been highlighted in recent, widely discussed reports on the quality of education in the United States. The excellence of the six papers in this volume and the importance of the policy problems they address indicate that the economics of education is presently one of the livelier fields of economic inquiry.

The recent decline in productivity growth in the U.S. economy has been dramatic. Although productivity in the private business sector grew at a rate of 2.0 percent annually in 1948 to 1973, according to the Bureau of Labor Statistics, the annual growth rate fell to 0.2 percent in 1973 to 1981. In 1982, productivity was lower than in 1978 (U.S. Department of Labor, BLS 1983).[1]

Slow productivity growth in the United States hampers its ability to compete in world markets. One study has concluded that output per hour in manufacturing in the United States has in recent years increased more slowly than in nine of eleven major international competitors. Only the United Kingdom and Canada experienced productivity growth as low as the United States (Alvarez and Cooper 1984). From 1973 to 1982, the average annual U.S. growth in manufacturing productivity was two percent less

I am indebted to most of the other contributors to this volume, as well as to Frederick Mulhauser and William Waldorf, for helpful comments. Richard Murnane and W. Lee Hansen provided especially detailed comments. David Mandel gave invaluable advice on the research program that led to these papers.

1

than the appropriately weighted productivity growth of the eleven trading partners.[2]

This introduction places the six contributions to this volume in a research, as well as policy, context. First, it provides an outline of recent research on the role of education in productivity growth and identifies several research problems presently facing investigators in this field. Second, it suggests priorities for policy-oriented research. The perspective adopted is quite focused: Given the state of U.S. education, and the state of economic research on U.S. education, what policy-oriented research would provide information and analyses most useful to policymakers and the interested public?

EDUCATION AS A SOURCE OF PRODUCTIVITY GROWTH: RESEARCH THROUGH THE MIDDLE 1970s

Early attempts to analyze the growth of output in the U.S. economy resulted in the discovery of a large "residual": an increase in output not due to increases in inputs or to measured increases in productivity. This residual was so large that researchers began to search for concrete ways to explain it. Several researchers pointed to improvements in the quality of the labor force, due mainly to increased education, as a major, previously unmeasured source of growth in education. Zvi Griliches, in a 1970 study based on methods he and Dale Jorgenson had developed in an earlier article, concluded that increased educational attainment accounted for one-third of the residual (Griliches 1970: 79; Jorgenson and Griliches 1967). Such conclusions seemed especially credible in light of the first results of the then recently developed human-capital literature. In the early 1960s, Gary Becker had estimated that the rate of return to investment in college education was high, higher in fact than the rate of return on alternative investments (Becker 1964: Chs. IV, V). Investment in college education, it appeared, had been insufficient to drive the rate of return down to the level of the return on other investments.

Edward Denison, in more recent and quite comprehensive studies, arrived at results broadly consistent with Griliches's and Jorgenson's work (Denison 1974; 1979). In 1948 to 1973, the growth in national income per person employed in the nonresidential business sector was 2.4 percent (Denison 1979: 94). Denison concluded that education accounted for 0.5 percentage points of this increase, about one-fifth of the total. However, this contribution reflects only the effect of education in improving the quality of the labor input; it does not reflect any influence of education on improvements in technology, management practices, or development of new products. Denison also found that "advances in knowledge and not elsewhere classified" accounted for 1.4 percentage points of productivity growth. These 1.4 percentage points were in fact Denison's residual: His use of the term "advances in knowledge" reflected his view that such advances accounted for most of the residual.

EDUCATION AS A SOURCE OF PRODUCTIVITY GROWTH: RECENT RESEARCH

In the late 1970s and early 1980s, research on the role of education in productivity growth provided few settled answers and raised many questions. Denison, among others, recently addressed the problem of explaining the slowdown in productivity growth (Denison 1983). He found that national income per person employed in the nonresidential business sector *fell* 0.2 percentage points annually in the period 1973 to 1981. He also found that improvements in the quality of labor due to education accounted for 0.6 percentage points in the growth of labor productivity—that is, more than the growth rate itself.

This large positive source of productivity growth was offset by other negative factors. Further, the residual itself had become negative: Taken at face value, "advances in knowledge and not elsewhere classified" accounted for a negative 0.3 percentage points. In another study presenting similar results, Denison wrote, "what happened is, to be blunt, a mystery" (Denison 1979: 4).

This puzzlement is widely shared: It has been noted that "Joseph Pechman, Herbert Stein, and Albert Rees have all termed the slump in productivity growth a mystery" (Maital and Meltz 1980).[3] Like Denison, however, other researchers have concluded that education has made a positive and/or growing contribution to productivity growth, even during the recent slowdown in productivity growth (Kendrick 1980; Norsworthy, Harper, and Kunze 1979). In light of these puzzling growth patterns, it is important to reexamine the role of education in productivity growth as well as the empirical procedures used to estimate education's contribution to growth.

IMPROVEMENTS IN GROWTH ACCOUNTING

A number of improvements in growth accounting have been suggested and, in some instances, implemented.

Weights for Returns to Education

Growth accountants generally use earnings of factors of production to estimate the marginal products of the factors. In particular, the relative contributions to output of workers with different amounts of education are
estimated by the relative earnings of workers in the different education
groups. In some studies, the relative contributions of different education
groups in one time period are estimated by their earnings in an earlier time
period. If earnings differences have diminished between the two periods,
and if the proportion of highly educated workers has increased, this procedure will result in an overestimate of education's contribution to productivity growth.

Interaction between Education and Other Factors
Influencing the Quality of Labor

Improvement in the quality of labor due to increased education can occur
simultaneously with changes in variables that reflect other dimensions of
labor quality. The statistical procedures chosen to estimate these separate
effects can make a great deal of difference to the estimated contribution of
education to productivity. Peter Chinloy (1980) calculated that the "main
effect" of education on labor quality in 1971 to 1974 was to cause an
increase in labor quality of 0.67 percent per year. However, if the impact
of education is computed net of interaction effects—involving interactions
of changes in education with changes in sex, employment class, age, and
occupation—this effect is reduced to 0.41 percent.

Dale Jorgenson, in the first half of his article in this volume, "The Contribution of Education to U.S. Economic Growth, 1948–73," provides
specific estimates of education's contribution to U.S. productivity growth.
These estimates reflect technical advances, introduced by Jorgenson and a
number of collaborators (including Chinloy), that solve or minimize the
effects of methodological problems such as the two described above. The
second half of Jorgenson's paper goes beyond the usual boundaries of
growth accounting studies to provide estimates of investment in education
in the United States for the period 1948 to 1973. Jorgenson's investment
estimates are based on discounted lifetime labor incomes of people with
different amounts of education and also account for nonmarket as well as
market returns to education. These estimates were the subject of spirited
discussion, including some skepticism, at the NIE conference on Education,
Productivity, and the National Economy held in Leesburg, Virginia, in
November 1982.

While a number of other outstanding problems in growth accounting deserve mention,[4] one rates special emphasis. The growth accounting work on education's contribution to productivity has concentrated on education's influence on the quality of the labor input. Education undoubtedly also has an effect on productivity through other channels, such as improving the efficiency of research and development activities or improving the speed with which managers introduce innovations into the production process. These effects may or may not be fully reflected in the earnings of the scientists, engineers, and managers involved in these activities. Research is needed on this question: If education's effects, through such channels, are not reflected in earnings, to what extent do existing growth accounting procedures understate education's contribution to productivity?[5] Similarly, growth accounting may not adequately take account of obsolescence of knowledge—in people's minds and as embodied in capital and production techniques.

A more fundamental question underlies these issues: What is it that education actually does to foster or retard economic growth? Do the information and skills learned in schools simply make people more productive? Or are more subtle benefits—for example, the development of good work habits, interpersonal skills, or heightened personal ambitions—the major contribution of schools to economic growth? Alternatively, is education's main economic benefit the development of flexible and imaginative future employees who can break bottlenecks and respond to unexpected opportunities? Is education, as an input into the growth process, highly complementary to other economic processes—for example, research and development—so that its contribution rises or falls depending on events occurring elsewhere in the economy?

CHALLENGES TO GROWTH ACCOUNTING

Some writers challenge the basic assumptions or the underlying models of growth accounting studies. The article in this volume by Mark Plant and Finis Welch, "Measuring the Impact of Education on Productivity," constitutes such a challenge, one which may well require important changes in the research methods used in this field. Plant and Welch argue that the questions asked by the current growth accounting literature are less fundamental than they appear and are poorly formed in the sense that they do not actually measure the contribution of education to output growth. Welch and Plant propose an alternative calculus, based on the concept of producer's surplus, for measuring the contribution of intermediate inputs such as education.

Other researchers have challenged the applicability of the assumptions of neoclassical economics to analyses of economic growth. Some question the assumption that the marginal products of the various factor inputs are equal to their earnings. And some note that growth accountants implicitly or explicitly assume equilibrium in product as well as input markets. (See, for example, Nelson 1981.) Research based on these assumptions might lead in unpromising directions if the causes of economic growth are to be found in the responses of businesses and individuals to market disequilibrium. For example, rising imports of inexpensive foreign products may stimulate domestic producers to introduce new products, techniques, or employee-relations policies.

Proponents of the "screening hypothesis" have questioned the growth accountants' argument that the relative earnings of workers in different educational groups reflect the contributions of differing amounts of education to output.[6] The observed correlation between earnings and educational attainment is due less, it is argued, to the productivity of education than to the use of educational credentials in screening job applicants. The high earnings of the highly educated are not due to their education.

This challenge—which is a challenge to human-capital theory as much as it is to growth accounting—comes in a variety of forms. Some writers believe that screening on the basis of education is consistent with the neo-classical assumptions relating to cost-minimizing behavior by employers: Employers believe that educational attainment conveys information about a person's raw abilities because only able people are capable of completing higher levels of schooling (Stiglitz 1975; Arrow 1973; Riley 1979). Yet others have argued that employers require extensive education when screening employees to ensure that they will have docile workers. Through education, it is claimed, people receive training in accepting the kind of authority relations that characterize the capitalist mode of production (Bowles and Gintis 1976).

NEW ISSUES, NEW PROCEDURES

For years, mainstream economists interested in education's role in productivity growth were likely to turn first to the investigations of the growth accountants and closely related topics on the research agenda of human-capital theorists. Much valuable work remains to be done through these approaches. Simultaneous exploration of alternative procedures and issues is also likely to prove instructive in the coming years. These approaches may provide new insights into the complex and multifaceted links between education and productivity growth and prove especially useful for policy formulation.

Robert Haveman and Barbara Wolfe, in "Education, Productivity, and Well-being," have provided a road map for those who would undertake such an exploration. Haveman and Wolfe examine links between education and productivity that operate through channels other than the inputs and outputs defined for national income accounting purposes. If education results in changes in people's economic well-being, as measured by their willingness to pay for these effects of education, then it has affected productivity, broadly and properly defined. Using this conceptual starting point, Haveman and Wolfe examine the effects of education on health, fertility, income distribution, time spent in household activities, and the diffusion of technology. These effects, they maintain, are productivity effects.

Macroeconomic work on education's contribution to productivity needs to be supplemented by research on the specific ways in which education affects productivity in particular industries and occupations. Studies of education's role in specific industries and occupations can help determine whether education plays an independent causal role in economic growth or whether its contribution is largely complementary to or dependent on activities in other sectors of the economy. Some of the areas that should be examined include the relative productivity of education imparted in different institutional settings (e.g., public versus proprietary vocational education); measurement of the quality of education, including vintage effects; and complementarity with other developments, including research and development and new computer technology.

Some researchers, not content to infer education's impact on productivity from the correlation between education and earnings, have attempted to measure directly the effects of education on work performance. Examples of such efforts include studies of the ship repair (Horowitz and Sherman 1980) and automobile (Wise 1975) industries, as well as work on the role of education in agricultural productivity. Results of these efforts are not conclusive: In some studies, the effects of education appear to be mixed (positive and significant in some instances, not so in others) while in others the measure of performance is suspect (e.g., supervisors' performance ratings). Further work along these lines is needed and should be informed by specific hypotheses concerning the influence of education on work performance.[7]

RESEARCH NEEDS FOR POLICY PROBLEMS

Priorities for policy-oriented research on education and productivity are best assessed from two complementary perspectives. First, what are the research problems, among those without immediate policy implications, most likely to yield understanding of the role of education in economic growth? This is the perspective that has informed the comments above.

Second, given the state of U.S. education and currently available research findings, what policy-oriented research is most needed to provide analysis useful to policymakers and the interested public? This question is addressed in what follows.

W. Lee Hansen's paper in this volume, "Economic Growth and Equal Opportunity: Conflicting or Complementary Goals in Higher Education," provides an instructive example of research directly focused on an important current policy issue: whether the considerable expansion in the 1970s of government-sponsored student financial aid resulted in increased college attendance by youths from lower-income families. Hansen explores this issue in the context of an examination of possible conflict between the goals of economic growth and redistribution in the provision and financing of higher education.

Three additional policy issues deserve exploration here: (1) education and training provided by employers and how it complements or substitutes for education in schools and universities; (2) skill requirements for the 1990s in light of current projections of rapid technological change and implications of these requirements for programs offered in educational institutions and corporations; and (3) the effectiveness of educational institutions and incentive structures currently affecting their effectiveness. New policies influenced by the results of research on these problems could improve the allocation of educational resources and the quality of education and thereby increase productivity.

Education and Training by Employers

Public discussion of education has generally ignored the substantial commitment of U.S. corporations and other private and public sector employers to the education and training of their employees. About 3.6 million private-sector employees received formal, employer-provided education or training in 1981 (University of Pennsylvania 1983). Though economists have conducted imaginative theoretical and empirical studies of on-the-job training (e.g., Mincer 1974; Mincer and Jovanovic 1981), these studies are not oriented toward specific policy issues. In these studies, employee training is usually measured by number of years' experience on the job, rather than by hours spent in training programs, total costs to employers, or completion of particular training programs. This literature also devotes little attention to such issues as the complementarity between employers' education programs and curricula in schools and universities or the desirable level of governmental support, direct or indirect, for such programs.

Far-reaching claims have been made regarding corporations' education and training programs: It is claimed that such education is growing very rapidly and that it is very badly needed; that schools provide poor education in basic language and computational skills; that adult employees' skills become obsolete rapidly, and companies simply must retrain them; that such retraining is essential for U.S. companies attempting to match the growing productivity and technical sophistication of workers in foreign countries; that there is underinvestment in training by companies because trained workers are hired, or "pirated" away, by competitors. On grounds such as these, proposals have been made for government intervention in the form of new tax credits or new requirements for spending by corporations or the federal government (e.g., Choate 1982).

The policy questions raised by discussion of corporations' and other employers' education and training programs could be better addressed in light of new information and analyses. What, in fact, is the current magnitude of employer education and training? What kinds of employees receive different amounts and kinds of training? (For preliminary information, see University of Pennsylvania 1983). If new definitions and measures of "training" are to be devised, what assumptions should guide this effort? Should we think of training mainly as formal programs of instruction, as informal hints and guidance by a trainee's more experienced co-workers, or as numbers of years of job experience? An examination of the claim that human-capital investment receives less favorable tax treatment than physical capital should take into account the fact that corporations can treat training expenses as a cost of doing business. It should also examine the degree to which tax treatment of physical capital investment renders it costless to some employers. Studies are needed of the comparative social rates of return to spending by schools and employers on training.

It would also be useful to examine this complex set of questions: Should schools reduce or eliminate vocational education programs, emphasize basic and advanced verbal and mathematical skills for almost all students, and leave to employers the task of providing occupation-specific training?

The impediments that now discourage close cooperation between corporations and university-based researchers give rise to additional research questions. Would increased corporate financial support for specific university-based research projects raise the rate of return on corporate R&D spending and help universities retain scholars who might otherwise depart for corporate employment? If so, at what cost (if any) to the quality of teaching and the independence of universities?

Future Skills Needs

Few doubt that as employers use increasingly sophisticated technology, the demands for highly skilled personnel will increase. Some observers, however, believe that revolutionary developments in computer and telecommunications technology are causing fundamental changes in skills requirements and creating a new "information society" (Bell 1981). Others believe that while there will be large percentage increases in employment in computer-related and other high-technology occupations, in absolute numbers the greatest employment growth will be in jobs requiring few advanced skills (Levin and Rumberger 1983; Riche, Hecker, and Burgan 1983).[8]

The concerns about future skills needs might be dismissed by economists who believe that supply and demand movements in the labor market send appropriate wage signals to potential students, their families, and educational planners. These signals, it is believed, cause impending shortages in each occupation to be met by appropriately increased enrollments or transfers between occupations. There are two appropriate responses to this position.

First, if this viewpoint is largely correct, then projections of future skills needs can provide information useful to the various decisionmakers (provided that the authors of the studies can correctly feed into their projections the supply and demand reactions of decisionmakers to the projections themselves). In this way, the shortages will be shorter in duration and less severe than if the studies, and public discussion of them, had not taken place.[9]

Second, real-life institutional conditions severely interfere with the supposed links between labor market signals and the educational decisions of students and educational planners. (1) The large government funding of elementary, secondary, and postsecondary public education and the substantial public support for private education result in differential supply impacts according to level of education, state and locality, and subject of study. For example, science courses are more expensive than most; students in small classes receive, in effect, larger government subsidies than those in large classes. Federal student-aid programs probably have encouraged student attendance at private more than at public institutions. (2) States and other governmental jurisdictions inhibit entry into a number of occupations by licensing or other requirements. (3) Public education enjoys a semimonopoly position because it is funded by taxation. Market forces, therefore, do not provide effective sanctions for the misallocation of resources by public school systems: School districts may suffer few consequences if ineffective teachers are retained or promoted, if courses are taught in outdated ways or with obsolete equipment, or if schools persist in offering vocational education courses in subjects for which the demand has greatly diminished.

Institutional factors, some would argue, retard only somewhat the educational improvements or other changes called for by rapidly changing technology or shifts in supply and demand. For example, proponents of the Tiebout hypothesis point out that parents who desire high-quality education can move to school districts with good schools. In general, it is claimed, the ability of citizens with similar tastes to live together will result in relatively little inefficiency in the provision of public goods. (See, e.g., Gramlich and Rubinfeld 1982; however, see also the provocative studies by Sonstelie 1982 and Owen 1983.)

The discussion to this point has provided two reasons why education's potential contribution to productivity can be enhanced through policy studies. First, the allocation of educational resources by individuals, companies, and educational institutions has been greatly influenced by existing structures of taxes and subsidies affecting corporations; current local, state, and federal systems for funding education; and existing public and private arrangements affecting occupational choice. These institutional influences may escape the attention of those who would offer straightforward proposals for increasing the skill levels of employees or providing skills for a society with an increasingly sophisticated technology. This caution applies to those who would advocate new governmental interventions as well as those who believe that a freely operating labor market will produce appropriate educational decisions. Second, the semimonopoly position of public education, particularly at the elementary and secondary levels, may well affect negatively the efficiency of public education as well as the ways in which labor market signals, such as changes in wage rates and unemployment levels, affect course offerings. For reasons such as these, policy-oriented research can also contribute to the effectiveness of our educational institutions and the quality of education.

The Quality of Education

The quality of education is undoubtedly greatly influenced by the quality of teachers. There is evidence that in the United States in recent years the quality of teachers has not been high and may be declining (Vance and Schlechty 1982; Weaver 1978); that teachers' salaries have declined in the last decade-and-a-half in real terms (U.S. Department of Education, National Center for Education Statistics 1980, 1982); that potential teachers' decisions to enter and remain in the profession and teachers' decisions to move between school districts are responsive to salary levels (Baugh and Stone 1982; Zabalza, Turnbull, and Williams 1979); and that teachers with high verbal abilities earn relatively high salaries (Antos and Rosen 1975; Levin 1968).[10] These findings suggest the hypothesis that declining teachers' salaries have contributed to a decline in the quality of teachers and hence the quality of education.

It is not clear that school administrators and taxpayers have strong incentives to attract and retain teachers of high quality. The departure of excellent teachers from a district does not directly threaten, for example, the district's financial viability.

The 1983 report of the National Commission on Excellence in Education and several other recent special reports of national organizations[11] have called attention to mediocrity in schooling. An effort to improve educational quality calls for an understanding of incentive structures affecting the decisions of teachers, administrators, parents, and students. The apparent past acceptability of low quality is not necessarily the result of mere absent-mindedness, parental acquiescence in their children's interest in television, or school administrators' acquiescence to calls for educational practices detrimental to student achievement. Research on incentive structures should also include examination of the effectiveness of legislated standards intended to improve performance, including legislated student achievement and teacher certification standards.

A comparison of the relative efficacy of legislated standards and altered incentives might be undertaken through a systems approach to education. Schooling can be viewed as a production process that yields various kinds of knowledge and skills. This process can be efficient or quite inefficient. Given the outputs of schooling, how are they valued in the marketplace? Given the way these outputs are valued in the marketplace, what feedbacks are produced that alter the production function or the inputs of schooling? Finally, what effects do legislated standards and altered incentives have on these feedbacks?

Economists interested in examining policies to improve educational quality should be prepared to raise awkward issues. For example, some commentators appear to assume that indefinitely large increases in teacher quality and teacher pay should be sought. In view of competing demands for limited resources, attention should be given to determining optimal teacher quality and the optimal teacher salary.

A second example of an important but difficult issue is provided by Murnane's (1981) examination of possible conflict between performance-based teacher pay systems and equal treatment of students of differing ability. Teachers paid on the basis of increases in student learning may confront an awkward realization: Their salaries might increase if they allocate more classroom time to those students for whom additional instructional time results in greater achievement increases. This may imply neglect of students whose test scores do not respond rapidly to additional inputs of teacher time.

The two concluding papers in this volume examine the first four papers in light of related research findings and policy problems.

Richard Murnane's paper, "Alternative Views of the Quality of U.S. Education," analyzes the first four papers in light of the pessimistic conclusions set forth in the recent special reports on the quality of U.S. education. He finds that the papers do not address directly the policy issues highlighted by these reports and that neither the reports nor the papers explore the implications of school districts' varying educational quality.

Jacob Mincer's concluding essay, "Overeducation or Undereducation?," examines outstanding problems in the economics of education, all pertinent to current policy issues. He warns against ready acceptance of the thesis that Americans are overeducated and against omissions in commonly used research procedures that lead to understatements of the returns to education. Finally, he reviews evidence that educational achievement in the United States is declining and is lower than achievement in other leading industrial countries.

EQUALITY OF EDUCATIONAL OPPORTUNITY

This book is devoted largely to education's links with economic productivity and efficiency. For generations, Americans of widely varying backgrounds have valued equality of educational opportunity. An overriding concern with economic efficiency and productivity, especially if accompanied by greatly increased reliance on market mechanisms to achieve efficiency, may or may not foster increased equality of opportunity; the outcome is, to say the least, not entirely clear. Hansen's study, in this volume, of student financial aid systems as well as Murnane's 1981 study of performance-based pay systems remind us how difficult it is to specify the terms of the tradeoff between efficiency and equality of opportunity in education. Economists cannot simply assume that other researchers or policymakers will carefully consider equality of opportunity. Such consideration deserves a place in economic research on education's links with efficiency and productivity.

NOTES

1. In this BLS report, productivity is measured by output per unit of combined and weighted inputs of capital and labor; this is referred to as multifactor productivity.

2. A trade-weighted index was used in making this comparison (see Alvarez and Cooper 1984).

3. Denison is one of several scholars who have attempted to solve the mystery (Denison 1979: Ch. 9).

4. Some of these problems may be outlined briefly.

    1. Growth accounting research takes the rates of return to specific factors as fixed data. In fact, however, the rates of return to factors, including the

rates of return to education of different types, are determined simultaneously with the rate of growth of productivity. If productivity declines or increases, the relative returns to different factors will be affected. Specifically, changes in productivity growth may widen or contract the relative earnings of people with different amounts of education. A more complete understanding of the role of education in productivity growth would be imparted by simultaneous estimation of the determinants of productivity growth. This would be a complex task, however, that might or might not provide greatly improved insights.

2. Several different procedures for measuring the capital input and its effects on productivity have been used. The procedures chosen for a specific study will affect the measurement of education's contribution.

3. Most authors have not been able to incorporate into the growth accounting framework a number of developments that probably help account for changes in productivity growth. These developments include trends in the ratio of hours worked to hours paid; the effect of rising energy prices; the effect of changes in the amount of spending on R&D; the effect of increased spending on compliance with governmental health and safety and pollution abatement requirements. Some authors, however, have been able to incorporate one or more of these developments into their particular frameworks.

Other issues may be mentioned still more briefly: (1) whether the outputs of government, nonprofit institutions, and households can be measured with fair accuracy; (2) the appropriate measure of output of the economy as a whole; (3) whether it is appropriate to treat "economies of scale" as a source of growth.

5. Edwin Mansfield's work is pertinent to new efforts in this direction (see, for example, Mansfield 1982).

6. It should be noted that some growth-accounting researchers have provided corrective adjustments to the education/earnings correlation by netting out the influence on this correlation of the link between ability and educational attainment. See, e.g., Denison's Appendix I in his 1974 study.

7. The empirical methods used in such studies should be able to withstand careful scrutiny, similar to that provided by Rosen (1977) in a review of the human-capital literature.

8. Several researchers have suggested that Americans are being overeducated. The returns to investment in postsecondary education, in particular, are supposed to have fallen relative to the returns to high school education. However, at least one proponent of this view expects a partial reversal of this trend by the end of the 1980s (Freeman 1976; 1981). Further, it has also been suggested that the overeducation hypothesis does not withstand an analysis that controls for employee work experience and age (Welch 1979).

Future skills needs are examined in studies undertaken by the Bureau of Labor Statistics and the National Science Foundation (U.S. Department of Labor, BLS 1980; Dauffenbach, Fiorito, and Folk no date). Unfortunately, most of these analyses are presented in terms not readily useful to university planners or state and federal officials responsible for educational policies.

9. The existence of lags in the adjustment process, as well as the need for some skepticism about the efficacy of governmental programs designed to prevent labor

market shortages, are illustrated by Richard Freeman's research on cob web responses and the National Defense Education Act (Freeman 1975; 1976).

10. There is also evidence that nonmonetary considerations play an important role in teachers' occupational decisions (Lortie 1975). Evidence from Brazil suggests that the effect of better-educated teachers on students' incomes is comparable to the effect of more years of schooling (Behrman and Birdsall 1983).

11. A list of recent reports is presented in Samuelson (1983).

REFERENCES

Alvarez, Donato and Brian Cooper. 1984. "Productivity Trends in Manufacturing in the U.S. and 11 Other Countries." *Monthly Labor Review* (January): 52–58.

Antos, Joseph R., and Sherwin Rosen. 1975. "Discrimination in the Market for Public School Teachers." *Journal of Econometrics* 3: 123–50.

Arrow, Kenneth. 1973. "Higher Education as a Filter." *Journal of Public Economics* 2, no. 3 (July): 193–216.

Baugh, William H., and Joe A. Stone. 1982. "Mobility and Wage Equilibration in the Educator Labor Market." *Economics of Education Review* 2, no. 3 (Summer): 253–74.

Becker, Gary S. 1964. 2d ed. 1975. *Human Capital*. New York: Columbia University Press.

Behrman, Jere and Nancy Birdsall. 1983. "The Quality of Schooling: Quantity Alone is Misleading." *American Economic Review* 73, no. 5 (December): 928–46.

Bell, Daniel. 1981. "The Social Framework of the Information Society." In *The Microelectronics Revolution,* edited by Tom Forester, 500–49. Cambridge, Mass.: M.I.T. Press.

Bowles, Samuel, and Herbert Gintis. 1976. *Schooling in Capitalist America*. New York: Basic Books.

Chinloy, Peter. 1980. "Sources of Quality Change in Labor Input." *American Economic Review* 70, no. 1 (March): 108–19.

Choate, Pat. 1982. "American Workers at the Rubicon: A National Human Capital Strategy." *Commentary* (Summer): 3–10.

Dauffenbach, Robert C.; Jack Fiorito; and Hugh Folk. No date. *A Study of Projected Supply/Demand Imbalances for Scientific and Technical Personnel.* Washington, D.C.: National Science Foundation.

Denison, Edward F. 1974. *Accounting for United States Economic Growth, 1929–1969.* Washington, D.C.: Brookings.

———. 1979. *Accounting for Slower Economic Growth: The United States in the 1970's.* Washington, D.C.: Brookings.

———. 1983. "The Interruption of Productivity Growth in the United States." *Economic Journal* 93 (March): 56–77.

Freeman, Richard B. 1975. "Supply and Salary Adjustments to the Changing Science Manpower Market: Physics, 1948–1973." *American Economic Review* 65, no. 1 (March): 27–39.

———. 1976. *The Over-Educated American*. New York: Academic Press.

———. 1981. "Implications of the Changing U.S. Labor Market for Higher

Education." National Bureau of Economic Research Working Paper No. 697. Cambridge, Mass.

Gramlich, Edward M., and Daniel L. Rubinfeld. 1982. "Micro Estimates of Public Spending Demand Functions and Tests of the Tiebout and Median-Voter Hypotheses." *Journal of Political Economy* 90, no. 3 (June): 536–60.

Griliches, Zvi. 1970. "Notes on the Role of Education in Production Functions and Growth Accounting." In *Education, Income and Human Capital,* edited by W. Lee Hansen, 71–127. National Bureau of Economic Research, Studies in Income and Wealth, Vol. 35. New York: Columbia University Press.

Horowitz, Stanley, and Allan Sherman. 1980. "A Direct Measure of the Relationship between Human Capital and Productivity." *Journal of Human Resources* 15, no. 1 (Winter): 67–76.

Jorgenson, Dale W., and Zvi Griliches. 1967. "The Explanation of Productivity Change." *Review of Economic Studies* 34, no. 3 (July): 249–83.

Kendrick, John W. 1980. "Productivity Trends in the United States." In *Lagging Productivity Growth: Causes and Remedies,* edited by S. Maital and N. Meltz, 9–30. Cambridge, Mass.: Ballinger.

Levin, Henry M. 1968. *Recruiting Teachers for Large City Schools.* Washington, D.C.: Brookings. Mimeo.

Levin, Henry M., and Russell W. Rumberger. 1983. "The Educational Implications of High Technology." Institute for Research on Educational Finance and Governance, Stanford University.

Lortie, Dan. 1975. *Schoolteacher: A Sociological Study.* Chicago: University of Chicago Press.

Maital, Shlomo, and Noah M. Meltz. 1980. "Summary and Conclusions." In *Lagging Productivity Growth: Causes and Remedies,* edited by S. Maital and N. Meltz, 265–74. Cambridge, Mass.: Ballinger.

Mansfield, Edwin. 1982. "Education, R&D, and Productivity Growth." Paper prepared for the National Institute of Education, Washington, D.C.

Mincer, Jacob. 1974. *Schooling, Experience and Earnings.* New York: Columbia University Press.

Mincer, Jacob, and Boyan Jovanovic. 1981. "Labor Mobility and Wages." In *Studies in Labor Markets,* edited by Sherwin Rosen, 21–63. Chicago: University of Chicago Press.

Murnane, Richard J. 1981. "Seniority Rules and Educational Productivity: Understanding the Consequences of a Mandate for Equality." *American Journal of Education* 90, no. 1 (November): 14–38.

National Commission on Excellence in Education. 1983. *A Nation at Risk: The Imperative for Educational Reform.* Washington, D.C.: U.S. Department of Education.

Nelson, Richard R. 1981. "Research on Productivity Growth and Differences." *Journal of Economic Literature* 19, no. 3 (September): 1029–64.

Norsworthy, J.R.; M.J. Harper; and K. Kunze. 1979. "The Slowdown in Productivity Growth: Analysis of Some Contributing Factors." *Brookings Papers on Economic Activity,* No. 2. Washington, D.C.: Brookings: 387–421.

Owen, John D. 1983. "Optimal Education in a Welfare State (An Overview)." Paper presented at 39th Congress of the International Institute of Public Finance, Budapest, Hungary, August.

Riche, Richard; Daniel Hecker; and John Burgan. 1983. "High Technology Today and Tomorrow: A Small Slice of the Employment Pie." *Monthly Labor Review* (November): 50–58.

Riley, John G. 1979. "Testing the Educational Screening Hypothesis." *Journal of Political Economy* 87, no. 5, pt. 2 (October): S227–S252.

Rosen, Sherwin. 1977. "Human Capital: A Survey of Empirical Research." In *Research in Labor Economics,* Vol. 1, edited by Ronald G. Ehrenberg, 3–39. Greenwich, Conn.: JAI Press.

Samuelson, Robert J. 1983. "Schools and Jobs." *National Journal* 15, no. 28 (July): 1426–46.

Sonstelie, Jon. 1982. "The Welfare Cost of Free Public Schools." *Journal of Political Economy* 90, no. 4 (August): 794–808.

Stiglitz, Joseph E. 1975. "The Theory of 'Screening,' Education, and the Distribution of Income." *American Economic Review* 65, no. 3 (June): 283–300.

U.S. Department of Education, National Center for Education Statistics. 1980, 1982. *The Condition of Education: Statistical Report* (annual). Washington, D.C.

U.S. Department of Labor, Bureau of Labor Statistics. 1983. "Multifactor Productivity Measures." BLS news release USDL 83-440 (October 13).

———. 1980. *Occupational Projections and Training Data, 1980 Edition.* Bulletin 2052. Washington, D.C.

University of Pennsylvania. 1983. *The Impact of Public Policy on Education and Training in the Private Sector.* A preliminary report to the National Institute of Education. Philadelphia, Pa., June.

Vance, Victor S., and Phillip C. Schlechty. 1982. "The Structure of the Teaching Occupation and the Characteristics of Teachers: A Sociological Interpretation." A Report to the National Institute of Education.

Weaver, W. Timothy. 1978. "Educators in Supply and Demand: Effects on Quality." *School Review* 86, no. 4 (August): 552–93.

Welch, Finis. 1979. "Effects of Cohort Size on Earnings: The Baby Boom Babies' Financial Bust." *Journal of Political Economy* 87, no. 5, pt. 2 (October): S65–S97.

Wise, David A. 1975. "Academic Achievement and Job Performance." *American Economic Review* 65, no. 3 (June): 350–66.

Zabalza, Antoni; Philip Turnbull; and Gareth Williams. 1979. *The Economics of Teacher Supply.* Cambridge: Cambridge University Press.

Chapter 1

Education, Productivity, and Well-Being: On Defining and Measuring the Economic Characteristics of Schooling

Robert H. Haveman and Barbara L. Wolfe

"Of late economists have been spending considerable time attempting to assess the economic contribution of education." So William Bowen begins his 1964 volume of essays on *Economic Aspects of Education*. Now, nearly two decades and hundreds of studies later, the statement is no less true.

This paper continues Bowen's struggle with both the definition and the measurement of the economic effects of schooling, but is more comprehensive than his. Extensive theoretical and empirical research on this issue during the two-decade lapse between Bowen's paper and this one has resulted in a more precise definition of the meaning of economic well-being, a more comprehensive understanding of the complex channels by which schooling alters human behavior (and, hence, well-being and productivity), and a far more extensive empirical literature on the behavioral effects of schooling.

Our opening discussion of schooling (or education) and economic productivity compares the standard measures of productivity to the ideal measure of productivity that would be employed if more extensive and complete information and data were available.[1] The standard measures are partial and, at best, serve as proxies for the ideal productivity measure. Standard measures of the economic effects of schooling are closely related to familiar productivity measures: The effects of schooling that typically are estimated are those embodied in the standard productivity measures. Hence, standard

The assistance of George Parsons is acknowledged, as are the helpful comments of Edwin Dean, W. Lee Hansen, Thomas Juster, Robert Lampman, Jacob Mincer, Theodore Schultz, Eugene Smolensky, and Burton Weisbrod. Support for this work was provided by the National Institute of Education.

measures of the economic effects of schooling are "partial" in the same way that familiar productivity measures are partial. This section outlines our focus on the full contribution of education or schooling to the output or productivity of the economy and on "economic well-being."

The next section briefly reviews both the human-capital (or returns-to-education) approach and the growth accounting approach to measuring the benefits of education and examines the serious weaknesses of both. The third section is a brief statement of the welfare economics notion of "benefits." This concept is based on the willingness of individuals to pay for the effects—either positive or negative—of an activity and is the monetary equivalent of the "compensating variation" concept of welfare economics. The willingness-to-pay concept is applicable to the private goods aspects of schooling, as well as to the external (or public goods) components of the benefits from schooling.

The fourth section distinguishes the numerous ways in which the effects of schooling can generate willingness to pay. Channels of impact beyond those perceived when Bowen wrote include health effects, fertility effects, income distributional effects, home time effects, and technology diffusion effects.

While we now have substantial evidence on the private returns to education as reflected in earnings differences, less is known about the other channels by which education affects economic well-being. The fifth section presents a partial review of recent evidence on some of the benefits of schooling not reflected in monetary private returns—in particular, the health and fertility effects of education, effects on the value of the home time of mothers, effects on criminal behavior, and effects deriving from the impact of education on the earnings distribution. Assessing the impact of schooling on economic well-being by focusing on only those private returns reflected in earnings differences neglects most of these other contributions, a number of which appear to be quantitatively large. The final section concludes with policy implications that derive from our discussion.

EDUCATION AND PRODUCTIVITY—FULL AND PARTIAL MEASURES

"Productivity" can be defined as the total output of an economy divided by the total inputs that contribute to producing that output. As such, it is among the most comprehensive indicators of the performance of the economy. In a very real sense, a productivity ratio is a benefit/cost ratio.

With complete data and information, statisticians could calculate productivity as a ratio of the total economic benefits generated by the economy divided by the value of the resources that entered into that production. An increase in productivity, then, would be an increase in benefits holding inputs constant, a decrease in costs holding output constant, or a simultaneous increase in benefits and a decrease in costs. And any phenomena—such as education, new technology, or weather—that increased the numerator of the ratio, decreased the denominator, or did both, would be said to increase productivity or to contribute to the growth in productivity.

In fact, data and information are not complete. As a result, statisticians have formulated a variety of surrogates for true productivity. Consider the most common (and official) measure, labor productivity. Instead of measuring the value of all of the outputs of the economy, the labor productivity index includes in the numerator only the outputs recorded in the nation's national income and product account. Indeed, in some measures only the output of the private nonfarm business sector is included. The contributions of the economy to nonmarketed benefits—for example, reductions in accidents and illnesses, increases in leisure, improvements in product quality, reductions in travel or waiting time—are all neglected in the standard productivity measures. Similarly, the labor productivity index includes only one input, labor, in the denominator. The contributions of capital, natural resources, or other nonlabor inputs to the economy are neglected.

A number of productivity measures that are more extensive than this simple, single-factor measure have been developed in recent years. The primary improvement adds factor inputs other than labor to the denominator of the productivity index. These are referred to as full-factor productivity measures and are represented primarily in work by Denison (1962, 1967, 1979), Kendrick (1961, 1977), Christensen and Jorgenson (1973), Christensen, Jorgenson, and Cummings (1981). Full-factor productivity measures are still partial. They still accept as the output numerator only those effects recorded in the national income accounts and in fact still neglect some real inputs to the economy. Recently, however, Jorgenson (this volume) has attempted to account for education's impact on the value of leisure and other home time in estimating the volume of educational investment.

The most common measures of the economic effects of education (or schooling) are the human-capital (or direct returns) and growth-accounting measures. These measures—which will be critiqued in detail in the next section—have problems very similar to those of the standard productivity measures. They measure only a portion of the full benefits of schooling and capture only a portion of the full costs of providing education services. In fact, some of the "rate of return" measures of the economic effects of education suffer from almost the same limitation as the standard productivity measures: The returns are measured as only those effects that are recorded in the nation's income and product accounts.

Both standard productivity measures and the commonly used measures of the economic effects of schooling are proxies for their more comprehensive counterparts. Because both are partial indicators of the phenomena that they are designed to reflect, the answers they provide may be misleading—indeed wrong. For example, true productivity—the ratio of the full economic outputs of the economy divided by all productive inputs to the economy—might well be rising at the same time that the standard, partial measures are suggesting that productivity is falling. This might be particularly true if leisure were increasing.

The discussion of the relationship of schooling to productivity in this study takes a comprehensive view of the measuring of productivity. The output measure that we will use is one that reflects the total output of the economy valued at what individuals are willing to pay for that output. It goes well beyond the gross national product measure of output or any of the other output measures used in the standard productivity indexes. Indeed, our output measure captures the contribution of the economy to what we call economic well-being. Our analysis of the contribution of education or schooling to productivity, then, is in terms of its contribution to this full measure of economic well-being. Before elaborating on this output concept, however, we will describe how estimates of the economic effects of schooling have been based on partial measures of output in the standard studies.

MEASURING THE ECONOMIC EFFECTS OF SCHOOLING

We have emphasized that economic well-being in a society is more than aggregate personal income or gross national product—that the full productivity of an economy is different from the official labor productivity index. To be sure, the money values reflected in GNP or private sector output are major components of well-being: For many purposes GNP may serve as a good proxy for economic well-being, and the standard productivity indices, for true economic productivity. Moreover, those variables that ultimately determine the aggregate level of economic well-being—education, health status, environmental amenities, the productive capital stock, the housing stock, the level of public sector infrastructure—may also be closely related to aggregate levels of gross income and product. This judgment underlies the primary efforts to measure the economic effects of schooling. Indeed, both the direct-returns approach and the growth-accounting approach reflect the view that the economic well-being effects of education are captured by the impact of education on measured income and product.

The Direct Returns Approach

The pioneering work on human capital was done by Mincer (1958, 1970) and Becker (1964).[2] In Mincer's formulation, the logarithm of earnings (Y)

is a linear function of the years of schooling (S) and a quadratic function of an experience variable (j), thought of as postschool investments in human capital and defined as age (A) less ($S+5$),

$$\log Y = a_0 + a_1 S + a_2 j + a_3 j^2 + \epsilon \qquad (1.1)$$

This basic formulation has several characteristics relevant to its use in estimating the direct economic returns to education:

1. It assumes implicitly that all private direct returns to education are reflected in measured earnings of individual recipients of educational services; no nonlabor market effects (e.g., nonmonetary differences in the quality of jobs) are admitted, nor are the consumption benefits of education admitted.
2. It assumes that, in the absence of postschool training, the age/earnings profile is flat and, hence, that the present value of individual earnings is constant across individuals with equal levels of schooling.
3. It posits that the rate of return to postschool training is constant irrespective of the age at which the training is obtained.
4. It assumes that the individual maximizes lifetime earnings, ignoring hours of work and hence hours of leisure.

The first of these assumptions is clearly not correct, as we argue later in this paper. As Blaug (1976) has pointed out, there are good empirical and theoretical reasons for doubting the remaining assumptions. If the first assumption does not hold, and if those effects of education on economic well-being that are not reflected in labor earnings are on balance positive, the estimates of the returns to education based on this direct returns framework are lower bound estimates. The implication of the inaccuracy of assumptions 2 through 4 is that empirical estimates of the benefits of education are not likely to be reliable; overestimates caused by some of the assumptions are offset by underestimates due to other assumptions in some unknown way.

In addition to these modeling issues, human-capital-based empirical estimates of the direct earnings effects of education are encumbered by serious data and specification problems. The concept of human capital—or, indeed, education—is unobservable, and as a result estimation of its impacts confronts problems of censored data and self-selection. The contribution of education services to earnings differences cannot easily be disentangled from differences in abilities, tastes, ambition, or "connections." Estimates of returns (or earnings inequality) impacts based on life cycle income concepts are different from and inconsistent with estimates based on a shorter accounting period. The effect of labor demand differences on earnings has not been effectively or reliably incorporated into earnings functions. Indeed, the definitions of human capital used in the various studies are inconsistent: Concepts of ability, schooling, skills, and the empirical counterparts of each are complex and have not been thoroughly developed in the literature. The complex structure by which truly exogenous factors can be identified and their effects on outcomes kept separate from that of other factors has not been clearly set forth. For example, schooling may change an individual's learning capabilities as well as earnings (Welch 1970). Finally, although the accumulation of human capital is an aspect of lifetime utility-maximizing choice in a framework of earning, consuming, and leisure-taking, it has been evaluated in a context in which life-cycle variation in work time has not been well accounted for.

The Growth Accounting Approach

The growth accounting framework is a national income account-based technique for evaluating the contributions of various factors to observed growth in output. Estimates of the contributions of education services to income growth have also been derived using this technique and compared to those obtained from the direct returns approach. Since the early 1960s, the application of the growth accounting approach has been pursued most forcefully by Denison (1962, 1967, 1979), who assigns education as one factor contributing to output growth.

In the growth accounting framework, factor inputs (and various elements that determine their productivity) are the determinants of national output (measured as national income or net national product valued at factor cost). The determinants of output demand or input supply are not explicitly considered. In the analysis, the determinants of output combine multiplicatively, and as a result their exponential rates of growth combine additively. For example, in the case of labor, the following components comprise the total input: number of persons employed; average hours (adjusted by various factors); age/sex composition; education; and unallocated. The contribution of labor to the growth rate of productivity (national income per person employed—NIPPE) is obtained by subtracting the contribution of the number of persons employed from the remainder of labor's contribution. In the 1948 to 1973 period, for example, the contribution of labor to the average annual growth rate of output was 1.42 percentage points, of which education was credited with 0.41 percentage points. Of the rate of growth of productivity of 1.52 percentage points per year during this period, education was again credited with 0.41 percentage points per year.

Throughout the various phases of Denison's work, the contribution of education to output growth has always been positive and has accounted for about 15 to 25 percent of growth in national income per person employed. As Table 1–1 indicates, Denison has estimated that the contribution of

Table 1-1. Changes in the Effects of Various Factors on Productivity Growth: Contributions in Percentage Points of Various Factors to the Growth Rate of Productivity in Recent Years Minus the Contributions in Past Years.

Factor/Author	Denison[a]	Denison[b]	Kendrick[c]
Cyclical effects, weather, work stoppages	0.2	−0.4	−0.6
Shifts from manufacturing to services	—	—	−0.1
Shift from farm to nonfarm and shift out of self-employment	−0.4	−0.3	−0.1
Changes in hours worked	−0.3	−0.1	—
Labor force composition	−0.1	−0.3	−0.3
Education	0.4	0.2	0.2
Health and vitality	—	—	0
Nonresidential structures and equipment	−0.1	−0.1	—
Inventories	−0.1	0	—
Economies of scale	−0.2	0	−0.2
Land	0	−0.1	−0.1
Pollution abatement and other regulations	−0.4	−0.2	—
Government services	—	—	−0.1
Diffusion of knowledge	—	—	−0.15
Residual factors ("advances in knowledge")	−2.1	0.2	0.2
Total change explained	−3.1	−1.0[d]	−1.5

[a] Compares nonresidential business income per employed person in 1973–76 versus 1948–69.
[b] Compares nonresidential business income per employed person in 1969–73 versus 1948–69.
[c] Compares private sector output per total factor input in 1966–76 versus 1948–66.
[d] The sum of the component parts does not equal the total because of rounding errors.

education to productivity growth has increased over time; that the contribution in 1973 to 1976 less that in 1948 to 1969 was 0.4 percentage points; that for 1969 to 1973 less that in 1948 to 1969 was 0.2 percentage points. Kendrick's analysis, also based on a growth accounting framework, suggests a similar pattern for education. The results of Denison's analysis, however, have been puzzling in recent years. The category of "residual factors" composed of advances in knowledge and components not classified elsewhere (and in many cases not even identified) contributed a change of −2.1 percentage points per year to productivity growth in 1973 to 1976 relative to 1948 to 1969, as opposed to a change of 0.2 percentage points per year in 1969 to 1973 relative to 1948 to 1969. As Denison stated, "It is possible, perhaps even probable, that everything went wrong at once [during the 1973 to 1976 period] among the determinants that affect the residual series" (Denison 1979: 145).

While Denison's results suggest a large and growing contribution of education to output growth, the unexplained behavior of the residual casts doubts on the reliability of this as well as the remainder of the estimates. As Stone (1980: 1540) has commented regarding the role of the residual: "This is a counsel of despair. The presence of a residual in any set of accounts is pernicious because it does away with the only constraint to which the data are subject." Abramovitz (1956: 11) called it "a measure of our ignorance."

The growth accounting framework, however, has still other weaknesses pertaining to the contribution of education to either output or productivity growth. First, education refers only to changes in the amount of *formal* education received by members of the labor force. As a result, it does not account for improvements in the quality of a year's worth of schooling or increases in a variety of educational services other than formal education. This criticism is similar to that levied at the estimates of the direct return to education provided by studies employing the human-capital framework. The second criticism is also similar to one discussed in connection with the human-capital framework—namely, the only output that is attributed to education is that recorded in the national income accounts; its effects on other components of economic welfare (for example, the consumption value of education) are neglected. Third, Denison's estimates of the contribution of education to measured output fail to account for the loss of experience attributable to education. Finally, several of the indirect effects of education—for example, its impact in increasing the labor-force participation rate—are not accounted for.

EDUCATION SERVICES AND ECONOMIC WELFARE

Neither of the two standard approaches to measuring the benefits of educational services—the direct-returns and the growth-accounting approaches—captures the full value of educational services. This is the fundamental criticism of both approaches. In this section, we inquire into the meaning of the economic well-being benefits of goods and services consumed by individuals, irrespective of the nature of the goods or services, following a brief description of the nature of educational services.

Education Services as Public and Private Goods

In some of its guises, educational services are privately demanded. Higher education services, for example, are not mandated; the amount consumed is at the discretion of individual consumers. The incentives for individual choice, however, are often altered by collective action. For example, higher education services at state institutions are offered at prices (tuitions) that are below marginal costs. Similarly, student assistance (whether publicly or privately offered) and subsidized loan arrangements seek to induce a greater demand for higher education services than would otherwise be observed.

Individual demands, apart from the special inducements, reflect the private gains that recipients of the services are likely to experience. Of the many possible private gains, we will distinguish but two. First, there are the private gains reflected in market incomes and gross national product; these productivity increases due to education are manifest in increases in the output of goods and services. A second form of private gain is a direct increase in utility attributable to education. For example, individuals may enjoy the process of being educated. In addition to these private effects, there are more widely dispersed—or "public" effects—of higher education services. These effects are not fully reflected in private demands. As a result, the quantity of higher education services privately demanded may exceed or fall short of demands that reflect both private and public effects. The extent to which full private and public benefits of education are not reflected in market demands is crucial in determining if, at the margin, the economic well-being benefits of education exceed or fall short of the economic costs of producing them.

The provision of education services at lower levels is not dominated by private choices. In the case of elementary and secondary education, for example, attendance is mandatory. For those students in public institutions—the substantial majority—the volume of education services provided is determined collectively. Only for the small proportion of children in private schools is the volume of education services a matter of private choice.[3] However, even in the case of publicly provided education, the education services provided are not pure public goods. As in the case of higher education, much of the benefit of educational services is privately appropriated;[4] in this case as well, however, spillover benefits accrue to the community at large in the form of public goods.

For all major forms of education services, then, private demands and provision are mixed in some fashion with collective provision and collective effects. In the higher education sector, collective provision plays a small role relative to that in sectors providing lower levels of education. Regardless of the level of education services provided, the output stream yields benefits in the form of both private and public goods, although in varying combinations. Evaluation of the full benefits of education must encompass benefits reflected in earnings increments, private benefits represented by direct utility changes, and public benefits of educational services.

The Concept of Economic Benefits

Contemporary welfare economics provides the conceptual underpinnings for defining the contribution of service flows (whether from public or private goods) to economic well-being. As depicted in formal analyses, both forms of service flows enter individual utility functions, and the utility impacts of each can be represented by marginal benefit functions. Such relationships, also known as marginal-willingness-to-pay functions, display for any quantity of the good consumed the value of other goods and services that would have to be received in order to compensate for the loss of one unit of the good in question.[5] The area under the curve from zero units to the amount of the good or service consumed is the total value to the individual of that amount of the good or service consumed—that commodity's contribution to the individual's well-being. This total value would be consumers' surplus if the specified quantity were secured at zero price. It equals the full contribution of the good or service to the individual's economic well-being. At a positive price, the total willingness to pay equals the amount actually paid plus the amount the individual would be willing to pay rather than go without the consumption of the good (the area under the curve from zero units to the amount of the good or service consumed but above the price).[6]

This willingness-to-pay concept of the contribution of various forms of consumption to total individual well-being applies to both private and public goods. The measurement of this willingness-to-pay value is quite different for the two types of goods, however. For pure private goods—those passing through a competitive market and for which a price can be observed—measurement of the economic benefits of consuming any traded amount requires estimation of a demand curve and the measurement of the appropriate areas under it.

For pure public goods, however, measurement of the contribution that consumption of the good or service makes to economic well-being is substantially more difficult. In this case, price/quantity combinations—from which willingness-to-pay functions are constructed—are rarely observed. Given the public-good nature of these goods, if these combinations were observed we would expect them to underestimate the true willingness to pay associated with each quantity. While a number of conceptually correct approaches have been proposed and evaluated—including direct survey questions regarding willingness to pay and the inferring of values from price/quantity relationships of commodities whose consumption is complementary with that of the public good in question—none is without serious problems. Further, all the empirical research that has sought to estimate the economic well-being benefits of public goods has confronted serious data and estimation problems.[7] Nevertheless, a full evaluation of the contribution of any good or service to economic well-being must be based on the estimation of this total willingness to pay—the sum of the amount actually paid and consumers' surplus—of all of the citizens benefiting from consumption of the good or service.[8] To the extent that provision of any identifiable service yields well-being effects of a variety of types, the willingness of citizens to pay for these benefits must be measured and aggregated over types.

This conclusion is particularly relevant in the case of educational services. They, as much as any other good or service, convey a wide variety of effects—some are of a public-good character, others are private goods, either in the form of monetary returns or direct consumption—that carry economic well-being implications. It is to this variety of effects on well-being that we now turn, in an effort to distinguish the primary channels by which educational services create or reduce economic well-being and their private and public good character.

The Effects of Education on Economic Well-Being: The Channels of Impact

Two primary points were emphasized in the last section. First, educational services, like other goods and services, affect the economic well-being of individuals and families and are valued by the willingness-to-pay concept of welfare economics. Second, the economic well-being effects of education services include private marketed and nonmarketed impacts as well as external or public impacts; estimates of the aggregate value of education services must encompass all of these. In this section, we attempt to identify the major channels of impact by which education services affect economic well-being and to indicate which of these impacts are captured by analyses based on the direct monetary returns and (to a more limited extent) the growth-accounting frameworks. This approach, then, grows out of the benefit/cost analysis framework of welfare economics. Its emphasis is on the total return from educational services and not on the marginal effect of a dose of educational services.

Human-Capital Based Effects of Education

1. *Earnings Differentials.* From the perspective of the human-capital framework, the principal effect of educational services is the increased productivity of the direct recipients of these services. Given perfect labor markets, labor services will be sold at their market prices and the productivity

Figure 1-1. The Effects of Education on Economic Well-Being: Channels of Impact.

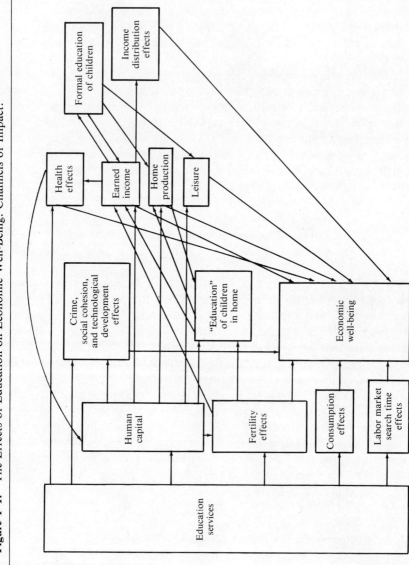

increase generated by education will be reflected in the wage rates and earned income of the recipients of educational services. Hence, wage differentials among education levels reflect the productivity returns to education services. These returns are captured in standard human-capital based estimates of education benefits; they are private returns, and under certain labor market conditions they are also social returns. They are shown in Figure 1-1.

2. *Labor/Leisure Choices.*   In addition to earnings increases, however, education services may generate other productivity-related impacts that also convey economic well-being. For example, increases in human capital, by enabling workers to command higher wage rates are also likely to induce alterations in labor/leisure choices. In particular, if leisure is a normal good, additional education is likely to induce an increase in the quantity of leisure chosen—the standard backward-bending portion of the labor supply curve. Individuals are willing to pay for this additional leisure, and it must therefore be credited as a well-being benefit to the education services that induce it. Although earnings may decrease because of this choice—and earnings differentials among education levels as well—economic well-being will tend to increase.[9] For others, education seems to lead to a preference for more work. To the extent this effect dominates, the earnings differential overstates the return to education, since the value of the loss of leisure is not subtracted from the earnings differential.

3. *Nonmarket Productivity Differences.*   Education may also influence the uses made of an individuals' leisure time. If education increases an individual's productivity, and hence labor market rewards, these same education services are likely to generate an increase in the value of the activities in which the person engages during leisure hours. This higher value must serve as the basis for the evaluation of leisure time. If these hours are spent in productive activities (e.g., do-it-yourself activities), the increased output in this nonmarket sector that is attributable to education should also be calculated and included in the value of leisure time.

The direction of the effect of education services on home production is not necessarily positive, however. For example, education may have the effect of increasing market work activities at the expense of home production activities. This effect has often been cited for women, for whom the increase in labor-force participation comes at the cost of reduced home time spent with children, fewer housework-type activities, and fewer do-it-yourself activities. More recent work suggests that educated women reallocate time away from housework and personal-care type activities but toward direct child-care.

4. *The Aggregate Return to Education with Disequilibrium Labor Markets.*
The direct productivity-related returns of education services are estimated
by assuming that the economy is a reasonably competitive, neoclassical
economy in which price and, in particular, wage adjustments serve to
equilibrate markets, and that such adjustments occur in response to changes
in supply and demand. In recent analyses, a disequilibrium framework
has been developed in which wage and price adjustments do not occur
in response to supply and demand changes. In this framework, unemployment—rather than wage rates—serves as the equilibrating mechanism.
Work by Todaro (1969), Harberger (1971), Sen (1972), Fields (1972), and
Stiglitz (1974), all of which concerns an economic situation in which substantial unemployment exists, is based on this framework. With reasonable
characterizations of this disequilibrium situation, it can be shown that the
net social benefit of educating one unskilled worker may be zero, the net
private benefit greater than zero, and the benefit as measured from observed
wage differentials greater than both. This conclusion assumes that educated
workers employed in the unskilled labor market are no more productive
than unskilled workers in that market and that educated workers in unskilled
jobs do not have a positive effect on the productivity of unskilled workers in
these jobs. If these assumptions are correct—if unemployment exists and if
wage rates do not equilibrate—standard estimates of the benefits of education based on observed wage differentials will overstate the true contribution of education to economic well-being.

Fertility Effects of Education

While the generally inverse relationship of education to fertility or child-
bearing has often been noted, its basis is not well understood. The relationship is complex since it involves demand for children, which in turn is
influenced by changes in tastes, increased ability to afford children, opportunity cost, biological or supply factors, and regulation of fertility. In terms
of demand, if it is assumed that utility depends on both consumption and
children, reductions in fertility (particularly female fertility) in response to
increases in human capital would be expected. The rewards of work increase
because of education, and simultaneously, the opportunity cost of home
time also increases. The incentive is to substitute market income—and the
consumption of goods that it affords—for the "consumption" of children
with its required home time.

The fertility response to education can also be understood apart from its
interaction with the acquisition of human capital. This would be the case if
education serves to directly change individual tastes for children, relative to
other forms of consumption. The taste effect could increase or decrease

demand for children, although evidence suggests it is primarily positive, at least at high levels of education. This taste alteration effect of education is difficult to deal with within an economic framework. Yet it seems unreasonable to deny that education, among all public services, is likely to change preferences for styles of life and relative consumption patterns.

Fertility is also influenced by supply-side phenomena such as probability of marriage, age of marriage, parents' health, infant mortality, and the possibility of fecundity. The directions of these effects are mixed: (1) More education tends to lead to older age at marriage and thus less exposure to conception; (2) more education leads to better health, which is associated with greater fecundity and lower infant mortality rates.

The dominant model of the relationship between fertility and women's education is the "new home economics" developed by Becker (1965), Willis (1973), and others. This model emphasizes the time-value effect—that is, the influence of education on the price of children—and uses a child quality/quantity maximizing framework where child services are hypothesized to enter the parental utility function. Parental utility also depends on the parent's own consumption of goods and services. Parents maximize their utility subject to production functions for child quality and commodities consumed by the parents and a full income constraint that depends on the time of parents, the value of the time of parents, other income sources, and market prices.[10]

Within the new home economics framework, education also plays a role in allowing a family to achieve its desired family size. If the net value of an additional child is negative, the household improves its well-being by lowering the probability of conception. One way to do this is to use contraceptives. Usage involves costs, however, in terms of expenditures on contraception, psychic costs, and costs of foregone sexual gratification, so that parents may demand more children than they would desire if contraception were less costly. Education is likely to reduce costs of using contraceptives through several channels: greater receptivity to new ideas, increased awareness of new techniques, increased efficiency in using any contraceptive, and increased efficiency in selection of contraceptives.

In Figure 1–1, two of these linkages between education and fertility are shown—one indirect through human capital accumulation and the other direct, reflecting a change in tastes. Changes in fertility behavior are also shown affecting economic well-being. The existence of this linkage is obvious: Estimation of the economic value of changes in completed family size is less straightforward. Yet, to the extent that fertility decisions are voluntary and do occur in the context of individual optimizing choices over a variety of consumption goods, these decisions will have positive economic well-being implications. If changes in standard-good consumption in response to changes in relative prices cause changes in net willingness to pay (consumer surplus), so too do changes in completed family size caused by changes in the prices of child bearing, contraceptive use, and child rearing relative to prices of other goods.

The economic well-being effects of fertility changes attributable to direct taste changes caused by education are more difficult to define. Irrespective of the magnitude or of the sign of the economic well-being effects of education operating through fertility changes, it is clear that neither the human-capital model nor the growth-accounting framework captures them in any systematic way.[11] Because education-induced changes in fertility are likely to generate some increases in economic well-being, particularly through increased ability to achieve desired family size, standard estimates of the benefits of education tend to be biased downward.

Health Effects of Education

Education services can also effect health and longevity. Such benefits occur through (1) information effects of education (e.g., awareness of potential benefits of prevention and avoidance activities); (2) effects of education on occupation (e.g., higher educated individuals tend to hold less dangerous jobs); (3) effects of the higher earnings associated with more education on the consumption of health care services; and (4) effects of education in selecting a better diet. These benefits will be reflected in the health status of both the direct beneficiaries of education services and their children.

In Figure 1-1, education is seen as directly affecting health status through the increased earnings associated with human-capital investments. Simultaneously, improved health status is a form of human capital and through this channel influences earnings.[12] While improved health status contributes to economic well-being through its effects on earnings, it directly affects economic well-being by providing nonmarketed services—increases in longevity, increases in the quantity and quality of well-time while living, and reductions in health care costs.[13] These contributions to economic well-being are captured in unobserved demand functions for nonmarketed goods. Although standard estimates measure education-related health effects that are manifest in increased earnings, they do not measure the contribution of education services to economic well-being through increases in longevity and well time (outside of work time) and decreases in health care costs. Moreover, to the extent that better health has externalities such as reducing contagious disease or influencing the well-being of others, some benefits spill over into the community. To this extent, standard estimates understate the full contribution of the benefits of education services to economic well-being.

Consumption Effects of Education

A classic example of a nonmarketed yet real effect of education is its value as a consumption good in its own right and its effect on the value of consuming other goods. An important component of the demand for education services, so the argument goes, is the value of these services as consumption goods. Individuals place a positive value on the experiencing of education—as though attending a lecture were like attending a concert. Moreover, it is further argued that through education the future enjoyment of other kinds of meritorious consumption activities—reading, music, art—will be increased, that these benefits also affect well-being, and hence that they should be attributed to the provision of education services. To the extent that the sign on them is positive, standard estimates of the benefits of education based on earnings differentials will be understated.[14]

Labor-Market Search-Time Effects of Education

The labor market functions efficiently to the degree that available workers with their skills are effectively matched to jobs with their requirements. These matches are made by a search process in which workers and employers try to secure the best match among the available options. This process is a costly one. The longer the time lapse between initiation of a search and securing of a match, or the poorer the match that is attained, the more costly the process.

Education services provided either to available workers or potential employers, it is hypothesized, reduce the time of search or improve the quality of matches attained. Individuals with more education could be expected to better perceive the requirements of an optimal match and proceed to it with less delay. As a result, the level of search and job-matching costs—essentially, transaction costs—would be reduced because of education. This reduction in costs is a social benefit appropriately attributed to education. It is a direct impact of education and is so depicted in Figure 1–1.

A related effect of education occurs through migration. Much migration is for improved job opportunities. Educated persons might be expected to be better informed about job opportunities in a wider geographic area and less likely to err in moving to improved opportunities (see DaVanzo 1983 for evidence on this point). Although some of the resulting cost saving or improved job matches may be captured in increased earnings and, hence, reflected in benefit measures based on wage differentials, it seems likely that most of these effects are not so captured. The true value of education services is, therefore, in excess of that implied by the standard measures.

Income-Distribution Effects of Education

As has been emphasized, one of education's primary effects is to create human capital and to increase the earnings of individuals who receive education services. Depending on who receives education services and the effect of these services on earnings, the distribution of income can be made more or less unequal because of education. To the extent there have been compensatory efforts in the provision of education services, individuals with weaker family background and lower earning capacities have tended to receive education services beyond what they would otherwise have received. For the most part, this sort of targeted education has been viewed as reducing income inequality.

Individuals have preferences for the degree of inequality existing in the community to which they belong. Some may be willing to pay a positive amount for decreases (or in some cases increases) in the degree of income inequality: The degree of inequality is an argument in their utility function. It is this perception that lies at the base of the "optimal redistribution" literature (see Hochman and Rogers 1969).

If, in fact, the provision of education services decreases inequality and if a reduction in inequality is of benefit to citizens, education services must be credited with this economic well-being benefit as well. In Figure 1-1, the channel of impact runs from education services to human capital to earnings effects and then to income distribution effects. This implies that it is only earnings inequality that enters the utility functions of members of the community; in fact, inequality in any dimension of well-being could be relevant. Identifying only one channel, then, is an oversimplification.

Other Effects of Education

Education services generate changes in economic well-being in a variety of other ways. These other effects will be briefly mentioned here:

1. Education services, it is claimed, reduce the level of external costs that individual behavior imposes on others. Holding all else constant, it is hypothesized that education reduces criminal activity and delinquency, reduces accidents causing harm to others or imposing increased health costs on others (e.g., automobile accidents), and increases community participation and social cohesion.
2. Education services, it has been suggested, facilitate and further the advance of technology and the diffusion of new technologies. In effect,

the link between invention and innovation becomes stronger, making isoquants more elastic and increasing the complementarity between research and development and capital investment.[15]

3. Finally, education has been viewed as a mechanism by which talented individuals can be identified and elevated to crucial positions of leadership. Alfred Marshall (1890), perhaps, expressed this best:

> We may then conclude that the wisdom of expending public and private funds is not to be measured by its direct fruits alone. It will be profitable as a mere investment to give the masses of the people much greater opportunities to get the start needed for bringing out their latent abilities. And the economic value of one industrial genius is sufficient to cover the expenses of a whole town.

In Figure 1–1 these effects are shown as stemming directly from education services; in fact, the impacts could be indirect, resulting from changes in any one of the other effects of the provision of education services. Again, standard estimates of the benefits of education based on earnings differences or the growth accounting framework will fail to capture these benefits of education services.

This discussion, then, emphasizes the partial nature of the well-being benefits of education estimated from direct returns based on earnings impacts. Such direct returns impacts may *under*estimate the true well-being effects of education services because they neglect a variety of effects of education not reflected in direct return measures. These include: (1) the value of leisure; (2) the value of home production; (3) future earnings of children; (4) health effects; (5) fertility effects, (6) consumption effects; (7) labor-market search effects; (8) income distribution effects; (9) criminal activity effects; (10) social cohesion effects; and (11) technological diffusion effects. However, other factors suggest that such direct returns estimates yield *over*estimates of the well-being effects of education. Reductions in mother's home time due to education reduce leisure and may reduce the productivity of home time reflected in children's future earnings. These effects of education—either positive or negative—are not reflected in direct returns estimates. Moreover, earnings impacts may not reflect the aggregate impact of education on productivity if labor markets are in disequilibrium and adjust via changes in unemployment levels rather than wage rates. Intuition, and it is only that, suggests that on balance the former factors far outweigh the latter ones—that the true economic well-being effects are substantially greater than those reflected in direct returns. It is to some of the evidence regarding these former factors that we now turn.

EDUCATION AND ECONOMIC WELL-BEING: SOME EVIDENCE ON INDIRECT CHANNELS OF IMPACT

As the last section emphasizes, the contribution of education to economic well-being is much broader than is reflected in increases in market wages or in measured economic growth. Evidence indicates that education influences home productivity (particularly efficiency in raising children), health of oneself and one's children (and thus aggregate health status), nutritional intake (which also influences personal and family health), fertility and contraception (permitting closer attainment of desired family size), amount and type of criminal behavior, and finally distribution of earnings and income. This section is a partial review of some of this evidence. The effects described represent the impact of education with tastes held constant. If, alternatively, education affects these variables by changing individual tastes, the welfare impacts of education are more problematic. In the following sections, we first review the literature on efficiency impacts not reflected in wage or earnings differences and then the contribution of education to economic well-being through altering the income distribution.

Fertility Effects of Education

Education increases the value of a person's time. Since children are relatively time-intensive goods—particularly for women—a rise in the value of a woman's time is likely to lead to a substitution away from children. One model of this relationship between fertility and women's education has been labeled the "new home economics" (Becker 1965; Mincer 1962; Willis 1973). In this framework, education is related to fertility by later marriage, later child bearing, closer spacing, and more efficient contraceptive use.

Empirical work based on this framework generally employs simple reduced form and linear specifications as approximations to estimate the equations of a complex system. The assumption is made that children are relatively intensive with respect to mothers' but not fathers' time. This suggests that a partial effect of increased women's education through the increase in the value of their time is a decrease in the demand for quantity of children (or substitution away from children). The increase in potential income resulting from increased education leads to a greater demand for normal goods—including children. Most evidence suggests a net negative association between women's education and fertility (that is, the quantity of children) (see Michael 1973; Willis 1973; and DeTray 1973).

In studies including wife's opportunity cost in addition to her education, Wolfe (1979) and Cain and Dooley (1976) find that opportunity costs have the expected negative sign but that education itself has a positive sign. This argues that the effect of education on fertility through changing tastes may well be positive. The negative effect through changing opportunities generally dominates, however.

A further set of effects emphasized by Pennsylvania School (see Easterlin, Pollak, and Wachter 1980) and World Bank researchers (see Cochrane, 1979) are biological or supply factors. More education tends to lead to later age at marriage and therefore less exposure to conception—an effect that is expected to reduce fertility. However, in terms of biological factors, more education tends to improve health and diet, factors that increase fecundity (the ability to successfully bear children). This indirect effect is likely to increase fertility.

In sum, the evidence suggests that education services lead to a reduction in completed family size (see Mincer 1974; Birdsall 1982; and Easterlin 1968). To the extent that this represents greater efficiency in achieving desired family size and greater efficiency in producing child services (through child quality), this represents an improvement in well-being.

Additional evidence on the effect of education on fertility is provided in the literature on contraceptive use. If "child services" (thought of as the quality-adjusted hours of children) are viewed as a consumption good entering parents' utility functions, it follows that securing the optimal amount of child services will maximize utility. In effect, because child services require monetary and time expenditure, parents weigh the benefits of a prospective child to the net expenditure in order to obtain their desired family size. If the net value of a conception is negative, the household will improve its well-being by lowering the probability of conception. One way to do this is to use contraceptives. However, contraceptive use involves costs (in terms of expenditures on contraceptives, foregone sexual gratification, or conflicts with religious beliefs) so that parents may demand more children (use fewer or less efficient contraceptives) than they would if contraception were less costly.

Better educated couples may be able to reduce the probability of conception at lower cost than less well-educated couples through greater receptivity to new ideas, increased awareness of new techniques, increased efficiency of use of any contraceptives (Michael 1973), and increased efficiency in the selection of contraceptives. Several studies (Whelpton, Campbell, and Patterson 1966; Ryder and Westoff 1971; Michael and Willis 1976; and Rosensweig and Seiver 1982) provide evidence that better educated women have more knowledge of contraceptives and employ more effective techniques. For example, Ryder and Westoff found that better educated couples use oral contraceptives more frequently, are more informed of the timing of the ovulatory cycle, and are more likely to approve of contraceptive use. Rosensweig and Seiver find that conditional on birth intentions, women with more schooling are more likely to adopt newer, more effective contraceptive techniques and are also more likely to use traditional contraceptive techniques compared to no contraceptive use. This, in turn, suggests that education helps families achieve their desired family size—a well-being benefit generally not recognized in the returns to education literature and not measured by observing education-related differences in labor market returns.

Infant Mortality, Child Health, and Child Quality Effects of Education

As suggested above, child services yield economic well-being, and one component of child services is the quality of children. To the extent that education increases efficiency in producing child quality, well-being is also affected. In the work on fertility and education, child quality and quantity are viewed as substitutes in the household production of child services; education's effect on child quality also influences fertility.

Moreover, because an experience of infant mortality decreases well-being, this is also a channel by which education generates a return not measured in earnings differences. A number of studies have found that education has a positive impact on child survival: Mothers with more education are more likely to have a child survive (Wolfe and Behrman 1982). Similarly, better educated mothers are less likely to have low birth-weight children (which tend to have a lower health stock) (Birch and Gussow 1970).

Mothers' education has a positive effect on the height and weight of young children, and among school-age children mothers' education is also associated with good health. Edwards and Grossman (1980), using the Health Examination Survey, a national sample of over 3,000 children collected in 1963 to 1965, found mothers' education to be the only socioeconomic factor associated with a large set of children's health measures among children 6–11. Measuring health as a latent variable within a simultaneous structural equation model, Wolfe and van der Gaag (1981) also find a significant, though small, positive effect of mothers' education on children's health. In another study using the HES data, Edwards and Grossman (1979) find an indirect positive effect of mother's education on child health and intellectual development. The path is from mother's education to improved child's health, which has a positive association with intellectual development.

Increases in parents' education are also likely to affect other dimensions of child quality. For example, another form of increased efficiency in home production is through production of nutrition. In a study of the United

States (Chernichovsky and Coate 1979) and another of a developing country (Wolfe and Behrman 1982), an additional year of a mother's education is associated with a significant improvement in nutrition for each family member, although in a study of Colombia, Heller and Drake (1979) find a more ambiguous effect of education on child nutrition and health.

Father's education is also a determinant of child quality. One early study (Morgan, David, Cohen, and Brazer 1962) found education of the father to be the most important determinant of the education of their children who are heads of households. Children of fathers with more education attain more education and all the benefits that go with it. In a 1972 study, Robert Michael, using the NBER/Census Bureau Consumer Anticipation Survey of about 4,500 households, found that parents with more education expected a higher education level for their children.

While a good deal of evidence indicates that education affects both the number and quality of children, there is little evidence of the effect of child services on either the well-being of parents (whose education level is at issue) or the social benefits of this component of education's effects. A few studies have tried to estimate the total social value of such intergenerational effects. These are limited to first-generation types of benefits generally included in the human-capital framework—namely, the increments in childrens' earnings attributable to parents' education. A study by Swift and Weisbrod (1965) found that benefits of elementary and secondary education increase by 7 percent when such intergenerational benefits are included. Spiegelman (1968) estimates still larger benefits by measuring both the traditional childrens' earnings benefits discounted back twenty years and private benefits of the parents attributable to utility increases associated with children's earnings increases, which he estimates as a fraction (0.3) of the children's earnings benefits. Both of these studies indicate that a full estimate of the social benefits of education (including intergenerational effects) is in excess of the private benefits related to market earnings differentials.

Thus, parents' education may influence many aspects of child quality—health, education, achievement, and future labor market success. Underlying these influences is a hypothesis that education increases the productivity of time spent in home production or at least in "child quality" production. Leibowitz (1975) has examined whether an increase in mother's education leads to an increase in home productivity. She assumes that in equilibrium, a woman will equate the value of her home time to her wage rate. As a result, observed differences in home time of women of different education levels with children of varying ages provides a basis for imputing the value of home time. The essence of her approach is to use the value of a mother's time in the market (her wage rate) to estimate the value of home time, based on the allocation of her time between the market and home.

She observes that for women with small children, education is positively related to *both* the number of hours of home time *and* the value of home production per hour. As a result, the value of home production relative to the market wage is greater for better educated women with small children than those with less education.

Leibowitz' results, estimated for 1959 based on the 1/1000 sample of the U.S. census, show that college-educated women with a child of three to five years work somewhat less than women with less education (three weeks less compared to those with a grade school education and 1.8 weeks less than high school educated women). There is a somewhat smaller differential for each child six to eleven years present. Women with high school and college education work about one week less than those with a grade school education.

This evidence suggests that the increase in market wages resulting from increased education underestimates the increase in women's total productivity attributable to education. When only actual earnings increases are included, women's time spent in child rearing will not be included in the measurement. To fully capture this effect, a full-time labor market equivalent value must be adjusted upward to reflect the fact that home time is valued above the market wage for more educated women with young children.

Gronau (1973) also finds that better educated women have a higher shadow-price or value of time with the presence of small children. The presence of a child under three years was found to increase the value of a woman's time by 30 percent if she is a college graduate. Hill and Stafford's (1980) results on time allocation are consistent with this implied increased value of home child-care among more educated women.

A final impact of education operating through nonmarket home production activities concerns the efficiency of the production process for home services. According to Michael (1976), education is like new technology in the home. Households of better educated individuals have more access to knowledge, facts, and ideas and hence are able to act more efficiently. This also may include more efficient market expenditures. This implies that families with more education can do the same home tasks more efficiently, implying that they are better off even if they have the same available time and money as less educated households. Michael tests this theory by comparing three representative households that vary by income and education.[16] On the basis of this comparison he finds that education improves a family's well-being just as income improves their well-being. This is interpreted as evidence of an increase in nonmarket productivity due to increased education.

Thus, there is other evidence that parental schooling, particularly that of the mother, has a widespread positive impact on child quality. These are additional gains from education that are generally not counted in estimates of the benefits of education. Increasing parents' education appears to increase home production in terms of infant and child health, child nutrition, child education (and thereby future market success), and the efficiency of the production process by which home services are produced. All of these impacts contribute to economic well-being.

Personal Health Effects of Education

Consistent with a human-capital framework, investment in education may be joint with investment in health status. Improved health status is human capital in its own right and, like education, will have some effects that are measured by earnings differences, some that are private but not captured in earnings differences, and some that are external to the individual. In recent years, substantial literature on the correlates of health status has appeared; education is often one of the relevant independent variables.

In an early paper, Michael Grossman (1975) set out a model to explore the effect of schooling on health. Health is treated as a stock (a type of capital) that can be increased through investment and depreciates over time. The stock of health increases available productive time. Education serves to increase the wage rate (and so the value of productive time); however, education also increases the productivity of time spent on the production of health.

Grossman's estimates, using the NBER-Thorndike data, suggest that each year of schooling increases health by 1 to 3.5 percent (depending on whether poor health was controlled for). A wife's education also has a positive influence on her husband's health, and, in fact, the coefficient is larger than husband's own schooling. Finally, using logit analysis, Grossman finds that schooling has a positive and statistically significant effect on the probability of survival. Indeed, it is the single most significant factor in an extensive list of independent variables (including intelligence and income). At the expected mortality rate, a one-year increase in education lowered the probability of death by 0.4 percentage points. Orcutt et al. (1977) found a similar relationship between education and probability of death.

These findings suggest that education has an important indirect effect on productivity that operates through an individual's own health status (see also Fuchs 1974; Feldstein 1979; Leigh 1981; Lee 1982). Only to the extent that this form of human-capital increment is reflected in market earnings will it be captured in standard estimates of the returns to education. These findings also suggest a positive return from wife's education to spouse's health—an effect likely to be captured in standard benefit estimates only to the extent that own and spouse's education are correlated. And the evidence suggests that education increases the probability of survival. To the extent this is so, a portion of the benefits of education from this source are increased lifetime earnings. For all of these health or survival effects—increased probability of survival, survival past retirement, and improved health over one's own lifetime—the willingness to pay of the individual is not captured. Nor are the external effects of improved health or survival effects (for example, spouse's or children's improved health due to an individual's improved health or the willingness to pay of family and friends for increased survival and better health of a loved one).

Crime Effects of Education

The decision to perform a criminal act can be viewed as a utility-maximizing response to economic opportunities and, as such, is likely to be affected by education. While education's effect on market wages is well-documented, Ehrlich (1975) suggests that education is also likely to increase the productivity of an individual in illegitimate activities, particularly in avoiding detection. Since expected lifetime legitimate earnings are increased through education, the "potential cost" of detection is higher. Hence, individuals with more education are likely to engage in "more profitable" illegitimate activities, if any, and not the most common property crimes.

Ehrlich surveys the limited evidence from a variety of studies to show that those who commit property crimes have relatively low education. However, the evidence is weak since, if his model is correct, criminals with more education are less likely to be detected. The effect of education on illegitimate activities is uncertain.

Income-Distribution Effects of Education

As has been emphasized, if people care about income distribution or income poverty, the effects of education on income distribution may contribute to or detract from economic well-being. If less inequality is valued, for example, and if education is equalizing, the benefits attributed to education must be supplemented for this reason. A basic question in measuring the benefits of education is whether education equalizes income or not. Education has been viewed for many years as a means of increasing economic mobility and therefore promoting income equality. However, a number of researchers (e.g., Mincer 1974; Chiswick 1974) have found that income is more unequally distributed as the result of education and the returns to education. Others (e.g., Marin and Psacharopoulos 1976; Tinbergen 1975; and Pechman 1970) conclude that education is an equalizer of the income distribution.

Marin and Psacharopoulos present an insightful way of seeing the source of different findings. Begin with a standard human-capital model measuring returns to education,

$$\log Y_s = \log Y_0 + \sum_{j=1}^{S} \log(1+r_j) + u, \tag{1.1}$$

and rewrite it in estimatable form:

$$\log Y_s = \log Y_0 + rS + u, \tag{1.1a}$$

where Y_s = earnings of person with s years of education,
$\quad\quad Y_0$ = earnings of person with zero schooling,
$\quad\quad r$ = rate of return,
$\quad\quad u$ = error term measuring the effects of omitted variables.

Then by dropping the variance and covariance of u and estimating $\text{Var}(\log Y_s) = \text{Var}(\log rS)$, one can obtain an estimate of the degree to which income inequality is associated with the current education distribution. In order for researchers to analyze and predict the impact of changes in education (and rates of return) on the income distribution, this equation can be approximated by one that disaggregates the right-hand side into its component parts:

$$\text{Var}(\log Y_s) = \bar{r}^2 \, \text{Var}(S) + \bar{S}^2 (\text{Var})r + 2\bar{r}\bar{S} \, \text{Cov}(r,s).$$

As Marin and Psacharopolous point out, some researchers (e.g., Mincer, Chiswick) simplify and assume that r and S are independent random variables. In this case, they estimate $\text{Var}(\log Y_s) = \bar{r}^2 \, \text{Var}(S) + \bar{S}^2 \, \text{Var}(r) + \text{Var}(S) \, \text{Var}(r)$. Since all of these terms on the right-hand side are positive, increases in the level of schooling must lead to increases in inequality. If, instead, r and S are allowed to be dependent[17] and if the covariance of r and S is negative, the income distribution can be made more or less equal through increases in S, depending on the relative size of the positive and negative terms.

Marin and Psacharopoulos perform estimates of the response of the $\text{Var}(\log Y_s)$ to changes in schooling assuming both independence and dependence. For a close approximation to the level of actual schooling in the United States, where the rate of return declines as schooling increases,[18] they find a one-year increase in schooling of the population leads to a 15 percent increase in income inequality assuming independence and a 10 percent decrease in income inequality assuming the rate of return declines as schooling increases (dependence). This suggests that a good deal of the dispute over the income-distributional effects of education stems from different underlying models or assumptions incorporated into the model and that, at best, the estimates are offering only clues, not clear answers.

Tinbergen (1975) uses an alternative model to conclude that education equalizes the income distribution. His model is based on a supply/demand race between technological shifts toward more highly educated labor on the demand side of the labor market and increases in education of the labor force on the supply side. Equalization depends on the relative rate of increase between the percentage of the population educated and the technology-based demand for educated workers. Reductions in inequality occur only if the expansion of education overtakes the technology's demand for better educated workers. He concludes that income inequality could be halved by either doubling the proportion of the population with higher education or increasing secondary school enrollment to 90 or 95 percent and doubling higher education enrollment.[19]

Dresch (1975) also analyzes returns to education and income distribution effects by examining technology's demand for educated workers. In his analysis, the continued high returns to education in the United States through the 1960s and early 1970s were due to technologically-based demand changes and rapid growth of sectors employing highly educated labor. Using estimates of substitution elasticities from a model employing fitted production functions, fairly nonrestrictive labor demand models, and a supply model sensitive to demographic and relative wage changes, Dresch estimates that the ratio of college graduate to nongraduate wages will decrease about 13 percent from 1970 to 1990 in response to the relative increase in higher education. This will equalize the income distribution. As with Tinbergen, Dresch finds that equalization depends on the relative rates of increase of educated persons and the technology-based demand for labor.

Others argue that schooling has little effect on income inequality. Even if schooling is targeted at "disadvantaged groups," Jencks (1972), Levin (1971), and Thurow (1972) argue, there will be little change in the inequality of the income distribution. According to Jencks, education alone explains little of the variation in men's incomes. Even if traditionally disadvantaged groups (e.g., nonwhites, women, and working-class whites) increase their education, their incomes will not increase substantially because of constraints on the access of these persons to highly paid positions. Because most of the financial benefit of education comes via access to more highly paid occupations, increasing or equalizing education for everyone would not equalize incomes since, in Jencks's words (1972: 224), "giving everyone more credentials cannot provide everyone with access to the best-paid occupations"; it follows that "equalizing everyone's educational attainment would have virtually no effect on income inequality."

Levin and Thurow also argue that education is not an effective means of equalizing income. According to Thurow, the labor market should be characterized as one of job competition rather than wage competition.

Education determines one's position in the labor queue, while productivity is determined by on-the-job training after one's position is attained. Since education affects only one's position, not productivity, educating an additional person leads to equalizing within an education group but may accentuate the differences between groups.

Evaluating the contribution of education to well-being via its impact on income inequality or poverty also requires evaluating the distribution of education services. Clearly, the distributional impact will be different if educational services are targeted on the disadvantaged population as opposed to, say, being distributed equally. One common view holds that the public/private financing of higher levels of education has a regressive effect on the income distribution insofar as the children of upper socioeconomic groups have a greater probability of attending college than children from less well-to-do parents. An alternative view is that public subsidies or loan programs allow lower-income children to attend institutions of higher education. This increase in socioeconomic mobility reduces income inequality, which should be included in any measure of social benefits.

Evidence on the mobility effect reveals limited response to subsidies, but the elasticity is low (approximately 0.3) (see R.A. Freeman 1969). Even if all individuals who attend colleges *only* if they receive subsidization are from low-income families, Freeman argues that 75 percent of the subsidies are allocated to students from higher-income families.

Rivlin (1975) has also addressed the question of the distributional effects of targeted education programs. In her view, even such targeting efforts will not substantially reduce income inequality: Only a limited number of the poor receive such subsidization, education does not have large income impacts, these income impacts are realized only over the long run, and the relative earnings of educated workers have begun to erode.

From this brief survey, then, it seems clear that evidence on the effect of education on income distribution is not conclusive. This is due to several factors: data limitations; lack of clarity about how the demand for educated labor interacts with the supply of educated labor; existence of a dependent relationship between the returns to education and the quantity of education; and distribution of additional education services. However, all of these studies only include the *earned* income effects of education in measuring the income distribution effects. The effect of education on the distribution of nonearned income or a more comprehensive definition of full income including the value of leisure time has not been analyzed. As a result, the influence of education on inequality in distribution of well-being is likely to be understated. In any case, it seems quite impossible at this stage of understanding to attribute any social well-being benefits to education operating through the income-distribution effects. Neither the social benefits of reduced inequality nor the equalizing effects of educational services are known.

In sum, then, the indirect effects of education on economic well-being that we have discussed point to the following conclusions. Education tends to reduce completed family size. This is partly explained by the increased ability to achieve desired family size through more efficient contraceptive use. In addition, education leads to more efficiency in producing higher quality children, in part through improved nutrition. Since the utility from children (according to the new home economics) derives from child services that depend on both child quantity and quality, more education leads to a reduction in the quantity of children desired through its effects in increasing child quality. Education improves several dimensions of child quality: child health, intellectual development, education, and expected income. Education also leads to greater efficiency in consumption. Thus, more education indirectly leads to greater utility through improved market expenditures. Still further, education improves own health and spouse's health and decreases expected mortality. To the extent that these changes do not lead to wage increases, their effects on well-being are not captured in standard estimates of the benefits of education. There is also some evidence that crime may be reduced due to increased education. Finally, evidence on the effect of education on the income distribution presents an unclear overall effect, although targeted education policies, or large increases in the college-educated, may decrease income inequality.

Evidence on other effects of education, such as social cohesion, leadership, and the speed of technological diffusion, are not discussed. The first two effects are not included because there is little documentation of these effects, the last because another paper in this series deals specifically with this issue.[20]

IMPLICATIONS FOR POLICY

Our discussion suggests that the provision of education services is likely to have a substantially larger impact on economic well-being than is estimated by studies based upon either the direct-returns or growth-accounting frameworks. The primary contributions to this overall impact, which are not reflected in the standard studies, include health and longevity related effects, fertility and child quality effects, income-distribution effects, and social cohesion effects. The conclusion that standard estimates understate the total effect of education services reflects the judgment that the overstatement of the well-being effects of education in the standard estimates (due to erroneous estimates of the value of the home time of spouses and the displacement effects emphasized in disequilibrium models) is exceeded by the health, fertility, home productivity, social cohesion, and distributional effects of education on well-being which are not measured in the standard estimates.[21]

This conclusion suggests that the total contribution of education to social well-being is in excess of that reported in the standard rate-of-return-to-education estimates. It does not by itself lead to any policy conclusion regarding the level of public support for education. The question of public support must rest on an appraisal of the public-good component of total educational benefits, externalities associated with the provision of education services, or other market failures restricting the ability of the private sector to optimally respond to the demands of individuals reflecting the private-goods benefits of education. The preceding discussion does not directly address this question, nor does this discussion shed much light on the optimal composition of resources allocated by educational services. The internal rate of return on marginal expenditures in various directions is required for judgments on this issue.

This discussion does suggest some policy-related conclusions. First, if those components of economic well-being generated by education services but not captured in the standard estimates (e.g., health and nutrition benefits) are private goods, private decisions will reflect them automatically, with no implication for public support.[22] This is so, of course, unless market failures (e.g., private capital market failures) restrict the ability of individuals to secure the desired level of education services privately. Many of the non-human-capital benefits we have identified have this private-good character: A large share of health and nutrition benefits, fertility benefits, and job search benefits are of this sort. Others, however, are dominated by externality or public-good traits. These include the income distribution and social cohesion effects, and some share of the health, technology, and fertility effects. To the extent that these channels of benefit comprise a larger share of total benefits than is commonly believed—and our review of the evidence does suggest major well-being effects through these channels—increases in public support toward education would be justified.

Second, to the extent that these less recognized channels of well-being effects are public-good or externality dominated (or if private good in character but constrained due to market imperfections), the allocation of resources within the education sector should emphasize these outputs. This implies that educational services that induce behavioral change related to fertility, health status, or labor market search or that secure desirable changes in the inequality of income (e.g., compensatory education) should be emphasized.

NOTES

1. We use the terms "schooling" and "education" interchangeably in this paper, while recognizing that the former concept—that generally used in empirical studies—is narrower than the latter.

2. See Rosen (1977) for a good survey of the empirical human-capital literature.

3. One could claim that by not choosing private schools the parents of public-school children are also making a private choice regarding the quantity of education services to be provided to their children. However, because public education services are provided at a zero price, the notion that an effective private choice has been made appears to stretch the meaning of that term.

4. The notion of private benefits in the case of elementary and secondary education is not straightforward. Clearly some of the benefit is appropriated by the student and will be reflected in labor market earnings or consumption benefits, as in the case of higher education. In this case, however, some private benefits will be received by the parents of the student. We will label both as private sources of benefit.

5. This definition of willingness to pay is that of the compensating variation—the amount the individual would have to be compensated to maintain utility constant in the case of, say, an increase in the price of a good or service, evaluated at the new set of relative prices.

6. This concept of well-being effects rests on the same theoretical basis as the concept of benefits in benefit/cost analysis (see Haveman and Weisbrod 1975).

7. Most of this research has focused on the benefits of changes in air and water quality, which are by their nature public goods. A review and critique of this research is found in A.M. Freeman (1979).

8. This conclusion is based on the assumption that aggregate willingness to pay equals the summation of that of all individuals benefitted by the good or service—that there are no weights other than unity attached to any individual benefits. This is a standard assumption (see Harberger 1971).

9. Education is also likely to affect nonmonetary differences among jobs—differences in the dirtiness, difficulty, and unpleasantness of jobs, as well as fringe benefits (see Duncan 1976; Lucas 1977). The willingness to pay for these job quality differences should, like leisure differences, be reflected in the aggregate benefits of education.

10. A stylized model of this form can be represented by

$$U = U(N, Q, Z),$$

where N, Q, and Z represent the number of children, child quality, and non-child sources of satisfaction. Q and Z are produced in the home according to production functions

$Q = f(T_c/N, X_c/N)$ where T_c = time spent on children,

X_c = market goods allocated to children,

$Z = g(T_Z, X_Z)$,   where T_Z = time spent on Z,

X_Z = market goods allocated to Z.

Under certain assumptions (e.g., linear homogeneous production), child services (C) is a function of average child quality:

$$C = NQ = f(T_c, X_c).$$

There is a time and income constraint: In full income terms,

$$I = \Pi_c NQ + \Pi_Z Z = \Pi_c C + \Pi_Z Z$$

where Π_i are shadow prices of C and Z, respectively.

11. Figure 1–1, however, does suggest that education-induced changes in fertility may affect productivity by affecting earnings and the quantity or quality of home time spent with children.

12. Increases in health status might also increase the value of home production and leisure time and, through them, the value of "home time" provided to children. These are ignored in the diagram.

13. The correct basis for measuring the well-being effects of increases in longevity also comprises the willingness-to-pay concept. Its use in evaluating the benefits of increases in longevity and well-time, irrespective of the source of the increase, is analyzed in Mishan (1971). Note that to the extent that health care costs are not individually borne, the benefits of improved health status in the form of reductions in health-care costs are not reflected in private willingness to pay. This component then must be estimated independently and added to willingness-to-pay benefits.

14. The sign on these effects is not unambiguously positive, however. While education may well increase the value of certain types of consumption (e.g., music), it is likely to decrease the value of other consumption forms (e.g., stock car races). Therefore, from society's point of view, the net well-being impact of education through this complementary consumption effect depends on the utility function of the evaluators.

15. As R. Nelson (1973: 467) stated: "The production and installation of new technology requires educated workers; further, in the absence of technological advance educated workers would be doing nothing different than uneducated workers and would not be more productive."

16. 1 has more income than other 2; 2 more education but same income as 3; and 3 the same education as 1 and same income as 2.

17. Dependency of r and S will exist if (1) r depends on the level of schooling, or (2) those expecting higher rates of return (r) select more schooling. Both of these seem quite likely and are consistent with research in the area.

18. They perform this estimation using a parameter derived from the quadratic formulation of Mincer.

19. The estimates are based on national data of developed countries.

20. This paper, while produced as part of the N.I.E. research program on education and productivity, is not printed here. See Mansfield (1982).

21. In a related study (Haveman and Wolfe 1984) we provide an empirical estimate and conclude that "standard rate of return estimates of the benefits of incremental schooling may capture only about three-fifths of the full (marketed plus non-marketed) value of education."

22. This might, however, explain the disparity between declining measured rates of return to higher education and continued high demand for higher education.

REFERENCES

Abramovitz, M. 1956. *Resources and Output Trends in the United States since 1870.* New York: National Bureau of Economic Research.

Becker, G. 1964. *Human Capital: A Theoretical and Empirical Analysis.* New York: Columbia University Press, NBER.

———. 1965. "A Theory of the Allocation of Time." *Economic Journal* 75 (September): 493–517.

Birch, H., and Gussow, J.D. 1970. *Disadvantaged Children: Health, Nutrition, and School Failure.* New York: Harcourt, Brace and World.

Birdsall, N.M. 1982. "The Impact of School Availability and Quality on Children's Schooling in Brazil." Working Paper no. 82–8. Washington, D.C.: The World Bank.

Blaug, M. 1976. "The Empirical Status of Human Capital Theory: A Slightly Jaundiced Survey." *Journal of Economic Literature* 14, no. 3 (September): 827–55.

Bowen, W. 1964. *Economic Aspects of Education: Three Essays.* Princeton: Princeton University, Economics Department, Industrial Relations Section.

Cain G., and Dooley, M. 1976. "Estimation of a Model of Labor Supply, Fertility, and Wages of Married Women." *Journal of Political Economy* 84, no. 4, pt. 2 (August): S179–S200.

Chernichovsky, D., and Coate, D. 1979. "An Economic Analysis of Diet, Growth and Health of Young Children in the United States." Cambridge, Mass.: NBER Working Paper 416.

Chiswick, B.R. 1974. *Income Inequality.* New York: Columbia University Press, NBER.

Christensen, L., and D. Jorgenson. 1973. "Measuring Economic Performance in the Private Sector." In *The Measurement of Economic and Social Performance,* edited by M. Moss. New York: National Bureau of Economic Research.

Christensen, L.; D. Jorgenson; and D. Cummings. 1981. "Relative Productivity Levels, 1947–1973: An International Comparison." *European Economic Review* 16, no. 1 (May).

Cochrane, S.H. 1979. *Fertility and Education: What Do We Really Know?* Washington, D.C.: World Bank, Staff Occasional Papers, 26.

DaVanzo, Julie. 1983. "Repeat Migration in the U.S.: Who Moves Back and Who Moves On?" *Review of Economics and Statistics* (May): 552–559.

Denison, E. 1962. *The Sources of Economic Growth in the United States.* New York: Committee for Economic Development.

———. 1967. *Why Growth Rates Differ.* Washington, D.C.: The Brookings Institution.

———. 1979. *Accounting for Slower Economic Growth: The United States in the 1970s.* Washington, D.C.: The Brookings Institution.

DeTray, D.N. 1973. "Child Quality and the Demand for Children." *Journal of Political Economy* 81, no. 2, pt. 2 (March/April): S70–S95.

Dresch, S. 1975. "Demography, Technology, and Higher Education: Toward a Formal Model of Educational Adaptation." *Journal of Political Economy* 83 (June): 535–69.

Duncan, G.J. 1976. "Earnings Functions and Non-Pecuniary Benefits." *Journal of Human Resources* 11, no. 4 (Fall): 464–83.

Easterlin, R.A. 1968. *Population, Labor Force and Long Swings in Economic Growth: The American Experience.* New York: National Bureau of Economic Research.

Easterlin, R.A.; R. Pollak; and M. Wachter. 1980. "Towards a More General Economic Model of Fertility Determination: Endogenous Preferences and Natural Fertility." In *Population and Economic Change in Developing Countries,* edited by R.A. Easterlin, pp. 81–135. Chicago: University of Chicago Press.

Edwards, L.N., and M. Grossman. 1979. "The Relationship Between Children's Health and Intellectual Development." In *Health: What Is it Worth?,* edited by S. Mushkin, pp. 273–314. Elmsford, N.Y.: Pergamon Press.

———. 1980. "Children's Health and the Family." In *Annual Series of Research in Health Economics,* Vol. 2, edited by R.M. Scheffler, pp. 35–85. Greenwich, Conn.: JAI Press.

Ehrlich, I. 1975. "On the Relation Between Education and Crime." In *Education, Income, and Human Behavior,* edited by F.T. Juster, pp. 313–38. New York: McGraw-Hill.

Feldstein, P.J. 1979. *Health Care Economics.* New York: John Wiley.

Fields, G.S. 1972. "Private and Social Returns to Education in Labor Surplus Economics." *Eastern Africa Economic Review* 4 (June): 41–62.

Freeman, A.M. 1979. *The Benefits of Environmental Improvement.* Baltimore: Johns Hopkins Press.

Freeman, R.A. 1969. "Federal Assistance to Higher Education through Income Tax Credit." In Joint Economic Committee, *The Economics and Financing of Higher Education in the United States,* pp. 665–83. Washington: Government Printing Office.

Fuchs, V. 1974. *Who Shall Live?* New York: Basic Books.

———. 1980. "Time Preference and Health: An Exploratory Study." Working Paper No. 539. Cambridge, Mass.: National Bureau of Economic Research.

Gronau, R. 1973. "The Effect of Children on the Housewife's Value of Time." *Journal of Political Economy* 81, no. 2, pt. 2 (March/April): S168–S199.

Grossman, Michael. 1975. "The Correlation between Health and Schooling." In *Household Production and Consumption,* edited by N.E. Terleckyj, pp. 147–211. New York: National Bureau of Economic Research.

Harberger, A.C. 1971. "Three Basic Postulates for Applied Welfare Economics." *Journal of Economic Literature* 9 (September): 785–97.

Haveman, R., and B.A. Weisbrod. 1975. "Defining Benefits of Public Programs: Some Guidance for Policy Analysts." *Policy Analysis* 2, no. 1: 169–96.

Haveman, R., and Wolfe, B. 1984. "Education and Economic Well-Being: The Role of Non-Market Effects," *Journal of Human Resources,* forthcoming.

Heller, P.S., and Drake, D. 1979. "Malnutrition, Child Morbidity, and the Family Decision Process." *Journal of Development Economics* 6 (October): 203–35.

Hill, C.R., and Stafford, F.R. 1980. "Parental Care of Children: Time Diary Estimates of Quantity Predictability and Variety." *Journal of Human Resources* 15 (Spring): 219–39.

Hochman, H.M., and J.D. Rodgers. 1969. "Pareto Optimal Redistribution." *American Economic Review* 59 (September): 542–57.

Jencks, C. 1972. *Inequality.* New York: Basic Books.

Kendrick, J. 1961. *Productivity Trends in the United States.* Princeton, N.J.: Princeton University Press.

———. 1977. *Understanding Productivity: An Introduction to the Dynamics of Productivity Change.* Baltimore: Johns Hopkins Press.

Lee, L. 1982. "Health and Wage: A Simultaneous Equation Model with Multiple Discrete Indicators." *International Economic Review* 23 (February): 199–222.

Leibowitz, A. 1975. "Education and the Allocation of Women's Time." In *Education, Income, and Human Behavior,* edited by F.T. Juster, pp. 171–98. New York: McGraw-Hill.

Leigh, J. 1981. "Hazardous Occupations, Illness and Schooling." *Economics of Education Review* 1, no. 3 (Summer): 381–88.

Levin, H.M. 1971. "Review of Private Wealth and Public Education." *Planning and Changing* 1 (January): 194–99.

Lucas, R. 1977. "Hedonic Wage Equations and Psychic Wages in the Returns to Schooling." *American Economic Review* 761 (September): 549–58.

Mansfield, Edwin. 1982. "Education, R&D, and Productivity Growth." Paper prepared for The National Institute of Education, Washington, D.C.

Marin, A., and G. Psacharopoulos. 1976. "Schooling and the Income Distribution." *Review of Economics and Statistics* 58 (August): 332–38.

Marshall, A. 1890. *Principles of Economics.* London: Macmillan.

Michael, R.T. 1972. "The Role of Education in Production within the Household." Paper submitted to the National Center for Educational Research and Development, Washington, D.C.

———. 1973. "Education and the Derived Demand for Children." *Journal of Political Economy* 81, no. 2, pt. 2 (March/April): S128–S164.

———. 1975. "Education and Consumption." In *Education, Income, and Human Behavior,* edited by F.T. Juster, pp. 235–52. New York: McGraw-Hill.

Michael, R.T., and R.J. Willis. 1976. "Contraception and Fertility: Household Production under Uncertainty." In *Household Production and Consumption,* edited by N.E. Terleckyj. New York: National Bureau of Economic Research.

Mincer, J. 1958. "Investments in Human Capital and Personal Income Distribution." *Journal of Political Economy* 66 (August): 291–302.

———. 1962. "On-the-Job-Training: Costs, Returns and Some Implications." *Journal of Political Economy* 70 (October): 50–79.

———. 1970. "The Distribution of Labor Incomes: A Survey." *Journal of Economic Literature* 8 (March): 1–26.

———. 1974. *Schooling, Experience, and Earnings.* New York: Columbia University Press.

Mishan, E. 1971. "Evaluation of Life and Limb: A Theoretical Approach." *Journal of Political Economy* 79 (July–August): 687–705.

Morgan, J.; M. David; W. Cohen; and H. Brazer. 1962. *Income and Welfare in the United States.* New York: McGraw-Hill.

Nelson, R. 1973. "Recent Exercises in Growth Accounting: New Understanding or Dead End." *American Economic Review* 63 (June): 462–68.

Orcutt, G.H.; S.D. Franklin; R. Mendelsohn; and J.D. Smith. 1977. "Does Your Probability of Death Depend on Your Environment? A Microanalytic Study." *American Economic Review* 67 (February): 260-64.

Pechman, J. 1970. "The Distributional Effects of Public Higher Education in California." *Journal of Human Resources* 5, no. 3 (Summer): 361-70.

Rivlin, A. 1975. "Income Distribution—Can Economists Help? *American Economic Review* 65 (May): 1-15.

Rosen, S. 1977. "Human Capital: A Survey of Empirical Research." In *Research in Labor Economics,* edited by R. Ehrenberg, pp. 3-40. Greenwich, Conn.: JAI Press.

Rosensweig, M.R., and D. Seiver. 1982. "Education and Contraceptive Choice: A Conditional Demand Framework." *International Economic Review* 23, no. 1 (February): 171-98.

Ryder, N.B., and C.F. Westoff. 1971. *Reproduction in the United States, 1965.* Princeton, N.J.: Princeton University Press.

Sen, A.K. 1972. "Control Areas and Accounting Prices: An Approach to Economic Evaluation." *Economic Journal* 82 (March Supplement): 486-501.

Spiegelman, R.G. 1968. "A Benefit/Cost Model to Evaluate Educational Programs." *Socio-Economic Planning Services* (February): 443-60.

Stiglitz, J. 1974. "Wage Determinations and Unemployment in LDC's. I: The Labor Turnover Model." *Quarterly Journal of Economics* 88 (May): 194-227.

Stone, R. 1980. "Whittling Away at the Residual: Some Thoughts on Denison's Growth Accounting." *Journal of Economic Literature* 18 (September): 1539-43.

Swift, W.J., and B.A. Weisbrod. 1965. "On the Monetary Value of Education's Intergenerational Effects." *Journal of Political Economy* 73 (December): 643-49.

Thurow, Lester. 1972. "Education and Income Inequality." *The Public Interest* 28 (Summer): 66-81.

Tinbergen, J. 1975. *Income Distribution: Analysis and Policies.* Amsterdam: North-Holland Publishing Co.

Todaro, M. 1969. "A Model of Labor Migration and Urban Unemployment in Less Developed Countries." *American Economic Review* 59: 38-48.

Welch, F. 1970. "Education in Production." *Journal of Political Economy* 78, no. 1 (January): 35-59.

Whelpton, P.K.; A.A. Campbell; and J.E. Patterson. 1966. *Fertility and Family Planning in the United States.* Princeton, N.J.: Princeton University Press.

Willis, R.J. 1973. "A New Approach to the Economic Theory of Fertility Behavior." *Journal of Political Economy* 81, no. 2, pt. 2 (March/April): 514-64.

Wolfe, B. 1979. "Child Bearing and/or Labor Force Participation: The Education Connection." *Research in Population Economics* 2, edited by J. Simon and J. DaVanzo, pp. 365-86. Greenwich, Conn.: JAI Press.

Wolfe, B., and J. Behrman. 1982. "Determinants of Child Mortality, Health and Nutrition in a Developing Country." *Journal of Development Economics* 11, no. 2 (December): 162-93.

Wolfe, B., and J. van der Gaag. 1981. "A New Health Status Index for Children." In *Health, Economics and Health Economics,* edited by J. van der Gaag and M. Perlman. Amsterdam: North-Holland Publishing Co.

Chapter 2

Economic Growth and Equal Opportunity: Conflicting or Complementary Goals in Higher Education?

W. Lee Hansen

One of the many explanations offered for economic growth slowdown in the 1970s and recent productivity declines is that redistribution policies begun in the middle and late 1960s diverted resources and attention from the ongoing task of stimulating economic growth. This explanation draws support from the considerable increase in national resources devoted to public programs, particularly those in the social welfare or human services realm, which are largely redistributive in character. If this explanation has any validity, we might expect to see some manifestations of it in the higher education sector, which historically played a major role in promoting economic growth but beginning in the mid-1960s became a testing ground for redistributive programs.

Whether the goals of economic growth and redistribution conflict in the provision and financing of higher education is not immediately clear. Economists normally assume such conflict and discuss it in the more general terms of efficiency and equity. The prevailing view is that tradeoffs must be made in the pursuit of these two quite different goals. At the moment, however, we have no good basis for assessing the extent to which there is a tradeoff or conflict between these goals in higher education. This issue has not received much attention of late because, with the acceptance by the

I am indebted to many people for their comments on all or parts of this paper, including Edwin Dean, Bella Rosenberg, Robert Lampman, Jay Stampen, Robert Haveman, Barbara Wolfe, and Wally Douma. I also thank seminar participants at the National Institute for Education and the University of Wisconsin for their perceptive questions. Lou Ann Karter assisted in the empirical work. Support for this project was provided by the National Institute of Education and the University of Wisconsin Institute for Research on Poverty.

executive and legislative branches of a broader set of redistributive goals since the early 1960s, there has been a tendency for many economists to take these redistributive goals as a given. Perhaps this is appropriate. But some sacrifices in efficiency occur as these redistributive goals are pursued.

Another view holds that equity and efficiency goals may be complementary, particularly when dealing with human investment programs such as higher education. Educating talented youth can contribute to the future growth of aggregate output. If these youth cannot finance their own education because of economic barriers, then a program of financial aid to help them overcome these barriers can be both equitable and efficient. Whether real-world situations meet this dual test of equity and efficiency is much more difficult to ascertain.

This paper examines our lack of knowledge about the nature, dimensions, and effects of the shift from efficiency to equity goals in the provision and financing of higher education. It begins with a review of this shift and then presents a brief history of the major student financial aid programs, their rationale, and expected effects. Attention is then directed to the major purpose of the paper, that of ascertaining the extent to which student financial aid changed the composition of young people attending and planning to attend college—whether it broadened access to higher education opportunities. The paper concludes with some observations on how the growing focus on redistributive policies within higher education has affected education's contribution to economic growth.

FROM GROWTH TO REDISTRIBUTION—AN OVERVIEW

Over the years college attendance has been viewed by young people, their parents, and substantial portions of society as a means of enhancing one's earning power, widening one's intellectual and social horizons, and contributing to the larger social welfare. This view, which had long been obvious to casual observers, was formally assimilated into economics during the late 1950s and early 1960s when college attendance came to be viewed as a form of "human investment" (Schultz 1960, 1961; Becker 1962). People deferred accepting fulltime jobs and instead attended college, increasing their knowledge, skills, and potential productivity so that they could gain higher earnings than if they had gone to work immediately. Of course, below-cost tuition enhanced the attractiveness of higher education, which was subsidized by taxpayers for students attending public institutions and by alumni and other donors for students attending private institutions. The economic benefits of college attendance were viewed by individuals and by society as sufficiently large relative to the costs of college to yield rates of return on these human investments that were at least comparable to those available from alternate investments (Becker 1960; Hansen 1963). These findings on private and social rates of return proved to be consistent with those of the growth economists who found educational investment to have been a prime generator of U.S. productivity growth over much of this century (Denison 1962).

Initial findings on the economic benefits of investing in human capital via education led to an explosion of research both here and abroad on the effects of schooling on individual earnings, on rates of return to investment in schooling, and on education's role in stimulating more rapid growth (Blaug 1966, 1970, 1978). Within a few years the economics of education emerged as a legitimate and flourishing specialty in economics.

While these developments were unfolding, it became apparent that substantial numbers of young people who were qualified for college did not attend because of inadequate financial resources and difficulties in getting access to needed resources (Wolfe 1954; Little 1958, 1959). Below-cost tuition was not sufficient to overcome these deterrents. Of particular concern was the so-called talent loss, reflecting the fact that many able but poorer young people could benefit from college but were unable to gain access because of their limited financial resources. The evidence also hinted that substantial numbers of qualified but financially poor high school graduates not planning to attend college had more promising futures ahead of them than did wealthier but less able students already enrolled. The very term "talent loss" suggested that removing the financial barriers to college attendance through a relatively small expenditure of public funds would be economically efficient and contribute to economic growth.

In another sense, however, this talent loss could be viewed as a distributional issue. Qualified young people from poor families deserve the same opportunities, it was claimed, as other young people even if the return to such investment might not be all that high. Everyone, by this line of argument, should have equal educational opportunities—that is, not be prevented from attending college for economic reasons. The attainment of such a goal would be reflected by smaller disparities in the probabilities of attending, persisting in, and completing college. While this view commanded some attention in the early 1960s, it lacked persuasiveness because it did not fit easily within the then-dominant policymaking concerns.

All of this was destined to change dramatically. The shift from a heavy emphasis on efficiency to equity began with the declaration of War on Poverty in 1964 and accelerated rapidly after that. One interpretation of this change follows: Because of rapid economic growth and the belief that the benefits of economic growth could and should be more widely shared, society had an obligation to help those of its members most in need, as reflected by their low incomes (Harrington 1962). But rather than merely transferring cash benefits to the poor, a more acceptable and, it was hoped, more powerful strategy was adopted (Economic Report of The President 1964). Education, training, and related services were to be provided to poor families and especially to their younger members so as to enhance their skills and knowledge and make it possible for them to earn their way out of poverty. A variety of antipoverty programs followed, many of which had strong educational and training components (Levin 1977).

Other influences were also significant. A strong push came with the release of the Coleman (1966) report, *Equality of Educational Opportunity*. This massive study directed attention to the concept of equality of educational opportunity. While the report dealt with the determinants of the cognitive achievement of elementary and secondary students, it stimulated efforts to generalize the concept of equal opportunity to higher education as well. Another important influence was the proposed negative income tax. Although not viewed as a means of assuring equal educational opportunity, it led to wider acceptance of the potential effectiveness of transfer payments in augmenting limited incomes to achieve some target level of consumption or to aid in the purchase of human investments, such as health and education, that would enhance the long-run earnings prospects of the recipients.

The shift to a more explicit focus on equity was exceptionally quick. Within the space of just a few years the question guiding policymakers changed from what would a program do to stimulate economic growth to what might it do to help the poor (Lampman 1974). In higher education the aim became that of assuring greater equality of educational opportunity as reflected in more equal enrollments rates not only across income groups but also among different race and sex groups. These developments led to the creation by both federal and state governments of student financial aid programs that increasingly used demonstrated financial need as a basis for allocating financial aid to students. The resources available grew quickly. By fiscal year 1980, federal resources for student financial aid amounted to almost $7 billion, with an additional 1 billion provided by state governments, and another $2 billion from institutions of higher education. The undetermined remaining costs were paid by students and their parents.

The focus of research also shifted. Greater attention was given to disparities in higher education spending and to differential access to college for different population groups (Folger 1970). Higher education came to be viewed by some as a mechanism that redistributed resources from the poor to the rich as a result of cost differences among institutions, selection processes that directed students of different backgrounds into different types of colleges, and the tax structure used to finance higher education (Hansen and Weisbrod 1969; Carnegie Commission 1973). The concept of equity soon became part of the jargon in the economics of higher education (Schultz 1972).

This brief account indicates the profound shift in both thinking and policy that occurred in the 1960s and 1970s—from a heavy focus on questions of efficiency prior to the middle 1960s to an almost exclusive focus on equity or income redistribution after that. The speed of this transformation is remarkable. Unfortunately, since no full treatment of the transformation exists, its details must be left for others to tell.

Now, after over a decade in which equity concerns dominated, we appear to be entering a new era. It is likely to be characterized by increasingly sharp conflict over the goals of efficiency and equity. The tradeoffs remain exasperatingly unclear because of the absence of systematic efforts to determine whether equity-oriented financial aid programs produced the effects they were designed and created to achieve. Have they stimulated greater proportions of lower-income students to attend college and to persist to graduation? Have they helped generate additional private and social benefits for their recipients and for the larger population? Or have they produced side effects that affect adversely the internal productivity of the educational sector? Have they undercut future growth possibilities for the economy as a whole?

These are the questions that come to mind as one reviews the experience of the past two decades. Unfortunately, these questions are difficult to answer because pertinent evidence is so hard to assemble. An effort is made in the next sections to narrow the scope of these questions so that some limited evidence can be provided.

TYPES OF AND RATIONALE FOR STUDENT FINANCIAL AID

Before proceeding, it is important to describe the major types of financial aid and the rationale for each of them. Financial aid for college students takes two principal forms. One is the less apparent and sometimes forgotten across-the-board subsidy that reduces tuition below the cost of instruction. This subsidy is provided by taxpayers who defray anywhere from two-thirds to three-fourths of the cost of instruction for students enrolled in public colleges and universities. Students attending some private colleges and universities also pay much less than the full cost of instruction and in effect are subsidized. The amount of the subsidy depends on the size of the institution's endowment, the generosity of alumni and others, and the ingenuity of colleges in raising funds; in some states, public support is also provided to private institutions. This means that private college students pay on average as much as 100 percent and as little as perhaps 40 percent of instructional costs. Considerable variation also exists among students at different institutions in the size of these subsidies.

Despite the existence of these subsidies, students and in most cases their parents must incur the direct costs of college attendance, including tuition, books, room and board, and related costs that may approximate the size of the tuition subsidy. This does not include the additional opportunity costs (earnings foregone) over and above maintenance costs (room and board).

A now all-but-disappeared form of financial aid for undergraduates is what used to be called scholarships. Scholarships were typically offered to freshman applicants and to continuing students with outstanding academic records. Often these funds were targeted to outstanding students who came from poor families. Given limited resources, scholarships rewarded talented students from poor families, in the apparent belief that emphasis should be put upon past academic performance *and* financial status rather than on financial need alone. Awards generally did not exceed the costs of attendance. Usually they were considerably less and were viewed as aid that by itself would harly be sufficient to permit scholarship recipients to enroll unless they had other resources.

The other major form of financial aid—grants, loans, and employment— goes directly or through institutions to individual students and is based almost exclusively on financial need. The amount of such aid ranges from nothing to 100 percent, and sometimes even higher, of the usually recognized costs of attending college (tuition, fees, books, and room and board). Because no one source of financial aid is large enough to meet the costs of college, and because of differing eligibility for these several types of aid, students receive a "package" of financial aid (i.e., some mix of grants, loans, and work) that may or may not fully meet their financial need. The distribution of financial aid reflects to a considerable extent the economic position of students and their families, the choice of students as to the college they attend, and the availability of financial aid resources. The extent to which student-directed financial aid represents a subsidy depends in part on type of aid received. Work/study offers no subsidy to students (the subsidy goes to employers) but does provide students with employment opportunities that otherwise might not exist. Grants represent a full subsidy for whatever proportion of the costs of attendance they meet. Loans carry different repayment obligations, with more favorable interest and repayment conditions for guaranteed loans than other loans from private lenders. Thus, loans provide subsidies to recipients and to the lending institutions that provide the loans.

Several purposes are served by financial aid, in addition to shifting part of the costs of college attendance from students (and their parents) to taxpayers. Across-the-board subsidies are justified by economists and others on the ground that without them a less-than-optimal amount of education would be demanded because individuals would take account only of the private returns they expected to receive as they made decisions about attending college. To the extent that higher education produces valuable external benefits that spill over to other people, the realization of these benefits can be assured only through subsidies that lower the cost to individuals and thereby encourage more young people to make larger purchases of higher education (Orwig 1971; Bowen 1977; Breneman and Finn 1978).

Need-based student financial aid is seen as (1) enhancing equality of opportunity, which is defined as (a) greater access to postsecondary education, (b) wider student choice among educational options, and (c) greater persistence in school; and (2) easing the financial burden of college costs for particular types of families, most notably low- or low- and middle-income families (Congressional Budget Office 1980). These terms are rather vague. Can we be more precise about what these terms mean? Under (1), "access" seems to mean that qualified students should not be denied the opportunity to attend college because of limited financial resources; "choice" means that cost differentials among institutions, both public and private, should not influence decisions of young people about which college they attend; "persistence" means that qualified students making acceptable progress should not by reason of limited financial resources be unable to complete their degrees. Another way to think about financial aid is to view it simply as reducing the price of higher education, thereby causing an increase in the quantity of education demanded. Under (2) there is little to be said. Obviously, low family incomes inhibit student access, choice, and persistence. Financial aid reduces the schooling costs that families might otherwise pay and thereby frees up money for other purchases.

"Greater" access, "wider" choice, and presumably "greater" persistence are laudatory goals, but since they are probably impossible to attain completely, what can we take as indicative of movement toward their attainment? Unfortunately, these terms have not been given operational meaning, thereby making it difficult to know whether these objectives have been attained.

Consider first the matter of "greater access." The typical pattern of attendance rates by parental income is shown by line *BB* in Figure 2–1, which already takes into account the presence of across-the-board subsidies: Line *AA* depicts presumed attendance rates by family income level in the absence of across-the-board subsidies. Now we introduce student financial aid. Direct student aid conditioned on family income is assumed to cause line *B* to pivot around some point, such as *D*, the breakeven point, with the new segment shown as line *C*. While this description seems plausible, little or no effort has ever been made to give empirical content to the pattern of enrollment with and without across-the-board subsidies and in the presence of student financial aid.

Much the same can be said about "wider choice" and "greater persistence." What would be the distribution of students by type of institution

Figure 2–1. Illustrative College Attendance Rates by Family Income with and without Student Financial Aid Programs.

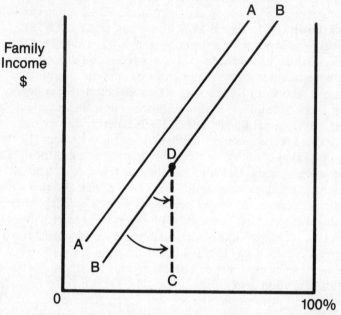

Percentage of Age Group or Eligibles Attending

AA = without financial aid
BB = with across-the-board financial aid
BDC = with need-based financial aid
D = breakeven point

(public versus private, two-year versus four-year versus university, small versus large, etc.) if wider choice and greater persistence were attained? Given the importance of tastes in selecting a college, there are enormous difficulties in trying to give operational meaning to these terms. As an example, does greater persistence mean that graduation rates should be similar for students irrespective of family income levels? Are we talking about persistence levels through the first year of college, the first two years, or the full four years and a diploma? How much change is required before we are convinced that student financial aid is accomplishing these objectives?

To sum up, these objectives and their operational meaning remain quite fuzzy. This creates great difficulties for anyone, including Congress, who attempts to evaluate the accomplishments of these programs. But even if the goals had been given more specific meaning, we would still experience difficulty figuring out what would have happened in the absence of these programs: that is, what is the counterfactual? Unless the conterfactual is spelled out beforehand—and this is both a difficult and hazardous under-taking—subsequent evaluators must try to reconstruct the expectations of those who decided these issues. This too is difficult and at times impossible to do satisfactorily.

We face the same difficulty in current discussions of student financial aid: If these programs are cut back or eliminated, what would be the effects on access, choice, and persistence? With respect to access, will the enroll-ment function in Figure 2–1 shift from the *BDC* function back to *BDB*? Or might it remain relatively unchanged? If it remained unchanged, would this reflect a shift in tastes or attitudes among low-income families about the desirability of higher education for their children? Or might it reflect great efforts on the part of students and their parents to offset cutbacks in financial aid by increasing work activity or drawing on assets?

EVOLUTION OF STUDENT FINANCIAL AID

A full account of the evolution of student financial aid has yet to be written. We do know that what was traditionally viewed as a matter of individual and family concern became transformed, in the mid- to late-1960s, to a gen-eral societal concern for assisting students largely through low-cost loans and work/study funds, and in the early 1970s, to a special concern for pro-viding cash grants to qualified but poor students so that they might attend college. These programs grew steadily, culminating with passage of the 1980 amendments to the Higher Education Act of 1965, which provided a detailed program for further expansion of federal support to the mid-1980s. The administration began to cut back these federal programs in 1981.

Until quite recently, parents traditionally played a major role in paying the college attendance costs of their children. Students also contributed, often earning much of their own expenses by working while attending school and in the summers; in some cases they found it necessary to spend a year or two working before enrolling in college. Colleges and universities typically maintained small scholarship and loan funds, often from bequests provided by former graduates and corporations, to help underwrite some part of the costs of attendance for a few able but financially poor stu-dents. In addition, there are heart-warming instances of friends, eminent townspeople, and others helping to send promising young people to college by paying a part of their expenses.

This informal system began to change in the early 1950s when competition for able students intensified. A number of private colleges, notably the Ivy League colleges, came to the conclusion that competing for the same students with their limited scholarship funds was not a wise approach and that more efficient methods of allocating their limited resources had to be established. This led them to begin taking into account the financial needs of students, with the help of a financial needs analysis system developed for them by the College Scholarship Service. Colleges and universities still made most of their financial aid awards, then called "scholarships," on the basis of academic merit.

With the advent of Sputnik and the subsequent enactment of the National Defense Education Act of 1958, a major shift took place. This legislation offered low-cost, federal loans to students entering certain academic programs in college. These loan obligations could be reduced considerably if individuals opted to enter into some critical training program or occupation after graduation. In making these awards, no consideration was given to financial need; the objective was to stimulate the flow of qualified young people into activities that were viewed as in the national interest.

Meanwhile, the perennial difficulties of mobilizing the resources required to support students while in college led a number of states to establish loan programs and, in some cases, guaranteed loan programs for residents. These subsidized programs, designed to facilitate human resource investment, sought to reduce if not eliminate the difficulties students experienced in obtaining loans from private lenders who were quite properly concerned about the lack of collateral for people planning to invest in the development of their intellectual skills.

Despite periodic discussion of the need for more federal support in the early 1960s, the first major legislation to provide substantial federal monies for student financial aid came with passage of the Higher Education Act of 1965. The purpose of this legislation was to establish a federal guaranteed student loan program. A variety of factors helped produce this legislation. New York's favorable experience with a guaranteed student loan program showed that such a program could work; loans for college students were seen by opponents of a tuition tax credit as a less costly and much more useful program to support higher education; and finally, strong support came from then-President Lyndon B. Johnson, who believed firmly in student loans but on a limited scale. One can also view the legislation as a political response to large successive waves of the baby boom reaching college age. In any case, the federal government entered the student aid business by providing subsidized loans guaranteed in case of student default, with eligibility limited to students from families with incomes of under

$15,000. Congress also incorporated into this legislation a part of the package of poverty proposals passed the year before, principally a small program of Economic Opportunity Grants targeted for low-income youth to help them pay the costs of college and the Work/Study Program, also for low-income youth.

It is interesting to note that Educational Opportunity Grants, while targeted on students from poor families, also emphasized that recipients should "show evidence of academic or creative promise." In other words, the focus on students from low-income families was conditioned on some measure of quality, a reflection of the continuing concern from the early 1960s over "talent loss."

The emphasis on the War on Poverty and on the plight of minorities quickly led to a recasting of priorities by higher education, which, after experiencing substantial injections of public funds for new buildings and research, wanted to gain federal support for institutional costs. The changing goals were reflected in several ways. First, the 1967 amendments to the Higher Education Act called for a study to recommend means of "making available a post-secondary education to all young Americans who qualify and seek it." The terms "qualify and seek" are quite different from the 1965 language "show evidence of academic or creative promise."

Second, and much more important, this new set of goals was reflected in a paper by Clark Kerr (1968) who had just assumed direction of the newly created Carnegie Commission on Higher Education. He called for a massive expansion of federal spending for higher education by 1976, with up to $5 billion for student financial aid to assure greater equality of educational opportunity. Shortly afterwards, Kerr's Carnegie Commission (1968) issued its first report, *Quality and Equality: New Levels of Federal Responsibility for Higher Education.* This was followed shortly thereafter by a report from a Task Force of the Department of Health, Education and Welfare (1969) directed by Alice Rivlin with a somewhat similar title: *Toward a Long Range Plan for Federal Support of Higher Education.* These reports called for a substantial expansion of federal monies for a need-based grant system, an expanded work/study program, an enlarged student loan program, direct institutional grants tied to the number of students receiving federal support, and related proposals. These two reports made it quite clear that a central purpose of their recommendations, which were carefully spelled out and costed, was to achieve greater equality of educational opportunity. Similar recommendations began to emerge from the various states, such as the full-fledged financial aid proposal for Wisconsin developed in 1969 by Hansen and Weisbrod (1971).

The weight of these recommendations, combined with redistributive sentiments and large cohorts of "baby boom" children of college age, brought action. Congress began to consider ways of providing institutional aid and, particularly, student financial aid that would be targeted to student need. Institutional aid was considered but quickly rejected. Instead, attention was concentrated on aid to students. There soon materialized the 1972 amendments to the Higher Education Act which established the Basic Educational Opportunity Grant (BEOG) program to provide direct grants to students based on financial need (Gladieux and Wolanin 1976).

Further changes in student financial aid programs were made through the 1970s, especially by the Middle Income Student Assistance Act of 1978 and the 1980 Higher Education Act Amendments. The former loosened slightly the income eligibility criteria for BEOG funds but even more important eliminated them completely for student loans. As a result, the careful targeting of federal student financial aid was reduced (Hansen and Lampman 1974, 1983). The 1980 amendments offered a four-year patterned program of increases in BEOG funds per student and also altered the eligibility criteria such that program costs could be expected to rise more sharply than they had in the past.

With the election of the Reagan administration and its program of substantial budget cuts, all bets for the future are off (Toma 1981). BEOG levels have been reduced, interest rates on student loans have been raised, and more budget cuts are anticipated. While the picture is still highly uncertain, it appears that major reductions will be made in what has been the substantial federal commitment of funds to support equality of educational opportunity (*Chronicle of Higher Education,* various issues).

As of late 1980 a variety of federal student financial aid programs were in place. These programs are described as they existed in late 1980.

1. *National Direct Student Loans* (NDSL).   Established under the National Defense Education Act of 1958, this program provides low-interest loans to students enrolled at institutions eligible for participation. These loans are made through institutions. Student eligibility is based on financial need. Interest is set at 3 percent, with the start of repayment deferred until nine months after a student completes school.

2. *Guaranteed Student Loans* (GSL).   The Higher Education Act of 1965 established a program of federally guaranteed loans offered by private and nonprofit lenders. For students from families with incomes of less than $15,000, loans were offered at subsidized rates of interest (6 percent originally and 7 percent since 1968) and in addition permitted the deferral of interest payments until after the borrower completed college. Students with higher family incomes could borrow but had to pay 7 percent interest from the date of the loan. Loan maximums were originally $1,000 per year but have since been raised to $2,500 per year. The most important changes in the program came in 1978 with the removal of the limit on family income;

all borrowers became eligible for the in-school subsidy as well as the much lower than market rate of interest.

3. *College Work Study* (CWS).   Although established by the Economic Opportunity Act of 1964, the work/study program was transferred to the Office of Education under the Higher Education Act of 1965. Work/study programs provide funds to colleges and universities, enabling them to pay up to 80 percent of the costs of employing students from low-income families in jobs primarily but not exclusively on campus. In recent years students could earn up to a maximum of $2,500 per year. In addition to providing earnings, it was hoped that the job experience gained would enhance the subsequent employability of CWS participants.

4. *Supplementary Educational Opportunity Grants* (SEOG).   This program, begun under the name of Educational Opportunity Grants in 1965 and recast slightly in 1972, provides funds to institutions for disbursement to students with exceptional financial need who also maintain a high level of academic performance (in the upper half of their class). Institutions are required to match the federal funds. Grants range from $200 to $1,500 per year, with a $4,000 maximum for the education of any particular student. Recipients must be enrolled at least half time.

5. *Basic Educational Opportunity Grants* (BEOG but renamed Pell Grants). Established by the 1972 amendments, the BEOG program provides grants to students enrolled at least half time in college or postsecondary education. The amount of these grants is based on financial need and originally could not exceed $1,400 or 50 percent of the cost of attending college, whichever was least. The amount of the grant is determined on the basis of financial need, which takes into account parental income, assets, family size, and other pertinent expenditures. Various changes have been made in this program over the years, principally through raising the maximum amount of the grant from $1,400 to $1,800, broadening eligibility by family income level from $15,000 to almost $28,000, and altering the elements in the formula for determining financial need.

6. *State Student Incentive Grants* (SSIG).   This program was also established in 1972, with the federal government matching state contributions to provide grants of up to $1,500 per academic year based on financial need.

7. *State and Institutional Programs.*   The dominance of federal legislation obscures the important role played by various states and by individual institutions. Not only did some develop their own student loan and grant programs well before the federal government, but the newly developed federal

Table 2–1. Growth of Appropriations for Major Federal Student Financial Aid Programs, Fiscal Years 1964 to 1982 (in millions of dollars).

Fiscal Year	NDSL (1)	GSL (2)	CWS (3)	SEOG (4)	BEOG (5)	SSIG (6)	Total Appropriations (7)[a]	GSL Loan Value (8)	Total Funds Available (9)[a]
1964	0	0	0	0	0	0	0	0	0
1965	0	0	56	0	0	0	56	0	56
1966	182	10	99	0	0	0	291	77	358
1967	192	43	134	0	0	0	369	248	574
1968	193	40	140	0	0	0	373	436	769
1969	193	75	140	0	0	0	408	687	1020
1970	195	73	152	0	0	0	420	840	1187
1971	243	161	158	0	0	0	562	1044	1445
1972	317	209	427	0	0	0	953	1302	2046
1973	293	292	270	0	122	0	977	1199	1884
1974	298	399	270	210	475	20	1672	982	2255
1975	329	594	420	240	840	20	2443	1208	3057
1976	331	808	390	240	1326	44	3139	1735	4066
1977	323	357	390	250	1904	60	3284	1470	4397
1978	326	480	435	270	2160	64	3735	1648	4903
1979	329	945	550	340	2431	77	4672	2250	5977
1980	301	1609	550	370	1718	77	4625	4840	7856
1981	201	2581	550	370	2604	77	6383	7300	11102
1982	308	2753	550	370	2486	77	6474	9479	13200

[a]Column 7 is the sum of columns 1 through 6; Column 9 is the sum of columns 1, 3 through 6, and 8.

Source: Office of Evaluation and Program Management, *Annual Evaluation Report.* vol. II, Fiscal Year 1980, U.S. Department of Education, 1981, pp. 135–88; 1982 figures are estimates.

programs were often tailored after already successful state and institutional programs. States and institutions operated what were essentially scholarship programs, but in the 1970s these were rapidly converted to need-based grant programs.

The growth of these programs is shown by Table 2-1. Until 1973 loan funds represented from 60 to 70 percent of all federal appropriations for student financial aid. But with the advent of SEOG and BEOG in the early 1970s, the balance shifted, with loan appropriations ranging between 30 and 40 percent of the total (the sum of columns 1 and 2 divided by column 7).

If instead we consider not loan appropriations but loan volume, then loans represented 70 to 80 percent of total federal aid until 1973, after which the proportion dropped to about 40 percent but climbed steeply to well over 60 percent as loan volume increased sharply beginning in 1979, after the family income limitation was removed (the sum of columns 1 and 8 divided by column 9).

The evolution of student financial aid programs can be summarized with the help of Figure 2-2, which shows a series of grids describing the college-age population by ability quartiles in the rows and economic status quartiles in the columns. The distribution of student financial aid funds is indicated by the slash marks.

Prior to 1965 student financial aid took the form of scholarships and loans that were distributed largely to high-ability students and especially among them to students from low-economic-status families. Beginning in 1965 a new focus was added, that of directing some aid to students from low-economic-status families, with some attention to ability. By about 1970 the scholarship concept was largely discarded, with those funds redirected to low-economic-status students without, or at least with less, regard to ability. The next transformation occurred in 1972 when need-based aid expanded greatly with passage of BEOG. The 1978 amendments further opened up eligibility for BEOG and made GSL loans available to virtually anyone who wanted them.

These changes are quite dramatic. Most apparent is the shift in targeting after 1965 and the move beginning in 1978 to spread eligibility much more broadly.

PREDICTED EFFECTS OF STUDENT
FINANCIAL AID

Two studies have been located that attempted to estimate the additional enrollment induced by national need-based programs of student financial

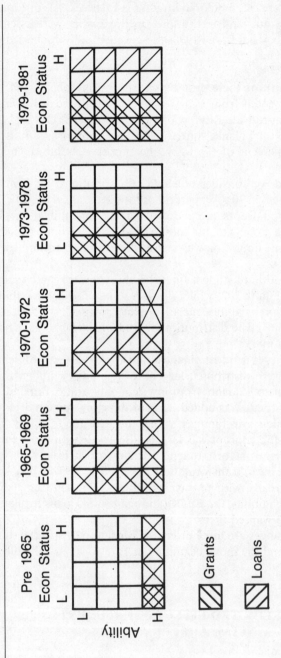

Figure 2-2. Evolution of Targeting of Student Financial Aid by Economic Status and Ability Quartiles, Pre-1965 to 1980.

aid. The first estimate was made by Folger, Astin, and Bayer (1970) based on Project Talent data for the early 1960s and reflects concern with the loss of talent. The second, by Hartman (1972), is an analysis of the BEOG program when it was under consideration by Congress.

Folger asked what effect a financial aid program would have if it met the financial needs of all students from the lowest SES (socioeconomic status) quintile who were also in the top half in ability. He estimated a 4 percent increase in total enrollment on the assumption that these students would behave like those similar in ability but in the top SES quintile. Of course, all of the enrollment increase would be for low-quintile SES students and hence low-income students. If we broaden Folger's approach to embrace the upper three quintiles in ability and the bottom three quintiles in SES, total enrollment would rise by 8 to 10 percent. If we assume instead that all students would be eligible for financial aid based on their SES but irrespective of their ability, the total enrollment increase would be even greater. Thus, Folger's approach suggests the potential enrollment effects of increased student financial aid.

Hartman's estimates are more pertinent to the focus of this paper in that he was concerned with the impact of the BEOG program as it was finally adopted. Working with enrollment rates by family income level, he showed that if the BEOG program brought the enrollment rates of youth from lower-income families up to the enrollment rate for the then $10,000 to $14,999 income class (based on the reasonable assumption that BEOG would give potential students the buying power of a family in this income class), the overall enrollment rate would increase by 20 percent. Enrollment rates for youths from lower-income families would rise by even more since all of the overall increase would be concentrated at the low end of the family income distribution. This means, for example, that the enrollment rates of youths from the lowest-income families (under $3,000 family income) would rise from 13 to 41 percent, a more than 200 percent increase. Hartman's more conservative assumptions produce overall enrollment rate increases of 13 and 9 percent; in these cases the enrollment rates of the lowest income group would rise by approximately 100 percent and 50 percent, respectively.

In sum, the predicted effects of financial aid programs, in particular their impact on enrollment rates of lower SES and lower-income high school graduates, were not small. They were clearly large enough to be reflected in any comparisons of pre- and postprogram data. Because other program changes also occurred, notably the removal of the income cap on eligibility for GSL funds, enrollment rates for youth from higher-income families would also have been expected to increase somewhat. It seemed quite clear that enrollment rates of low-income youth were expected to rise relative to those of higher-income youth.

EVALUATION OF STUDENT FINANCIAL AID
PROGRAM EFFECTS

The Department of Education has made continuing efforts to evaluate the effectiveness of federal student financial aid programs in promoting the goal of greater equality of opportunity, particularly the dimensions of access and choice. The evidence used is summarized here to set the stage for the subsequent sections of this paper (Office of Evaluation and Program Management 1981: vol. II).

The first type of evidence examined is enrollment rates of young people, 18 to 24 years old, from the early and mid-1970s through 1978 (the most recent year spanned by that report). It is pointed out that (1) enrollments of blacks and Hispanics rose somewhat relative to whites and (2) enrollments of dependent students from families with incomes of $15,000 and above fell off while enrollment rates for youth from lower-income families maintained themselves. The report is properly cautious in not drawing any conclusions about access or choice from these data. Nevertheless, the inclusion of these data could suggest that the results are viewed as mildly supportive of the access objective.

The second type of evidence is less direct. It is based on an assessment of the difficulty students are likely to experience in financing the student burden—that part of the cost of attendance that remains after taking account of parental contributions and grant funds. This student burden can be met by loans, earnings from part-time work while in school, and summer savings. Two types of conclusions are drawn from these calculations of student burden. One is that the size of the burden is quite manageable at two-year and four-year public institutions for both dependent and independent students. This means that the access objective has been reasonably accomplished. The other is that students at private institutions would have to incur greater debt and make greater sacrifices but this would not impose unmanageable burdens on them. Thus, the choice goal is to a large extent being achieved.

These conclusions have to be qualified when the full range of student expense budgets is considered, including the "over $6,000" category where the student burden is quite substantial. The analysis assumes that parental contributions were forthcoming in the stipulated amounts, that part-time employment yielded as much as $1,350 based on working at the minimum wage for fifteen hours a week during the school year, and that summer work yielded $500 in savings for college. However, no information is provided about whether these various funds materialized and whether students did indeed avail themselves of the various loans available to them. On the other hand, because estimates of the student burden are based on the financial aid information of students already enrolled at these high cost schools and receiving financial aid, this indicates that the student burden, whatever its size, is somehow being financed and, thus, it cannot be an unmanageable burden! Unfortunately, we are offered no data on students who are not receiving financial aid; such data would permit us to compare their burdens with those of aid recipients. It is entirely possible that these students not receiving aid could be more heavily concentrated at lower-cost schools where their burden would be less; their inability to qualify for financial aid would manifest itself in the choice of less expensive institutions. It is also unfortunate that we lack information on young people not attending college, either because they could not afford it in the beginning or because they had been forced to drop out for lack of adequate financial resources.

In short, the conclusions about the effects of student financial aid programs on access and choice speak only to the allocation of the costs of attendance among already enrolled students. Whether additional students might have been drawn into higher education is not addressed in the Department of Education analysis.

A CLOSER LOOK AT ACCESS

Two standards can be used to assess the effectiveness of student financial aid programs in widening access to college. These standards involve comparing enrollment rates to ascertain whether and to what extent the composition of college-age youth attending or planning to attend college has changed as a consequence of the greater availability of federally provided student financial aid.

The first of the standards compares enrollment rates for college-age youth from above- and below-median income families with dependents age 18–24, on the assumption that need-based financial aid should raise the enrollment rates of lower-income relative to higher-income youths. This follows from the discussion of Figure 2–1 above, which suggested that the establishment of financial aid programs would produce a twist in the relationship between family income and enrollment rates, with a rise in the ratio of enrollments of lower-relative to higher-income students.

The second standard compares planned and realized enrollment rates for high school seniors by socioeconomic status and ability. This follows up on the presentation surrounding Figure 2–2, which shows how the evolution of student financial aid programs might be expected to have altered the composition of college students.

Application of these standards requires examining several sources of pertinent data and making comparisons over time periods that are most likely to reveal the effects of more abundant student financial aid. The data we employ come from two sources: One is the annual October Current Population Survey on school enrollments, which provides extensive information for dependent youth age 18 to 24 on their enrollment by race, sex, and family income. The other source of data is two longitudinal surveys of high school seniors. The 1972 *National Longitudinal Study of the High School Class of 1972* (NLS) provides extensive baseline and followup data over the rest of the decade. The survey titled *High School and Beyond—A National Longitudinal Study of the 1980s* began in 1980; its first followup was undertaken in 1982. This paper examines enrollment expectations, comparing data from the 1972 and 1980 baseline years.

To make the data analysis as comparable as possible, we utilize CPS data for the early 1970s (an average of October 1971 and 1972) and the late 1970s (an average of October 1978 and 1979, the most recent years for which data were available). The initial period in both data sets precedes implementation of the BEOG program, whereas the end period partly reflects the changes resulting from the Middle Income Student Assistance Act (1978).

Enrollment Rates by Family Income Levels Based on CPS Data

The impact of student financial aid should manifest itself by raising the enrollment rates of low-income college-age youth relative to high-income college-age youth. Isolating such changes is difficult because family incomes have risen sharply, largely as a result of the inflationary environment of the 1970s. Hence, enrollment rates for particular family income classes are not directly comparable over time. To circumvent this difficulty enrollment rates have been calculated for young people age 18 to 24 from families with incomes above and below the overall median level of income for all those families whose children are eligible or qualified to attend college. The use of median income makes this a rather crude analysis. While the lower family-income quartile could have been used, the results would have been more heavily affected by the linear interpolation procedures that must be applied to the published data that groups families by rather wide income classes. On the other hand, because eligibility for student financial aid extends up to at least the level of median income, this cutoff seems more appropriate than using the bottom quartile.

Several comments need to be made about the quality of the data. Aside from the usual hazards of working with survey data whose standard errors are large because of the relatively small number of observations in each cell, family-income data are available only for those college students who are classified as dependents. However, the "dependent" definition used in the

CPS does not necessarily coincide with the dependent definition used in determining eligibility in student financial aid programs. To the extent that young people may now be leaving home earlier than in the past, there could be some systematic bias in the data. Difficulties also arise because of the broad age category used, age 18 to 24. Since college lasts no more than four years for most young people attending college, enrollment rates will reflect graduate enrollments to some extent, difference in persistence, and difference in the duration of student programs (two-year versus four-year programs). For these and other reasons, the data are at best only roughly indicative of the true enrollment patterns that are of interest here.

Enrollment Rates for Family Units with Dependent Students. Table 2-2 displays the various enrollment data that will be used in this analysis. Here the focus is on college enrollment rates for families with one or more dependents age 18 to 24. No allowance is made for the number of dependents per family; thus, this is a less precise indicator than the evidence on dependents in the next section.

The top two lines show how enrollment rates changed through the 1970s. Overall, there was a sizeable drop in the enrollment rate from 37.9 to 33.8 percent. White enrollment rates fell considerably while those for blacks

Table 2-2. College Enrollment Rates for Families with One or More Dependents Age 18 through 24.[a]

	Whites	Blacks	Whites + Blacks
Overall Enrollment Rates			
1. 1971/1972	40.4%	22.5%	37.9%
2. 1978/1979	35.7	24.0	33.8
Enrollment Rates for Below- and Above-Median Income Families			
3. 1971/1972 Below	28.1	20.0	26.6
4. 1971/1972 Above	50.4	33.6	49.7
Enrollment Rates for Below- and Above-Median Income Families			
5. 1978/1979 Below	24.8	20.4	24.0
6. 1978/1979 Above	44.1	40.1	43.9
Ratios of Below- to Above- Rates			
7. Line 3/4	0.56	0.60	0.54
8. Line 5/6	0.56	0.51	0.55

[a] The unit of observation is families with dependents age 18 through 24.

Source: Calculations by author from data published in annual October reports of U.S. Department of Commerce, Bureau of the Census, *Current Population Reports; Population Characteristics—Social and Economic Characteristics of Students.* Data for 1971 (Series P-20, no. 241) are from Table 13, p. 38; for 1972 (Series P-20, no. 260) from Table 11, p. 39; for 1978 (Series P-20, no. 346) from Table 12, p. 39; for 1979 (Series P-20, no. 360) from Table 12, p. 36.

Table 2-3. College Enrollment Rates for Dependents from Families with Dependents Age 18 through 24.[a]

	Whites	Blacks	Whites + Blacks	Males	Females	Males + Females
Overall Rates						
1. 1971/1972	26.4%	18.4%	25.5%	31.2%	20.6%	25.5%
2. 1978/1979	25.9	20.0	25.1	26.8	23.8	25.2
Rates for Below- and Above-Median Family Income						
3. 1971/1972 Below	16.0	16.1	16.0	19.8	12.4	16.1
4. 1971/1972 Above	35.1	25.2	34.4	40.5	29.6	34.9
Rates for Below- and Above-Median Family Income						
5. 1978/1979 Below	15.3	17.1	15.7	17.9	15.2	16.4
6. 1978/1979 Above	34.9	29.8	34.6	37.9	38.1	38.0
Ratios of Below- to Above- Rates						
7. Line 3/4	0.46	0.64	0.47	0.49	0.42	0.46
8. Line 5/6	0.44	0.57	0.45	0.47	0.40	0.43

[a]The unit of observation is dependents age 18 through 24.

Source: October *Current Population Reports;* see Table 2. Data for 1971 (Series P-20, no. 241) are from Table 14, p. 40; for 1972 (Series P-20, no. 260) from Table 12, p. 42; for 1978 (Series P-20, no. 346) from Table 13, p. 41; for 1979 (Series P-20, no. 360) from Table 13, p. 38.

displayed a partially offsetting increase. The next four lines (3 to 6), show-ing enrollment rates for below- and above-median income families in both periods, indicate that from 1971 to 1972 through 1978 to 1979 white enroll-ment rates fell for both categories of families, while for blacks the enroll-ment rate for high-income families rose appreciably. The roughly offsetting magnitudes of change, shown in the bottom two lines (7 and 8), caused the white ratio of below- to above-median income enrollment rates to remain constant. For blacks, by contrast, it dropped substantially.

These results are difficult to interpret. It is clear that we do not observe a general rise in the enrollment rates of lower- to higher-income students as we might have expected. And the sharp rise in the enrollment rate of high-income blacks seems unlikely to have resulted from student financial aid, given that such aid is for the most part heavily targeted to lower-income students. So, though our expectations did not materialize, we have no obvious interpretation for the results in Table 2-2.

Enrollment Rates for Dependent Students.   In Table 2-3 emphasis is shifted to enrollment rates for dependent students age 18 to 24 rather than for families with dependents. Looking first at the data by race, we observe that white enrollment rates fell a bit while those for blacks rose. But whereas white enrollment rates fell for students in both below- and above-median income families, the enrollment rates for below- and above-median income black students rose, particularly for above-median blacks in 1978 to 1979 (lines 3 to 6). As a consequence, the ratios of enrollment rates in lines 7 and 8 drop slightly for whites and by over one-tenth for blacks. Hence, it is not clear over this period that youth from lower-income families were pulled into college relative to students from higher-income families.

Shifting our focus now to gender differences, we find a somewhat dif-ferent story. Enrollment rates for males fell while those for females rose. Whereas enrollment rates of below- and above-median income students fell for men and rose for women, the net effect in lines 7 and 8 is a decline in the overall ratio for men and women combined. Once again, the trends run counter to our expectation that student financial aid would increase enroll-ments of lower-income youth.

Enrollment Rates for Dependents Who Are High School Graduates.   The use of all dependents age 18 to 24 as a basis for the preceding calculations ignores the reality that some of these dependents are not eligible for college because they did not graduate from high school. To clarify what happened, enrollment rates have also been calculated for dependents who are high school graduates. The results that are shown in Table 2-4 parallel those in Table 2-3.

Table 2-4. College Enrollment Rates for Dependents from Families with Dependents Age 18 through 24 Who Are High School Graduates.[a]

Overall Rates	Whites	Blacks	Whites + Blacks	Males	Females	Males + Females
1. 1971/1972	32.8%	28.8%	32.4%	40.1%	26.1%	32.5%
2. 1978/1979	31.9	29.9	31.6	34.6	29.5	31.9
Rates for Below- and Above-Median Family Income						
3. 1971/1972 Below	22.5	26.7	23.3	30.9	17.8	23.5
4. 1971/1972 Above	41.9	34.3	41.5	48.4	35.1	41.5
Rates for Below- and Above-Median Family Income						
5. 1978/1979 Below	21.5	27.3	22.5	25.8	20.7	22.9
6. 1978/1979 Above	40.9	37.9	40.7	42.1	39.6	40.9
Ratios of Below- to Above- Rates						
7. Line 3/4	0.54	0.78	0.56	0.64	0.51	0.57
8. Line 5/6	0.53	0.72	0.55	0.61	0.52	0.56

[a]The unit of observation is dependents age 18 through 24 who are high school graduates.

Source: See Table 2–3.

Several results deserve comment. First, the enrollment rates shown in Table 2–4 are all higher than those shown in Table 2–2; this is because we subtract from the denominator those dependents who are not high school graduates. The higher the fraction of dependents age 18 to 24 who are not high school graduates, the larger the increase in the enrollment rates. Thus, the overall enrollment rates (lines 1 and 2) rise for blacks relative to whites and for males versus females, given that high school completion rates are lower for blacks and for males.

Second, and more important, whereas female enrollment rates are in all cases lower than those for males, overall as well as for those above and below the median income level, we note a different pattern for blacks versus whites. Enrollment rates for black high school graduates from families with below-median incomes are actually higher than for similar whites (see lines 3 and 5 for whites and blacks). This is not the case, however, for black high school graduates from above-median income families. More surprising is the fact that while the enrollment rate for lower-income black high school graduates rose slightly from 1971 to 1972 through 1978 to 1979, the enrollment rate for higher-income black high school graduates rose by a considerably greater margin. The net effect is a sharp decline in the enrollment ratio for blacks (lines 7 and 8) and a much smaller decline for whites, with no real change for whites and blacks combined.

Third, the story for women is roughly the same as in Table 2–3. Enrollment rates fell over the period for men and they rose for women (lines 1 and 2). The ratios of the below to above median enrollment rates (lines 7 and 8) indicate that despite heavily targeted financial aid, the enrollment ratio for women showed no real change while that for men dropped somewhat. Again, these patterns run counter to our expectations.

Summary.   This initial foray into the widely used and readily available CPS data indicates no clearcut effect of student financial aid in causing enrollment rates to increase more markedly for youth from lower-income families relative to higher-income families.

Enrollment Plans by Income, Socioeconomic Status, and Academic Ability

We next want to consider other ways that the composition of college enrollments changed from the early to the late 1970s. In particular, we are interested in knowing whether the growing availability of need-based financial aid stimulated the enrollment of academically promising young people from lower-income or lower socioeconomic status families. This question is important because it reflects a long-standing concern about talent loss—that is, the extent to which financial aid helps the more academically able high school students from lower socioeconomic status to attend college.

We now shift attention from the CPS data to longitudinal data, namely the *National Longitudinal Study of the High School Class of 1972* (NLS) and *High School and Beyond—A National Longitudinal Study of the 1980s* (HSB). As noted earlier, these studies gathered exhaustive information on high school seniors while they were still in high school. The NLS base-year data base has been augmented through periodic followup studies. The HSB study completed its first two-year followup in spring 1982, the results of which were not available when this paper was written. This means that for now we can only compare college plans, not actual enrollments. Although planned and actual enrollments are likely to differ, and for a variety of reasons, there is no reason to expect systematic differences from 1972 to 1980.

One other comparable body of data is available but will not be utilized here. This is the Project Talent (PT) study, which also surveyed a substantial number of high school seniors in 1960 and followed their careers over the next sixteen years. While some published tables are available from the PT study, most of them differ from those presented here. Moreover, because of difficulties in getting access to the PT data, a detailed examination of them is deferred for another time.

The NLS and HSB studies differ slightly, but they are in close enough agreement to permit comparisons of data from them; such comparisons have already been made (National Center for Education Statistics 1981). Individuals are classified by socioeconomic status, family income, academic ability as measured by a brief test, and the usual demographic variables such as sex and race. Information on college plans came from the following questions. In 1972 seniors were asked "... circle one number for the highest level of education ... you plan to attain." In 1980 seniors were asked, "As things stand now, how far in school do you think you will get?" These questions are viewed here as being equivalent for purposes of comparison. It should be pointed out that because some seniors either did not know or report their plans, they have been excluded in producing the various tables that follow. Also excluded are seniors who did not report on the particular variables used in constructing the tables.

Enrollment Expectations by Family Income.   Our first comparison follows the format of those in the previous section by displaying enrollment plans for high school seniors from below- and above-median income families for 1972 and 1980, based on the two longitudinal studies. Table 2-5, Panel A, shows information for high school seniors expecting to obtain a four-year degree or more, and Panel B shows information for high school seniors who expect to participate in any kind of postsecondary education. The key data are in the form of the ratios of expected enrollment rates for youths from below- to above-median income families (lines 7 and 8).

Table 2-5. Percentages of High School Seniors Expecting to Obtain Various Amounts of Postsecondary Education by Race and Gender, 1972 and 1980.

	Whites	Blacks	Males	Females
A. *Completing a Four-Year Degree or More*				
Overall Rates				
1. 1972 4-year degree or more	52.5	52.0	56.8	46.6
2. 1980 4-year degree or more	46.7	49.0	48.4	45.8
Rates for Below- and Above-Median Family Income				
3. 1972 Below	45.0	48.7	45.5	37.3
4. 1972 Above	69.7	69.5	66.9	64.0
Rates for Below- and Above-Median Family Income				
5. 1980 Below	35.0	45.5	37.9	36.3
6. 1980 Above	57.2	59.3	57.8	57.1
Ratios of Below- to Above-Median Family Income				
7. 1972 Below/1972 Above	0.65	0.70	0.68	0.58
8. 1980 Below/1980 Above	0.61	0.77	0.66	0.64
B. *Attending Some Form of Postsecondary Education*				
Overall Rate				
1. 1972	82.2	84.2	85.2	78.4
2. 1980	80.8	83.6	80.1	82.5
Rates for Below- and Above-Median Family Income				
3. 1972 Below	75.7	82.8	79.3	73.4
4. 1972 Above	88.1	91.8	90.6	84.4
Rates for Below- and Above-Median Family Income				
5. 1980 Below	73.8	81.8	73.3	73.3
6. 1980 Above	87.1	88.6	86.1	88.6
Ratios of Below- to Above-Median Family Incomes				
7. 1972 Below/1972 Above	0.86	0.90	0.88	0.87
8. 1980 Below/1980 Above	0.85	0.92	0.85	0.83

Source: Calculations by author from data files for *National Longitudinal Study of the High School Class of 1972,* U.S. National Center for Education Statistics (NCES), Princeton, N.J.: Educational Testing Service; Triangle Park, N.C.: Research Triangle, 1973; and from *High School and Beyond: Student File 1980,* Chicago: National Opinion Research Center, 1981. Distributor for both files is NCES, Washington, D.C.

For those planning to complete four-year degrees or more, the ratios of those from below- to above-median family incomes drop for whites and for males whereas they rise for blacks and women. Our expectation is that the ratios would have risen for all groups because of the greater availability of student financial aid funds. It is conceivable that financial aid was more heavily targeted to blacks and that financial aid provided a greater inducement to women than to men. We have no way, however, of verifying such possibilities with these data.

For those planning to enter some kind of postsecondary education, the data in Panel B provide conflicting results. The ratios of expected enrollment rates are down somewhat for whites, males, and females, and are up only slightly for blacks. Most surprising is the higher percentage of blacks than whites expecting to enter postsecondary education in both 1972 and 1980 (and also to complete at least four-year degrees but only in 1980; see Panel A). This may be the most startling finding from these data. One can conclude from these data that no sharp changes occurred in enrollment expectations from 1972 to 1980 despite widespread publicity about the availability of financial aid to help students from low-income families.

Overall Enrollment Expectations by SES, Ability, Sex, and Race.   Comparable published information is available from the NLS and HSB on the educational expectations of high school seniors categorized by ability and socioeconomic status. The data showing the percentages of seniors expecting to complete at least a four-year degree are in Table 2-6. By ability level we observe little or no absolute or relative change from 1972 to 1980. The same can be said when seniors are classified by SES. The percentages rose slightly for blacks and Hispanics but dropped a bit for whites. By sex, the male percentage went down while that for females rose. Again, the changes from 1972 to 1980 are not so large as to suggest responses that can easily be associated with the greater availability of student aid. Surprisingly, these widely available data have been ignored by most commentators.

Detailed Enrollment Expectations by SES and Ability.   We now turn to more detailed data on the enrollment expectations of high school seniors tabulated simultaneously by SES and ability. We follow the format of Table 2-6 by collapsing the middle two SES and ability quartiles as is done by the National Center for Education Statistics (1981). This serves to highlight changes in the top and bottom SES and ability quartiles. Admittedly, this approach may hide some changes that occur from 1972 to 1980 but with the offsetting gain of reducing the amount of data to be scanned.

Before turning to the results, it is important to indicate our expectations as to what we might find. As with the data on enrollments and enrollment expectations by family income level, we would expect financial aid to reduce the barriers to attendance among students from the lowest SES quartile relative to the highest SES quartile. This would lead to a relative rise (i.e., relative to the highest quartile) in the percentages of seniors from the lowest SES quartile planning to complete or attend the various levels of postsecondary education.

Table 2-6.   Percentages of High School Seniors Expecting to Complete at Least a Four-Year Degree, by SES, Ability, Race, and Sex, 1972 and 1980.

	1972	1980
All	45.9	46.0
SES		
Low quartile	26.3	26.2
Middle two quartiles	40.4	41.9
High quartile	74.2	75.8
Ability		
Low quartile	18.6	19.6
Middle two quartiles	41.2	42.1
High quartile	77.4	79.1
Sex[a]		
Male	51.6	47.2
Female	41.5	44.9
Race[a]		
White	47.2	45.6
Black	46.2	47.5
Hispanic	34.1	36.0

[a] These percentages differ from those in Table 2-5. The latter are restricted to seniors who reported family income levels while those here are not so restricted.

Source: National Center for Education Statistics, *The Condition of Education, 1981,* U.S. Department of Education, Table 3.1, p. 126.

Our expectations as to changes in enrollment plans by ability are less clear. There is nothing in the way financial aid programs are structured to suggest that they select on any measure of academic ability, other than that youths seeking admission must meet the academic standards of the college or university they expect to attend and, once there, maintain some minimum grade-point average. Because four-year schools have stricter admission standards than two-year colleges, we would expect to find smaller changes at the middle and higher ability levels for youth planning to complete four or more years of college. By contrast, the lesser selectivity of two-year colleges and the complete absence of selectivity for other postsecondary institutions implies greater relative increases at the middle and low ability levels.

What about possible changes by gender and race? By gender, it is conceivable that the availability of financial aid enables larger proportions of low SES women to attend college, through overcoming the barrier frequently imposed by limited family resources and preferences, which in the past often resulted in greater educational outlays for sons than daughters.

Table 2–7. Percentages of High School Seniors Expecting to Obtain Various Amounts of Postsecondary Education, by SES and Ability, 1972 and 1980.

		1972				1980		
Expectations		SES				SES		
and								
Ability		L	M	H		L	M	H
A.	*Expect to Complete at Least a Four-Year Degree*							
	L	18	19	34		15	18	39
	M	28	39	65		29	38	67
	H	60	69	90		57	72	91
B.	*Expect to Enter a College Program*							
	L	29	33	52		28	34	62
	M	40	56	80		46	58	82
	H	70	80	95		73	84	96
C.	*Expect to Enter Some Form of Postsecondary Education*							
	L	57	64	76		55	66	81
	M	66	79	92		71	82	94
	H	86	91	98		85	94	99

Source: See Table 2–5.

By race, it is possible that the growth of special programs for minority students has encouraged more blacks relative to whites to attend some kind of postsecondary education. Thus, we might expect more pronounced changes in enrollment expectations for low-SES females and blacks than for low-SES males and whites.

We turn now to the results. Data on enrollment expectations of seniors classified jointly by SES and ability in 1972 and 1980 are presented in Table 2–7. The data of most interest are in the left-hand columns of each panel; These show expected enrollment rates of seniors from the low SES quartile by ability grouping—the bottom, middle two, and high quartiles. For these low SES seniors expecting to complete at least four years of college (Panel A), there are slight declines from 1972 to 1980 for the top and bottom quartiles. For those planning to enter a college program (including those with plans to complete a four-year degree), shown in Panel B, there is a perceptible increase for the middle ability group and a small increase for the top-ability quartile. For seniors who plan to enter some form of postsecondary education (including vocational, trade, or business schools, as well as college programs and completion of a four-year degree), shown in Panel C, there is a mild increase only for the middle-ability group. The most dramatic and consistent change elsewhere in the table is for the high SES/low ability cells in all three panels. We should not fail to note some slight increases scattered elsewhere: Panel A, medium SES/high ability; Panel B, middle SES/high ability; and Panel C, middle SES/middle ability.

What can we conclude from these results? One interpretation is that the availability of financial aid did have some effect, though still rather slight, on only middle-ability students from low-SES families. The small increases for middle-SES seniors in the middle- and high-ability groups are also at least partly consistent with this view, inasmuch as some financial aid goes to the middle-SES group. At the same time, the increases for high-SES/low-ability students are not at all consistent with this interpretation (an alternative interpretation of this unexpected change is that high-SES parents with not too talented children want them to attend college as a kind of defensive measure, in hopes that the resulting credential will overcome limited ability). Some of the other small increases for high-SES/middle-ability seniors are also not consistent with the financial aid explanation. After reviewing all of the evidence, however, one can hardly make a persuasive case that the availability of financial aid had any dramatic effect on the composition of high school seniors planning further education. Indeed, the enrollment plans of seniors from low-SES families still remain well below those from middle- and higher-SES families.

Similar data by gender are shown in Table 2–8. For males a reduction

Table 2–8. Percentages of High School Seniors Expecting to Obtain Various Amounts of Postsecondary Education, by SES, Ability, and Gender, 1972 and 1980.

	1972						1980					
	Males			Females			Males			Females		
Expectations and Ability	SES			SES			SES			SES		
	L	M	H	L	M	H	L	M	H	L	M	H
A. Expect to Complete at Least Four Years of College												
L	21	21	37	16	17	30	12	15	40	17	20	38
M	33	46	69	25	32	61	30	38	67	28	38	68
H	59	76	92	60	63	88	59	74	91	56	69	92
B. Expect to Enter a College Program												
L	30	36	51	28	31	53	23	28	56	31	41	69
M	44	61	81	36	51	79	41	53	79	49	62	84
H	68	85	97	71	75	93	73	83	95	73	86	96
C. Expect to Enter Some Form of Postsecondary Education												
L	58	67	80	56	60	71	49	61	77	59	70	85
M	71	83	93	62	74	90	69	79	94	73	84	95
H	87	95	99	86	88	98	86	94	99	85	94	99

Source: See Table 2–5.

occurred from 1972 to 1980 in plans to attend postsecondary education, with the largest absolute declines for low-SES seniors occurring among the low- and middle-ability groups, at all levels of schooling. The declines also show up clearly for the middle-SES groups except for high-ability seniors. For low-SES females, we note sizeable increases in enrollment expectations for middle-ability students, except for those planning to complete four years of college. We also note substantial increases for females in the middle- and high-SES groups, without respect to ability. All of this evidence confirms the narrowing of gender differences in enrollment expectations, brought about by a combination of decreased expectations for males and increased expectations for females. How much of the change for females is due to the greater availability of student financial aid is not clear, given that the effects for similarly situated men are so different.

We turn finally to the data by race, shown in Table 2–9. It is difficult to make a strong case that lower-SES white seniors experienced sharp increases in enrollment expectations. The gains for middle-ability students in Panels B and C are countered by declines for low- and high-ability students in Panel A. Again, the gains for high-SES/low-ability students show up clearly. The results for low-SES blacks are essentially unchanged in Panel A

Table 2–9. Percentages of High School Seniors Expecting to Obtain Various Amounts of Postsecondary Education, by SES, Ability, and Race, 1972 and 1980.

	1972						1980					
	Whites			Blacks			Whites			Blacks		
Expectations and Ability	SES			SES			SES			SES		
	L	M	H	L	M	H	L	M	H	L	M	H
A. *Expect to Complete at Least Four Years of College*												
L	9	16	31	32	42	70	6	12	34	27	41	56
M	22	38	65	55	72	91	22	35	66	57	67	84
H	58	69	91	85	89	85	53	71	91	83	86	89
B. *Expect to Enter a College Program*												
L	17	30	51	45	61	70	16	28	59	43	57	79
M	33	55	80	62	77	91	40	56	81	72	77	90
H	68	79	95	87	94	100	70	84	96	90	96	97
C. *Expect to Enter Some Form of Postsecondary Education*												
L	44	61	73	76	85	90	43	61	79	70	83	94
M	61	78	91	88	94	95	66	81	94	91	93	96
H	85	92	98	100	97	100	84	94	99	97	100	100

Source: See Table 2–5.

and Panel C; the only sizable change is for middle-ability students in Panel B. The 1972 and 1980 cells show no overall increases for middle- and high-SES blocks. All this suggests no apparent change for blacks relative to whites as a result of the greater abundance of financial aid.

Summary. This review of data on enrollment expectations has failed to produce any substantial evidence that the greater availability of student financial aid from 1972 to 1980 altered the college enrollment plans of high school seniors differentially by SES and ability. While some of the minor increases for low-SES relative to high SES students are consistent with possible positive effects of financial aid, there are enough other changes for middle- and high-SES students to cloud any conclusion that might be drawn about the efficiency of student financial aid in affecting access.

CONCLUDING OBSERVATIONS

On the basis of the foregoing discussion, what can we say about the relationship between education and economic growth? The most we can do is offer several suggestions about this relationship.

First, the evidence assembled here suggests that expansion of federal financial aid programs and their targeting toward youth from lower-income and lower-status families did not alter to any appreciable degree the composition of postsecondary students or the college enrollment expectations of high school seniors over the 1970s. While enrollment rates have risen somewhat for blacks and for females, it is not obvious that these changes reflect responses primarily to increased student financial aid.

Second, the failure of enrollments and enrollment plans to move in directions consistent with greater student financial aid resources is difficult to explain. One possibility is that student financial aid is not sufficiently generous to prompt any appreciable response—that is, to attract into college young people who might not otherwise have attended or planned to attend. Estimates made elsewhere of the effects of student financial aid on the internal rate of return to the educational investment of individuals indicate that, at most, the rate of return to financial aid recipients might have risen by 1.5 to 2 percentage points (Hansen 1982). It is not obvious that such increases are sufficient to evoke any substantial response in attracting additional young people into college.

Another possibility is that if there had not been increases in financial aid, over the 1970s, enrollment rates and enrollment expectations for students from lower-income families would have been lower than they were in the late 1970s. This possibility requires more systematic investigation. Still another possibility is that the data are confounded by the tendency of more young people to seek "independent" status for purposes of gaining financial aid. Those who would profit most from this change are not youth from low-income families who would qualify for aid anyway but rather those from higher-income families who could obtain financial aid only by severing their link to their parents (Hansen and Lampman 1983).

As usual, then, we are left with a new set of questions that must be pursued before we can be satisfied that we understand what happened and why it happened. We must still start with the failure to observe more pronounced changes in enrollment patterns that would be consistent with the increased provision of student financial aid. As noted earlier, this came as a surprise to this writer and to many other observers of the program. To the extent that these expectations have not been fulfilled, and assuming that there is no other explanation for the absence of change, it may be that student financial aid simply operated as a transfer program—that by substituting public for private funds it reduced the financial burden of college for parents and students without inducing additional enrollments or even changing the mix of present enrollments.

Aside from the lack of discernible impact, the program has entailed real costs. These include the administrative costs and the time costs (of students) associated with these programs. Another cost originates in the diversion of funds via the tax system to finance the redistributive student financial aid programs; in the absence of these expenditures and had taxes been reduced because of this, there is the presumpion that these resources would have been used more efficiently in providing people with what they as individuals wanted. Because of these additional costs the development of federal student financial aid programs may have retarded somewhat the pace of economic growth. In addition, it can be argued that our focus on greater equality of opportunity in higher education has led to disappointment because of the gap between our expectations and what has been accomplished. Thus, it appears that economic efficiency has been sacrificed in the pursuit of greater equity.

It is impossible, however, to offer any estimate of how much economic growth may have been slowed in the recent past—or is likely to be slowed in the future—because of these redistributive efforts. We simply do not know enough about these linkages to warrant making statements one way or the other. At the same time one senses that the tremendous energy and attention given to pursuing the objective of greater equality of educational opportunity has diverted attention from improving the quality of the higher education enterprise.

Whatever may have occurred over the past two decades of concern with issues of equity rather than efficiency, there appears to be a return to concerns about efficiency and economic growth. This will no doubt begin manifesting itself in the way we view higher education. What this will mean for the composition of college enrollments—and, more important, for the subsequent achievement of those who attend college—remains unclear. Will this redirection of activity spur economic growth? If it does, what is the mechanism by which schooling stimulates growth? These are old questions that have in recent years received too little consideration.

POSTSCRIPT

Since this paper was completed, Francis (1982) has argued that adjustment of family income size classes for price-level increases and use of a 1974 to 1980 comparison period leads to opposite conclusions from those reported here, implying that federal financial aid has opened access to enrollment. Lee (1983), following the price-level adjustment procedure of Francis and using data for the 1974 to 1981 period, offers a more cautious judgment, namely that federal financial assistance may have affected access and choice but that the evidence is not clearcut. Manski and Wise (1982), using a conditional logit model, analyze the 1972 NLS data and conclude that financial aid is an important determinant of postsecondary school attendance only for students attending two-year and vocational technical schools.

REFERENCES

Becker, G.S. 1960. "Underinvestment in College Education." *American Economic Review* (May): 345–354.

———. 1962. "Investment in Human Capital: A Theoretical Analysis." *Journal of Political Economy:* Supplement (October): 9–49.

Blaug, Mark. 1966. 2d ed. 1970; 3d ed. 1978. *Economics of Education: A Selected Annotated Bibliography.* New York: Pergamon Press.

Bowen, Howard R. 1977. *Investment in Learning.* San Francisco: Jossey-Bass.

Breneman, David, and Chester Finn. 1978. *Public Policy and Private Higher Education.* Washington, D.C.: The Brookings Institution.

Carnegie Commission on Higher Education. 1968. *Quality and Equality: New Levels of Federal Responsibility for Higher Education.* New York: McGraw-Hill.

———. 1973. *Higher Education: Who Pays? Who Benefits? Who Should Pay?* New York: McGraw-Hill.

Coleman, James S., et al. 1966. *Equality of Educational Opportunity.* Washington, D.C.: U.S. Government Printing Office.

Congressional Budget Office. 1980. *Federal Student Assistance: Issues and Options.* Washington, D.C.: U.S. Government Printing Office.

Denison, Edward F. 1962. *The Sources of Economic Growth and the Alternatives Before Us.* Committee for Economic Development, Supplementary Paper No. 13. New York: CED.

Economic Report of the President 1964. 1964. Washington, D.C.: U.S. Government Printing Office.

Folger, John K.; Helen S. Astin; and Alan E. Bayer. 1970. *Human Resources and Higher Education.* New York: Russell Sage Foundation.

Francis, Carol, 1982. "Trends in College-Going Rates by Income Level." Paper prepared for the National Commission on Student Financial Assistance, Washington, D.C.: November 9, 1982.

Gladieux, Lawrence E., and Thomas R. Wolanin. 1976. *Congress and the Colleges.* Lexington, Mass.: D.C. Heath.

Hansen, W. Lee. 1963. "Total and Private Rates of Return to Investment in Schooling." *Journal of Political Economy* (April): 128–140.

———. 1982. "Student Financial Aid and the Returns to Educational Investment." Department of Economics, University of Wisconsin-Madison.

Hansen, W. Lee, and Robert J. Lampman. 1974. "Basic Opportunity Grants for Higher Education." *Challenge* (November/December): 46–50.

———. 1983. "Good Intentions and Mixed Results: An Update on the BEOG Program Eight Years Later." In *Public Expenditure and Policy Analysis,* edited by Robert H. Haveman and Julius Margolis, pp. 493–512. New York: Rand McNally.

Hansen, W. Lee, and Burton A. Weisbrod. 1969. *Benefits, Costs, and Finance of Public Higher Education.* Chicago: Markham.

Hansen, W. Lee and Burton A. Weisbrod. "A New Approach to Higher Education Finance," in M.D. Orwig (ed.), *Financing Higher Education: Alternatives for the Federal Government.* Iowa City: American College Testing Program, 1971.

Harrington, Michael. 1962. *The Other America: Poverty in the United States.* New York: Macmillan.

Hartman, Robert W. 1972. "Higher Education Subsidies: An Analysis of Selected Programs in Current Legislation." From *The Economics of Federal Subsidy Programs,* compendium of papers submitted to the Joint Economic Committee, Part 4, *Higher Education and Manpower Subsidies,* 92nd Cong., 2d Sess. 1972, Washington, D.C.: U.S. Government Printing Office.

Kerr, Clark. 1968. "New Challenges to the College and University." In *Agenda for the Nation,* edited by Kermit Gordon, pp. 237–276. Washington, D.C.: The Brookings Institution.

Lampman, Robert J. 1974. "What Does It Do for the Poor? A New Test for National Policy." *The Public Interest* (Winter): 66–82.

Lee, John. 1983. "Changes in College Participation Rates and Student Financial Assistance 1969, 1974, and 1981." Washington, D.C.: Applied Systems Institute.

Levin, Henry M. 1977. "A Decade of Policy Developments in Improving Education and Training for Low-Income Populations." In *A Decade of Federal Antipoverty Programs: Achievements, Failures, and Lessons,* edited by Robert H. Haveman, pp. 123–88. New York: Academic Press.

Little, J. Kenneth. 1958. *A Statewide Inquiry into Decisions of Youth about Education Beyond High School.* Madison: School of Education, University of Wisconsin.

———. 1959. *Explorations into the College Plans and Experience of High School Graduates.* Madison: School of Education, University of Wisconsin.

Manski, Charles E. and David A. Wise. 1983. *College Choice in America.* Cambridge: Harvard University Press.

National Center for Education Statistics. 1981. *The Condition of Education.* Washington, D.C.: Department of Education.

Office of Evaluation and Program Management. 1981. *Annual Evaluation Report, Fiscal Year 1980,* Vols. I and II. Washington, D.C.: Department of Education.

Orwig, M.D., ed. 1971. *Financing Higher Education: Alternatives for the Federal Government.* Iowa City: American College Testing Program.

Schultz, T.W. 1960. "Capital Formation by Education." *Journal of Political Economy* (December): 571–583.

————. 1961. "Investment in Human Capital." *American Economic Review* (March): 1–17.

————. 1972. "Investment in Education: The Equity-Efficiency Tradeoff." *Journal of Political Economy,* Supplement (May/June): S2–30.

Task Force of the Department of Health, Education, and Welfare. 1969. *Toward a Long Range Plan for Federal Financial Support of Higher Education.* Washington, D.C.: Department of Health, Education, and Welfare.

Toma, Eugenia Froedge. 1981. "Education." In *Agenda for Progress: Examining Federal Spending,* edited by Eugene J. McAllister, pp. 197–215. Washington, D.C.: The Heritage Foundation.

Wolfle, D. 1954. *America's Resources of Specialized Talent.* New York: Harper and Bros.

Chapter 3

The Contribution of Education to U.S. Economic Growth, 1948–73

Dale W. Jorgenson

INTRODUCTION

This paper analyzes the contribution of education to U.S. economic growth during the years 1948 to 1973. This remarkable quarter century was dominated by a powerful upward thrust in the level of U.S. economic activity. In 1973 the output of the civilian economy stood at $1.306 trillion in constant dollars of 1972; output in 1948 was only 498 billions. The increase in the level of economic activity from 1948 to 1973 was greater than the rise over the whole previous course of American history.

The growth record of the U.S. economy over the period 1948 to 1973 is all the more striking in view of the experience of the two preceding decades. The years from 1929 to 1948 were dominated by the Great Depression of the 1930s and the Second World War. For this period Christensen and Jorgenson (1970) have estimated the rate of growth of the U.S. private domestic economy at 2.1 percent per year. For the period 1948 to 1960 the U.S. growth rate rose to 3.6 percent per year; from 1960 to 1973 the growth rate averaged 4.3 percent, more than double the average from 1929 to 1948.

In this paper we employ a novel perspective on postwar U.S. economic growth. We show that the driving force behind the massive expansion of the U.S. economy between 1948 and 1973 was a vast mobilization of capital and labor resources. The most important single contribution to U.S. economic growth during this period was made by the growth in capital input. The contribution of capital input averaged 1.5 percent per year for the period

Financial support for this work was provided by the National Institute of Education.

1948 to 1973. The contribution of labor input was another important source of U.S. economic growth, averaging 1.1 percent per year from 1948 to 1973.

Capital and labor inputs combined contributed 2.6 percent per year to the growth rate of 3.9 percent for the output of the U.S. civilian economy from 1948 to 1973. These two inputs accounted for two-thirds of the growth of output that took place. By contrast advances in the level of technology contributed only 1.3 percent per year to the growth of output, half the combined contributions of capital and labor inputs. Accordingly, we have emphasized the mobilization of capital and labor resources rather than advances in the level of technology in analyzing postwar U.S. economic growth.

Increases in hours worked through gains in employment contribute to the growth of labor input. In addition, labor input grows through increases in the proportion of hours worked by more productive members of the work force. We identify this component of growth in labor input with growth in labor quality. In our approach the growth of labor input is the sum of growth in hours worked and growth in labor quality. The contribution of education to economic growth takes place through enhancement of the productivity of individual members of the labor force. Change in the educational composition of the labor force is a very important source of growth in labor quality. However, the contribution of education must be separated from the impact of changes in the composition of the labor force by sex, age, employment status, and occupation.

To implement our approach to the analysis of sources of U.S. economic growth we have developed a methodology based on an explicit model of production and technical change. This methodology is based on an aggregate production function giving output as a function of capital and labor inputs and time.[1] To identify the role of education in economic growth we represent labor input as a function of types of labor input that differ in marginal productivity. We combine the production function and labor input as a function of its components with necessary conditions for producer equilibrium. These conditions make it possible to identify the marginal product of labor input with the ratio of the wage rate to the price of output. Similarly, we can identify the marginal product of each type of labor input with the ratio of its wage rate to the wage rate of labor input as a whole.

To analyze the sources of U.S. economic growth and to identify the contribution of education we first allocate the growth of aggregate output between contributions of capital and labor inputs and changes in the level of technology.[2] We then separate the contribution of each input between growth in an unweighted sum of its components and growth in input quality.[3] Labor quality is defined as the ratio between the labor input index and the unweighted sum of hours worked. To identify the role of education we first represent labor input as a function of types of labor input broken down by characteristics of individual workers such as sex, age, education, employment status, and occupation.[4] We then allocate the growth of the quality of labor input among the contributions of changes in the composition of the labor force by characteristics of individual workers. This analysis enables us to separate the contributions of education to economic growth from the contributions of other changes in composition of the labor force.

First we analyze the sources of U.S. economic growth for the period 1948 to 1973. We show that the contribution of labor quality is a very important source of U.S. economic growth, accounting for 0.45 percent per year of a total contribution of labor input of 1.09 percent per year. The quality of labor input grows through increases in the proportion of hours worked by the more productive members of the labor force. In the next section we analyze the contribution of education to the growth of labor input in the U.S. economy. We show that the contribution of education accounts for 0.67 percent per year of a total growth in the quality of labor input of 0.72 percent per year. The contribution of education takes place through enhancement of the productivity of individual members of the labor force.

While the contribution of education to U.S. economic growth is obviously highly significant, our analysis of the sources of economic growth is subject to very important limitations. The most critical limitation is that educational investment in any year contributes to growth in the quality of the labor force in that year, but also enhances the productivity of individual workers in future years. A second limitation is that measures of labor input focus attention exclusively on market labor activities—hours worked and wage rates of employed persons. Education also contributes to social welfare through nonmarket activities of individuals employed in the labor market and through the activities of individuals not participating in the labor market.

In the next section we attempt to overcome some of the limitations of our analysis of education as a source of economic growth by presenting a measure of investment in education. The most important innovations in our measure of investment in education are these: First, our concept of human capital is based on lifetime labor incomes for all individuals in the U.S. population. Second, we incorporate both market and nonmarket activities into our measures of labor incomes. This makes it possible to provide measures of lifetime labor incomes for individuals employed in the labor market and for individuals not involved in the labor market. Third, our measures of investment in education are based on a system of demographic accounts that includes accounts for school enrollment. Fourth, we combine these accounts with economic accounts for the value of all available labor time to obtain measures of investment in education for the U.S. economy as a whole. Finally, we compare our approach to the analysis of sources of U.S. economic growth and investment in education with alternative approaches.

To implement our methodology for analyzing the sources of U.S. economic growth we have constructed a complete set of U.S. national accounts for capital and labor inputs as well as for output at the aggregate level. This system of accounts complements the existing U.S. national accounts for output developed by the Bureau of Economic Analysis (1977). Our accounts can be integrated with existing national accounts for capital formation and wealth in the form of nonhuman capital developed by Christensen and Jorgenson (1969, 1970, 1973a, 1973b). Our accounts can also be integrated with a new system of U.S. national accounts developed by Jorgenson and Pachon (1983a, 1983b) that includes capital formation and wealth in the form of human capital.

SOURCES OF U.S. ECONOMIC GROWTH

In this section we allocate the growth of aggregate output between growth in capital and labor inputs and changes in the level of technology. We construct data on the rate of technical change by combining price and quantity data for value added, capital input, and labor input. We employ a translog quantity index of the rate of technical change, equal to the difference between the change in the logarithm of value added from period to period and a weighted average of changes in the logarithms of capital and labor inputs.[5] The weights are given by average shares of each input in value added for the two periods.

The quantity of value added is the sum of the quantities of value added in all sectors:

$$V = \sum V_i.$$

We can define the price of value added for the economy as a whole p_V in terms of prices of value added in all sectors $\{p_V^i\}$:

$$p_V V = p_V \sum V_i,$$
$$= \sum p_V^i V_i.$$

Value added for the economy as a whole is equal to the sum of value added over all sectors. The quantity index of value added, the corresponding price index, and value added in all sectors are presented for the period 1948 to 1973 in Table 3-1.

Our next objective is to implement an index of productivity for the economy as a whole empirically. We assume that value added V can be expressed as a translog function of capital input K, labor input L, and time T. The corresponding index of productivity growth is the translog index of the rate of technical change $\bar{v}_T$:

Table 3-1. Aggregate Value Added, 1948–73.

Year	Price	Quantity	Value Added
1948	0.535	498.420	266.613
1949	0.527	497.007	261.742
1950	0.544	539.467	293.227
1951	0.582	578.305	336.845
1952	0.599	597.858	358.356
1953	0.600	621.816	372.991
1954	0.617	620.042	382.434
1955	0.622	664.014	413.164
1956	0.633	692.491	438.434
1957	0.645	707.485	456.351
1958	0.667	705.689	470.376
1959	0.674	748.836	504.652
1960	0.689	771.174	530.978
1961	0.695	788.039	547.613
1962	0.706	828.168	584.367
1963	0.708	867.460	614.488
1964	0.722	914.627	660.355
1965	0.743	967.928	719.641
1966	0.773	1020.897	789.336
1967	0.794	1049.774	833.063
1968	0.823	1101.789	906.418
1969	0.876	1134.840	993.783
1970	0.904	1137.615	1027.976
1971	0.948	1168.719	1108.318
1972	1.000	1233.220	1233.220
1973	1.065	1306.251	1391.316

$$\bar{v}_T = \ln V(T) - \ln V(T-1) - \bar{v}_K [\ln K(T) - \ln K(T-1)]$$
$$- \bar{v}_L [\ln L(T) - \ln L(T-1)],$$

where weights are given by average shares of capital and labor inputs, $\bar{v}_K$ and $\bar{v}_L$, in value added for the economy as a whole:

$$\bar{v}_K = \tfrac{1}{2}[v_K(T) + v_K(T-1)],$$
$$\bar{v}_L = \tfrac{1}{2}[v_L(T) + v_L(T-1)],$$
$$\bar{v}_T = \tfrac{1}{2}[v_T(T) + v_T(T-1)],$$

and

$$v_K = \frac{p_K K}{p_V V},$$

$$v_L = \frac{p_L L}{p_V V}.$$

The value shares are computed from data on the quantities of value added, capital input, and labor input and the corresponding prices, p_V, p_K, and p_L.

We assume that capital input and labor input can be expressed as translog functions of individual capital inputs $\{K_k\}$ and individual labor inputs $\{L_l\}$:[6]

$$\ln K(T) - \ln K(T-1) = \sum \bar{v}_{Kk}[\ln K_k(T) - \ln K_k(T-1)],$$

$$\ln L(T) - \ln L(T-1) = \sum \bar{v}_{Ll}[\ln L_l(T) - \ln L_l(T-1)],$$

where weights are given by average shares of quantities of capital input and labor input in the values of the corresponding aggregates:

$$\bar{v}_{Kk} = \tfrac{1}{2}[v_{Kk}(T) + v_{Kk}(T-1)], \qquad (k = 1, 2 \ldots p),$$

$$\bar{v}_{Ll} = \tfrac{1}{2}[v_{Ll}(T) + v_{Ll}(T-1)], \qquad (l = 1, 2 \ldots q),$$

and:

$$v_{Kk} = \frac{p_{Kk} K_k}{\sum p_{Kk} K_k}, \qquad (k = 1, 2 \ldots p),$$

$$v_{Ll} = \frac{p_{Ll} L_l}{\sum p_{Ll} L_l}, \qquad (l = 1, 2 \ldots q).$$

The value shares are computed from data on capital inputs and their prices $\{p_{Kk}\}$ and labor inputs and their prices $\{p_{Ll}\}$.

We next compare the rate of technical change and growth in capital and labor inputs as sources of growth in value added. We present annual growth rates for value added, capital input, and labor input for the period 1948 to 1973 in Table 3-2. The rate of growth of value added is the sum of the average rate of technical change and a weighted average of rates of growth of capital and labor inputs with weights given by the average value shares of the inputs. We present the share of capital input in value added in Table 3-2. The value share of labor input is equal to unity less the value share of capital input. Applying these weights to the rates of growth of the corresponding input identifies the contribution of each input to economic growth. We present the weighted growth rates of capital and labor inputs and the average annual rate of technical change in Table 3-2.

Value added grew rapidly throughout the period 1948 to 1973 with declines in 1949, 1954, and 1958 and a very low but positive growth rate in 1970. The declines lasted for a single year and were followed by sharp recoveries in 1950 to 1951, 1955, and 1959. Turning to the growth of capital input, we find that declines in value added during the period 1948 to 1973 were followed by reductions in the rate of growth of capital input one period later. By comparison with the growth of capital input, the growth of labor input was considerably more uneven. While the growth rate of capital input was positive throughout the period, substantial declines in labor input

Table 3-2. Contributions to Growth in Aggregate Output, 1948–73.

Year	Value Added	Capital Input	Labor Input	Average Value Share of Capital Input	Contributions to Growth in Aggregate Value Added: Capital Input	Labor Input	Technical Change
1949	−0.0028	0.0630	−0.0346	0.3470	0.0215	−0.0226	−0.0017
1950	0.0819	0.0375	0.0390	0.3610	0.0137	0.0247	0.0434
1951	0.0695	0.0710	0.0516	0.3576	0.0247	0.0337	0.0110
1952	0.0332	0.0555	0.0262	0.3492	0.0198	0.0165	−0.0031
1953	0.0392	0.0340	0.0175	0.3470	0.0118	0.0114	0.0160
1954	−0.0028	0.0389	−0.0285	0.3523	0.0136	−0.0186	0.0020
1955	0.0685	0.0316	0.0311	0.3677	0.0122	0.0194	0.0378
1956	0.0419	0.0530	0.0211	0.3648	0.0193	0.0139	0.0086
1957	0.0214	0.0416	0.0013	0.3541	0.0148	0.0005	0.0059
1958	−0.0025	0.0348	−0.0278	0.3572	0.0121	−0.0174	0.0027
1959	0.0593	0.0153	0.0356	0.3675	0.0061	0.0223	0.0308
1960	0.0293	0.0347	0.0281	0.3723	0.0129	0.0178	−0.0014
1961	0.0216	0.0320	−0.0101	0.3720	0.0115	−0.0064	0.0165
1962	0.0496	0.0234	0.0374	0.3714	0.0088	0.0229	0.0178
1963	0.0463	0.0363	0.0110	0.3721	0.0132	0.0073	0.0257
1964	0.0529	0.0350	0.0263	0.3748	0.0134	0.0163	0.0231
1965	0.0566	0.0407	0.0348	0.3801	0.0151	0.0211	0.0203
1966	0.0532	0.0549	0.0424	0.3801	0.0210	0.0265	0.0055
1967	0.0278	0.0594	0.0162	0.3758	0.0222	0.0103	−0.0046
1968	0.0483	0.0456	0.0236	0.3705	0.0167	0.0146	0.0169
1969	0.0295	0.0469	0.0259	0.3655	0.0172	0.0162	−0.0038
1970	0.0024	0.0470	−0.0041	0.3562	0.0165	−0.0025	−0.0116
1971	0.0269	0.0305	0.0031	0.3518	0.0107	0.0015	0.0146
1972	0.0537	0.0346	0.0233	0.3596	0.0123	0.0147	0.0266
1973	0.0575	0.0469	0.0421	0.3621	0.0171	0.0273	0.0130

coincided with declines in value added in 1949, 1954, and 1958; declines in labor input also took place in 1961 and 1970. Finally, the pattern of technical change, like that of labor input, was relatively uneven, with declines in the level of technology in 1949, 1952, 1960, 1967, and 1969 to 1970. Rapid growth in the level of technology is associated with recoveries in the growth of value added in 1950, 1955, and 1959. Rapid growth in the level of technology also took place during the period 1960 to 1966; this period was characterized by unusually rapid growth of value added, capital input, and labor input.

The average value share of capital input was very stable over the period 1948 to 1973, ranging from 0.3470 in 1949 and 1953 to 0.3801 in 1965 and 1966. Accordingly, the cyclical pattern relating growth in value added to the contributions of capital and labor inputs is virtually identical to the patterns relating growth in value added to growth in capital and labor inputs. Comparing the contributions of capital and labor inputs and the rate of technical change as sources of growth in value added, we find that the contribution of capital input was positive throughout the period from 1948 to 1973 and relatively even. By contrast, the contributions of labor input and the rate of technical change were negative for five and six of the twenty-five periods, respectively, and relatively uneven.

The contribution of capital input provides the largest single contribution to the growth of output in ten of the twenty-five periods from 1948 to 1973. The contribution of labor input provides the largest single contribution in four of these periods. Finally, the rate of technical change provides the largest contribution in ten periods. We find that the contribution of capital input is greater than that of labor input in fourteen of the twenty-five periods. The contribution of capital input is greater than the rate of technical change in thirteen of the twenty-five periods. Finally, the contribution of labor input is greater than the rate of technical change in only eleven of the twenty-five periods.

We have allocated the sources of growth in value added among growth in capital and labor inputs and the rate of technical change. We next decompose the rate of growth of capital input between rates of growth of capital stock A and quality of capital stock Q_K. Similarly, we decompose the rate of growth of labor input between rates of growth of hours worked H and quality of labor hours Q_L. Using indexes of the quality of capital stock and hours worked, we can decompose the rate of growth of value added as follows:[7]

$$
\begin{aligned}
\ln V(T) - \ln V(T-1) = \bar{v}_K [\ln Q_K(T) - \ln Q_K(T-1)] \\
+ \bar{v}_K [\ln A(T-1) - \ln A(T-2)] \\
+ \bar{v}_L [\ln Q_L(T) - \ln Q_L(T-1)] \\
+ \bar{v}_L [\ln H(T) - \ln H(T-1)] + \bar{v}_T.
\end{aligned}
$$

Table 3-3. Contributions to Growth in Aggregate Input, 1948–73.

Year	Quality of Capital Stock	Capital Stock	Quality of Hours Worked	Hours Worked
1949	0.0093	0.0122	0.0004	− 0.0230
1950	0.0058	0.0079	0.0085	0.0161
1951	0.0107	0.0140	0.0077	0.0259
1952	0.0083	0.0115	0.0126	0.0038
1953	0.0041	0.0076	0.0052	0.0062
1954	0.0053	0.0083	0.0032	− 0.0218
1955	0.0038	0.0073	0.0011	0.0183
1956	0.0073	0.0119	0.0042	0.0097
1957	0.0051	0.0097	0.0066	− 0.0060
1958	0.0044	0.0076	0.0033	− 0.0208
1959	0.0013	0.0047	0.0048	0.0175
1960	0.0042	0.0086	0.0140	0.0037
1961	0.0036	0.0078	− 0.0032	− 0.0031
1962	0.0025	0.0063	0.0110	0.0118
1963	0.0043	0.0089	0.0016	0.0056
1964	0.0033	0.0100	0.0060	0.0103
1965	0.0040	0.0110	0.0019	0.0191
1966	0.0073	0.0137	0.0079	0.0186
1967	0.0080	0.0141	0.0047	0.0055
1968	0.0055	0.0111	0.0043	0.0103
1969	0.0055	0.0116	0.0005	0.0156
1970	0.0052	0.0113	0.0067	− 0.0092
1971	0.0029	0.0077	0.0011	0.0004
1972	0.0027	0.0095	− 0.0038	0.0186
1973	0.0051	0.0119	0.0034	0.0239

The rate of growth of value added is the sum of a weighted average of the rates of growth of capital stock and hours worked, a weighted average of the rates of growth of quality of capital stock and hours worked, and the rate of technical change. In Table 3-3 we present weighted averages of rates of growth of the quality of capital stock and hours worked for the period 1948 to 1973. We also present rates of growth of capital stock and hours worked for the same period.

We find that the growth of capital quality is an important source of growth of capital input but that it is dominated by the growth of capital stock. Both components of the growth of capital input have positive rates of growth throughout the period 1948 to 1973. The slowdowns in the growth of capital input in 1950, 1955, 1959, and 1971 were associated with declines in rates of growth of both capital stock and its quality. Growth in the quality of hours worked is an important source of growth of labor input, with positive rates of growth in every year from 1948 to 1973, except for 1961 and 1972. By comparison the growth in hours worked is considerably more erratic with declines in 1949, 1954, 1957 to 1958, 1961, and 1970. Only

Table 3-4. Aggregate Output, Inputs, and Productivity: Rates of Growth, 1948–73.

Variable	*(Average Annual Rates of Growth)*						
	1948–73	*1948–53*	*1953–57*	*1957–60*	*1960–66*	*1966–69*	*1969–73*
Value added	0.0385	0.0442	0.0323	0.0287	0.0467	0.0352	0.0351
Capital input	0.0418	0.0522	0.0413	0.0283	0.0371	0.0506	0.0398
Labor input	0.0173	0.0199	0.0063	0.0120	0.0236	0.0219	0.0161
Contribution of capital input	0.0151	0.0183	0.0147	0.0103	0.0138	0.0187	0.0142
Contribution of labor input	0.0109	0.0127	0.0038	0.0076	0.0146	0.0137	0.0103
Rate of technical change	0.0125	0.0131	0.0136	0.0107	0.0182	0.0028	0.0107
Contribution of capital quality	0.0052	0.0076	0.0054	0.0033	0.0042	0.0063	0.0040
Contribution of capital stock	0.0098	0.0106	0.0093	0.0070	0.0096	0.0123	0.0101
Contribution of labor quality	0.0045	0.0069	0.0038	0.0074	0.0042	0.0032	0.0018
Contribution of hours worked	0.0063	0.0058	0.0001	0.0001	0.0104	0.0105	0.0084

the decline in hours worked that took place in 1957 failed to coincide with a decline in labor input. The growth of hours worked exceeded the growth of the quality of hours worked as a source of growth in labor input in seventeen of the twenty-five periods from 1948 to 1973.

We have analyzed the sources of growth of aggregate value added in the U.S. economy over the period 1948 to 1973 on the basis of annual data from the aggregate production account presented in Tables 3-2 and 3-3. Next we summarize these data for the period as a whole and for six subperiods—1948 to 1953, 1953 to 1957, 1957 to 1960, 1960 to 1966, 1966 to 1969, and 1969 to 1973—in Table 3-4. The first part of this table provides data from Table 3-2 on growth in output and inputs. The second part summarizes data from Table 3-2 on the contributions of capital input, labor input, and the rate of technical change to the growth of output. The third part presents decompositions of both the contribution of capital input into components associated with capital quality and capital stock and the contribution of labor input into components associated with labor quality and hours worked.

For the period 1948 to 1973 aggregate value added grew at 3.85 percent per year, while capital input grew at 4.18 percent per year, indicating that the ratio of capital input to output has risen during the period. By contrast labor input grew at only 1.73 percent per year while the rate of aggregate technical change averaged 1.25 percent per year. The average annual rate of growth of value added reached its maximum at 4.67 percent during the period 1960 to 1966, grew at an average annual rate of 4.42 percent in 1948 to 1953, and fell to a minimum of 2.87 percent per year during the period 1957 to 1960. The average annual rate of growth of capital input reached a maximum of 5.22 percent from 1948 to 1953, grew at 5.06 percent per year during the period 1966 to 1969 and fell to a minimum of 2.83 percent per year in 1957 to 1960. The rate of growth of labor input reached its maximum during the period 1960 to 1966 at 2.36 percent per year, grew at 2.19 percent per year during the period 1966 to 1969, and fell to a minimum of 0.63 percent per year in 1953 to 1957.

To analyze the sources of U.S. economic growth for the period 1948 to 1973, we next consider the contributions of capital and labor inputs, and the rate of technical change as sources of growth in value added. For the period as a whole the contribution of capital input averaged 1.51 percent per year, the contribution of labor input averaged 1.09 percent per year, and the rate of technical change averaged 1.25 percent per year. Capital input is the most important source of growth in four of the six subperiods—1948 to 1953, 1953 to 1957, 1966 to 1969, and 1969 to 1973. Technical change is the most important source of growth during the two subperiods 1957 to 1960 and 1960 to 1966. Our overall conclusion is that capital input is the most important source of growth in value added, technical change is the next most important, and labor input is the least important. This conclusion is supported by our analysis of growth for the period as a whole, by data for subperiods given in Table 3-4, and by the annual data presented in Table 3-2.

In order to analyze the contributions of capital and labor inputs in more detail, we consider data on the contributions of capital stock and its quality and hours worked and their quality for the period as a whole and for the six subperiods presented in Table 3-4. For the period 1948 to 1973 the contribution of capital stock accounts for almost two-thirds of the contribution of capital input. This quantitative relationship between capital stock and its quality characterizes most of the period. The average contribution of capital quality reached its maximum at 0.76 percent per year in 1948 to 1953, averaged 0.63 percent per year during the period 1966 to 1969, fell to a minimum of 0.33 percent per year in 1957 to 1960 and averaged 0.40 percent per year in 1969 to 1973. The contribution of capital stock reached its maximum at 1.23 percent per year in 1966 to 1969, averaged 1.06 percent per year during 1948 to 1953, and fell to a minimum of 0.70 percent per year in 1957 to 1960.

For the period as a whole the contribution of hours worked exceeded the contribution of labor quality. For the first half of the period the contribution of hours worked fell below the contribution of the quality of hours worked. For the last half of the period the contribution of hours worked accounts for more than two-thirds of the contribution of labor input. The average contribution of labor quality reached its maximum at 0.74 percent per year in 1957 to 1960 and declined steadily to a minimum of 0.18 percent per year in 1969 to 1973. The contribution of hours worked reached its maximum of 1.05 percent per year from 1966 to 1969, averaged 1.04 percent per year during the period 1960 to 1966 and only 0.01 percent per year during the periods 1953 to 1957 and 1957 to 1960.

THE CONTRIBUTION OF EDUCATION

The previous section presented a production account for the U.S. economy as a whole, including measures of aggregate value added, capital input, and labor input. We have utilized these data to allocate the growth of aggregate output among the rate of technical change and the contributions of capital and labor inputs. This section analyzes the growth of labor input in greater detail in order to identify the contribution of education to U.S. economic growth. We assume that aggregate labor input can be expressed as a translog function of individual types of labor inputs, cross-classified by sex, age, education, employment status, and occupation. A measure of aggregate labor input can be constructed as a translog quantity index number.

For each of the components of labor input the flow of labor services is proportional to hours worked. Defining aggregate hours worked as an unweighted sum of its components, we can define the aggregate index of the quality of hours worked as an index that transforms aggregate hours worked into the translog index of aggregate labor input. This quality index reflects changes in the composition of aggregate hours worked by sex, age, education, employment status, and occupation. To analyze the sources of quality change in aggregate labor input, we introduce partial indexes of labor input, adding hours worked and the share of labor compensation over some characteristics of the labor force and constructing a translog index over the remaining characteristics.[8]

To analyze the sources of changes in the quality of aggregate labor input we introduce the contributions of each characteristic of labor input as the difference between the rate of growth of the corresponding partial index of labor input and the rate of growth of aggregate hours worked. For example, the contribution of education to the quality of aggregate labor input is defined in terms of the rate of growth of a partial index of labor input obtained by adding hours worked and the share of labor compensation over all other characteristics of the labor force—sex, age, employment status, and occupation—and constructing a translog index over educational groupings.

To construct an index of aggregate labor input we assume that aggregate labor input, say $L(T)$, can be expressed as a translog function of its individual components, so that the translog quantity index of aggregate labor input takes the form:

$$\ln L(T) - \ln L(T-1) = \sum \bar{v}_{Ll}[\ln L_l(T) - \ln L_l(T-1)],$$

where weights are given by the average shares of the individual components in the value of aggregate labor compensation:

$$\bar{v}_{Ll} = \tfrac{1}{2}[v_{Ll}(T) + v_{Ll}(T-1)], \qquad (l = 1, 2 \ldots q)$$

and:

$$v_{Ll} = \frac{p_{Ll} L_l}{\sum p_{Ll} L_l}, \qquad (l = 1, 2 \ldots q).$$

The value shares are computed from data on hours worked $\{L_l\}$ and compensation per hour $\{p_{Ll}\}$ for each component of aggregate labor input, cross-classified by sex, age, education, employment class, and occupation of workers.

In quantifying the effect of changes in the composition of hours worked we begin with the recognition that the relationship between labor services and hours worked is not the same for all categories of labor input. For each of the components of aggregate labor input $\{L_l(T)\}$ the flow of labor services is proportional to hours worked, say $\{H_l(T)\}$:

$$L_l(T) = Q_{Ll} \cdot H_l(T), \qquad (l = 1, 2 \ldots q),$$

where the constants of proportionality $\{Q_L\}$ transform hours worked into flows of labor services. Each of the scalars $\{Q_{Ll}\}$ is specific to a given category of labor input but is independent of time. It necessarily follows that the translog quantity index of aggregate labor input can be expressed either in terms of its components $\{L_l\}$ or in terms of the components of hours worked $\{H_l\}$:

$$\ln L(T) - \ln L(T-1) = \sum \bar{v}_{Ll}[\ln L_l(T) - \ln L_l(T-1)],$$

$$= \sum \bar{v}_{Ll}[\ln H_l(T) - \ln H_l(T-1)].$$

We form the aggregate index of labor input from data on hours worked by workers cross-classified by sex, age, education, employment class, and occupation. Changes in the logarithms of hours worked for each component are weighted by average shares in the value of aggregate labor compensation.

The relation between aggregate labor input and aggregate hours worked is a function of the changing composition of aggregate hours worked. More precisely, it depends on the factor of proportionality that transforms aggregate hours worked into aggregate labor input. We can define *aggregate hours worked,* say $H(T)$, as the unweighted sum of its components,

$$H(T) = \sum H_l(T).$$

We can then define the *aggregate index of the quality of hours worked,* say $Q_L(T)$, as an index that transforms aggregate hours worked into the translog index of labor input:

$$L(T) = Q_L(T) \cdot H(T).$$

It follows that the growth rate of the aggregate index of the quality of hours worked can be expressed in the form:

$$\ln Q_L(T) - \ln Q_L(T-1) = \sum \bar{v}_{Ll}[\ln H_l(T) - \ln H_l(T-1)]$$

$$- [\ln H(T) - \ln H(T-1)].$$

The quality index reflects changes in the composition of aggregate hours worked by workers classified by sex, age, education, employment class, and occupation.

The aggregate index of labor input, the corresponding price index, and the index of the quality of hours worked are presented for the period 1948 to 1973 in Table 3-5. Annual data for employment, weekly hours per person, hourly compensation, and total labor compensation and hours worked are also reported. The important conclusion to be derived from Table 3-5 is that 43 percent of the average annual rate of growth of labor input is accounted for by a shift in the composition of hours worked. The remaining growth in labor input is due to growth in unweighted annual hours reported in the last column of Table 3–5. Labor input increases at an average rate equal to 1.73 percent per year. The aggregate quality and unweighted hours indexes increase at average annual rates equal to 0.72 and 1.01 percents, respectively.

Our next objective is to analyze the effects of changes in the composition of total hours worked. For this purpose we consider the components of hours worked, say $\{H_{saeco}(T)\}$, cross-classified by sex, age, education, employment class, and occupation. Previously, we have used a single subscript l to represent categories of labor input cross-classified by all five characteristics. The subscript has represented 1,600 categories of labor input. In our new notation labor input is cross-classified by two sexes represented by the subscript s, eight age groups represented by a, five education classes represented by e, two employment classes represented by c, and ten occupational groups represented by o. The five education classes are (1) one to eight years of grade school, (2) one to three years of high school, (3) four years of high school, (4) one to three years of college, and (5) four or more years of college. We also consider the shares of the components of labor input in the value of labor compensation for the economy as a whole, say $v_{saeco}(T)$, cross-classified by sex, age, education, employment class, and occupation.

Our analysis begins with the construction "partial" indexes of labor input. We can define a partial index of labor input by adding hours worked and value shares over some characteristics of the labor force and constructing a translog index over the remaining characteristics. More specifically, we can define a *first-order index of labor input* corresponding to each characteristic of labor input by adding hours worked and value shares over all other characteristics of labor input and constructing a translog index over the single characteristic of interest. Since there are five characteristics of labor input—sex, age, education, employment class, and occupation—there are five first-order indexes of labor input. For example, the first-order index of labor input corresponding to sex, say L_s, can have its growth rate expressed in the form:

$$\Delta \ln L_s = \sum_s \bar{v}_s \, \Delta \ln H_s,$$

$$= \sum_s \bar{v}_s \, \Delta \ln \sum_a \sum_e \sum_c \sum_o H_{saeco},$$

where

$$\bar{v}_s = \tfrac{1}{2}[v_s(T) + v_s(T-1)],$$

$$v_s = \sum_a \sum_e \sum_c \sum_o v_{saeco},$$

Table 3-5. Aggregate Labor Input, 1948–73.

Year	Labor Input				Employment (thousands)	Weekly Hours per Person (hours)	Hourly Compensation (dollars)	Hours Worked (millions)
	Price (index; 1972= 1.000)	Quantity (billions of constant dollars of 1972)	Outlay (billions of current dollars)	Quality (index; 1972= 1.000)				
1948	0.330	531.760	175.676	0.839	61,639	39.3	1.39	126,132
1949	0.330	513.668	169.354	0.840	60,145	38.9	1.39	121,752
1950	0.346	533.910	184.967	0.850	61,688	38.9	1.48	124,977
1951	0.392	562.669	220.288	0.861	64,278	38.9	1.69	130,137
1952	0.402	577.204	232.060	0.878	64,981	38.7	1.77	130,888
1953	0.418	587.404	245.519	0.885	65,982	38.5	1.86	132,154
1954	0.427	570.791	243.599	0.890	64,533	38.0	1.91	127,715
1955	0.440	588.601	259.246	0.892	66,178	38.1	1.97	131,392
1956	0.468	601.721	281.856	0.897	67,730	37.9	2.11	133,555
1957	0.492	602.283	296.058	0.907	67,880	37.4	2.24	132,181
1958	0.511	586.070	299.483	0.911	66,416	37.0	2.34	128,028
1959	0.522	607.191	317.024	0.918	68,028	37.2	2.41	131,678
1960	0.533	624.684	333.009	0.940	68,742	37.0	2.52	132,325
1961	0.557	618.309	344.329	0.935	68,823	36.7	2.61	131,684
1962	0.572	641.354	367.153	0.951	70,127	36.8	2.74	134,198
1963	0.594	648.869	385.582	0.954	70,830	36.7	2.85	135,415
1964	0.617	666.053	411.233	0.963	72,332	36.5	2.99	137,660
1965	0.644	689.197	444.015	0.966	74,617	36.5	3.13	141,988
1966	0.683	719.392	491.534	0.979	77,717	36.2	3.36	146,317
1967	0.713	731.399	521.153	0.986	79,098	35.8	3.53	147,633

1968	0.767	748.674	574.124	0.993	81,010	35.6	3.83	150,090
1969	0.822	768.102	631.543	0.994	83,247	35.5	4.11	153,844
1970	0.876	765.146	670.183	1.004	83,245	35.0	4.42	151,636
1971	0.931	767.025	714.139	1.006	83,510	34.9	4.71	151,767
1972	1.000	784.888	784.888	1.000	85,885	34.9	5.02	156,246
1973	1.086	819.269	889.484	1.005	89,310	34.9	5.48	162,217

and the Δ notation signifies first differences in the associated variable, for example:

$$\Delta \ln L_s = \ln L_s(T) - \ln L_s(T-1).$$

The resulting first-order index corresponds to sex, but not to age, education, employment class, or occupation.

We can define a *second-order index of labor input* corresponding to any two characteristics of labor input by adding hours worked and value shares over other characteristics and constructing a translog index. The second-order index corresponding to sex and age, for example, reflects changes in the composition of aggregate hours worked by sex and age, but not by education, employment class, or occupation. There are ten second-order indexes of labor input generated by combinations of two of the five characteristics of labor input. All second-order indexes are defined in Table 3–6 together with the five first-order indexes.

Similarly, we can define *third-, fourth-, and fifth-order indexes of labor input* corresponding to any three, four, or to all five characteristics of labor input. Continuing our example, the third-order index corresponding to sex, age, and education reflects changes in the composition of aggregate hours worked by these characteristics, but not by employment class and occupation. The fourth-order index corresponding to sex, age, education, and class of employment, reflects changes in the composition of aggregate hours worked by these four characteristics. The ten third-order, and five fourth-order indexes are defined in Table 3–6 as is the single fifth-order index, which reflects compositional shifts among all characteristics of labor input.

Special attention must be focused on the fifth-order index of labor input corresponding to all characteristics of labor input. This index corresponds to the index of aggregate labor input $L(T)$ defined above. Recall that the growth rate of the index can be expressed in terms of the components of hours worked $\{H_l\}$:

$$\ln L(T) - \ln L(T-1) = \sum \bar{v}_{Ll}[\ln H_l(T) - \ln H_l(T-1)].$$

In terms of our new notation, this expression has the equivalent form:

$$\Delta \ln L = \sum_s \sum_a \sum_e \sum_c \sum_o \bar{v}_{saeco} \, \Delta \ln H_{saeco}.$$

This index reflects changes in the composition of labor input by all five characteristics of individual workers.

To complete the set of partial indexes of labor input we add hours worked over all characteristics of the labor force to obtain an index of aggregate hours worked. This index does not reflect any change in the composition of labor input. The single index of aggregate hours worked is defined in Table 3–6. There is a total of thirty-two partial indexes of labor input,

Table 3-6.   Partial Indexes of Labor Input.

Hours worked (one index):

$$\Delta \ln H = \Delta \ln \sum_s \sum_a \sum_e \sum_c \sum_o H_{saeco}.$$

First-order (five indexes):

$$\Delta \ln L_s = \sum_s \bar{v}_s \, \Delta \ln H_s,$$

$$= \sum_s \bar{v}_s \, \Delta \ln \sum_a \sum_e \sum_c \sum_o H_{saeco}.$$

Second-order (ten indexes):

$$\Delta \ln L_{sa} = \sum_s \sum_a \bar{v}_{sa} \, \Delta \ln H_{sa},$$

$$= \sum_s \sum_a \bar{v}_{sa} \, \Delta \ln \sum_e \sum_c \sum_o H_{saeco}.$$

Third-order (ten indexes):

$$\Delta \ln L_{sae} = \sum_s \sum_a \sum_e \bar{v}_{sae} \, \Delta \ln H_{sae},$$

$$= \sum_s \sum_a \sum_e \bar{v}_{sae} \, \Delta \ln \sum_c \sum_o H_{saeco}.$$

Fourth-order (five indexes):

$$\Delta \ln L_{saec} = \sum_s \sum_a \sum_e \sum_c \bar{v}_{saec} \, \Delta \ln H_{saec},$$

$$= \sum_s \sum_a \sum_e \sum_c \bar{v}_{saec} \, \Delta \ln \sum_o H_{saeco}.$$

Fifth-order (one index):

$$\Delta \ln L_{saeco} = \sum_s \sum_a \sum_e \sum_c \sum_o \bar{v}_{saeco} \, \Delta \ln H_{saeco}.$$

corresponding to the five characteristics of the labor force. We present these thirty-two partial indexes of labor input annually for the period 1948 to 1973 in Appendix Table 3-1. These indexes form the basis for our analysis of the effects of the changes in the postwar composition of aggregate hours worked.

Our next objective is to identify the contributions of the changing sex, age, education, employment class, and occupation composition of total hours worked to aggregate economic growth. For this purpose, we first define an index of total labor quality that captures the effect of all changes in the composition of hours worked. This index is defined in terms of the aggregate hours worked and fifth-order partial index we have described. The rate of growth of the index of total labor quality is defined as the difference between the rate of growth of the fifth-order partial index of labor input and the rate of growth of aggregate hours worked. To analyze the effects of changes in the quality of hours worked, we can decompose the index of total labor quality into components corresponding to the contributions of changes in the composition of labor input.

The partial indexes of labor input derived in the last section and reported in Appendix Table 3–1 are instrumental in identifying the first- and higher-order contributions of the five characteristics of labor input. We can define the *first-order contribution* of each characteristic of labor input to the rate of growth of total labor quality as the difference between the rate of growth of the corresponding partial index of labor input and the rate of growth of aggregate hours worked. For example, the first-order contribution of sex to the rate of growth of labor quality, say Q_{Ls}, takes the form:

$$\Delta \ln Q_{Ls} = \Delta \ln L_s - \Delta \ln H.$$

This index reflects the effect of changes in the composition of aggregate hours worked by sex on the rate of growth of labor quality. There are five first-order contributions to the rate of growth of labor quality corresponding to the five characteristics of labor input.

We can define the *second-order contribution* of each pair of characteristics to the rate of growth of labor quality as the difference between the rate of growth of the corresponding partial index of labor input and the rate of growth of aggregate hours worked, less the sum of the two first-order contributions of these characteristics to the rate of growth of labor quality. For example, the second-order contribution of sex and age, say Q_{Lsa}, takes the form:

$$\Delta \ln Q_{Lsa} = \Delta \ln L_{sa} - \Delta \ln H - \Delta \ln Q_{Ls} - \Delta \ln Q_{La},$$
$$= \Delta \ln L_{sa} - \Delta \ln L_a - \Delta \ln L_s + \Delta \ln H.$$

This index reflects the effect of changes in the composition of aggregate hours worked by sex and age on the rate of growth of labor quality, exclusive of the effects already reflected in the first-order contributions of sex and age. There are ten second-order contributions to the rate of growth of labor quality. These second-order contributions together with the five first-order contributions are defined in Table 3–7. We can similarly define *third-, fourth-, and fifth-order contributions* of characteristics of hours worked to the rate of growth of the quality of labor input by extension of our definitions of first- and second-order contributions. There are ten third-order indexes, five fourth-order indexes, and one fifth-order index. All are defined in Table 3–7.

By summing the contributions of all orders corresponding to a given set of characteristics of labor input we obtain the partial index of labor quality

Table 3-7.   Contributions to the Growth of Labor Quality.

First-order (five indexes):

$$\Delta \ln Q_{Ls} = \Delta \ln L_s - \Delta \ln H.$$

Second-order (ten indexes):

$$\Delta \ln Q_{Lsa} = \Delta \ln L_{sa} - \Delta \ln L_a - \Delta \ln L_s + \Delta \ln H.$$

Third-order (ten indexes):

$$\Delta \ln Q_{Lsae} = \Delta \ln L_{sae} - \Delta \ln L_{sa} - \Delta \ln L_{se} - \Delta \ln L_{ae}$$
$$+ \Delta \ln L_s + \Delta \ln L_a + \Delta \ln L_e - \Delta \ln H.$$

Fourth-order (five indexes):

$$\Delta \ln Q_{Lsaec} = \Delta \ln L_{saec} - \Delta \ln L_{sae} - \Delta \ln L_{sac} - \Delta \ln L_{sec} - \Delta \ln L_{aec}$$
$$+ \Delta \ln L_{sa} + \Delta \ln L_{se} + \Delta \ln L_{sc} + \Delta \ln L_{ae} + \Delta \ln L_{ac} + \Delta \ln L_{ec}$$
$$- \Delta \ln L_s - \Delta \ln L_a - \Delta \ln L_e - \Delta \ln L_c + \Delta \ln H.$$

Fifth-order (one index):

$$\Delta \ln Q_{Lsaeco} = \Delta \ln L_{saeco} - \Delta \ln L_{saec} - \Delta \ln L_{saeo} - \Delta \ln L_{saco} - \Delta \ln L_{seco} - \Delta \ln L_{aeco}$$
$$+ \Delta \ln L_{sae} + \Delta \ln L_{sac} + \Delta \ln L_{sao} + \Delta \ln L_{sec} + \Delta \ln L_{seo}$$
$$+ \Delta \ln L_{sco} + \Delta \ln L_{aec} + \Delta \ln L_{aeo} + \Delta \ln L_{aco} + \Delta \ln L_{eco}$$
$$- \Delta \ln L_{sa} - \Delta \ln L_{se} - \Delta \ln L_{sc} - \Delta \ln L_{so} - \Delta \ln L_{ae}$$
$$- \Delta \ln L_{ac} - \Delta \ln L_{ao} - \Delta \ln L_{ec} - \Delta \ln L_{eo} - \Delta \ln L_{co}$$
$$+ \Delta \ln L_s + \Delta \ln L_a + \Delta \ln L_e + \Delta \ln L_c + \Delta \ln L_o - \Delta \ln H.$$

corresponding to those characteristics. For example our aggregate index of labor quality presented in column 4 of Table 3-5 is the partial index of labor quality corresponding to all characteristics of labor input. We can represent this index in the form:

$$\Delta \ln Q_L = \Delta \ln Q_{Ls} + \Delta \ln Q_{La} + \Delta \ln Q_{Le} + \Delta \ln Q_{Lc}$$
$$+ \Delta \ln Q_{Lo} + \Delta \ln Q_{Lsa} + \Delta \ln Q_{Lse} + \Delta \ln Q_{Lsc}$$
$$+ \Delta \ln Q_{Lso} + \Delta \ln Q_{Lae} + \Delta \ln Q_{Lac} + \Delta \ln Q_{Lao}$$
$$+ \Delta \ln Q_{Lec} + \Delta \ln Q_{Leo} + \Delta \ln Q_{Lco} + \Delta \ln Q_{Lsae}$$
$$+ \Delta \ln Q_{Lsac} + \Delta \ln Q_{sao} + \Delta \ln Q_{Lsec} + \Delta \ln Q_{Lseo}$$
$$+ \Delta \ln Q_{Lsco} + \Delta \ln Q_{Laec} + \Delta \ln Q_{Laeo} + \Delta \ln Q_{Laco}$$
$$+ \Delta \ln Q_{Leco} + \Delta \ln Q_{Lsaec} + \Delta \ln Q_{Lsaeo} + \Delta \ln Q_{Lsaco}$$
$$+ \Delta \ln Q_{Lseco} + \Delta \ln Q_{Laeco} + \Delta \ln Q_{Lsaeco}.$$

This index is the sum of five first-order contributions, ten second-order contributions, ten third-order contributions, five fourth-order contributions, and one fifth-order contribution to the rate of growth of labor quality. This index incorporates the effects of changes in the composition of aggregate hours worked among all characteristics of labor input.

We apply the formulas of Table 3–7 to the disaggregated labor data described above. The resulting quality indexes for each year in the period 1948 to 1973 are presented in the second through last columns in Appendix Table 3–2. The first column of this table reports the quality index representing the total contribution made by all sources. It is formed by summing over all first- and higher-order contributions corresponding to all five characteristics of labor input.

The analysis of variance provides an analogy useful in interpreting the first- and higher-order contributions of the characteristics of labor input to the rate of growth of labor quality. Each of the characteristics of hours worked corresponds to a factor in the analysis of variance. The decomposition of the rate of growth of labor quality by all five characteristics corresponds to a five-way layout in the analysis of variance. The first-order contribution of each of the five characteristics corresponds to the main effect of the factor in the analysis of variance. The second-order contribution of any two of the five characteristics corresponds to the interaction effect of the two factors in the analysis of variance. The third-, fourth-, and fifth-order contributions to the rate of growth of labor quality correspond to higher-order interactions in the analysis of variance.

The indexes reported in Appendix Tables 3–1 and 3–2 imply that the shifting demographic and occupational composition of the labor force historically has been a very significant source of postwar economic growth. The fifth-order index of labor input given in the last column of Appendix Table 3–1 increases at an average annual rate of 1.73 precent for the period 1948 to 1973. This represents the sum of the growth rates of aggregate hours worked and the index of total quality change. Forty-two percent of this growth was due to quality change; the quality index given in the first column of Appendix Table 3–2 increases at 0.72 percent per year. Hours worked account for the remaining 58 percent, growing at an average annual rate equal to 1.01 percent.

If the postwar period is partitioned at 1960, we observe that the importance of quality change in labor input has declined in both absolute and relative terms. On average, the total quality index increased 0.95 percent per year over the 1948 to 1960 period and 0.51 percent per year between 1960 and 1973. At the same time, the importance of compositional change declined substantially relative to increases in hours worked. Between 1948 and 1960, hours worked increased at an average 0.40 percent annual rate; quality change accounted for nearly 71 percent of the growth in the index of labor input. After 1960, the economy experienced a surge in hours worked. The unweighted hours index grows at an average rate equal to 1.56 percent; labor quality is responsible for approximately 25 percent of the growth in the fifth-order index of labor input. An analysis of the most recent subperiod, 1969 to 1973, suggests that the decline in the absolute and relative importance of quality change has continued. While unadjusted hours worked increased at a 1.34 percent rate during 1969 to 1973, labor input grew at a 1.61 percent annual rate. The difference is the rate of growth in the labor quality index. It increases at an average annual rate of only 0.28 percent, accounting for only 17 percent of input growth.

The sources of the postwar change in aggregate labor input can be determined from the quality indexes reported in Appendix Table 3-2. Comparing the main effects, only sex and education have smooth persistent trends over the 1948 to 1973 period. The former, reflecting the high rate of entry of women into low paying jobs, has a negative effect averaging −0.17 percent per year; the latter, caused by the increasing proportion of highly educated workers, is positive, increasing at an average annual rate equal to 0.67 percent. The main effects of employment class and occupation are positive— 0.17 percent and 0.39 percent per year, respectively—but peak in the middle of the 1960s. The postwar shift of workers to high-paying occupations slows considerably by the end of the 1960 to 1966 period. Consequently, this characteristic has little effect on total quality change after 1966. Between 1966 to 1973, the main effects of class and occupation are 0.07 percent and 0.18 percent, respectively. The main effect of age reverses itself after 1960. The effect is positive through 1960, averaging 0.24 percent per year; after 1960, the effect turns negative, declining at an average annual rate equal to −0.32 percent. This reversal reflects the entry into the employed labor force of a large number of young laborers who were born immediately following World War II. Their low wages and low imputed productivity account for the negative effect of age on labor quality.

Although the second- and higher-order interaction effects are small, their aggregate effect is quantitatively important. The annual average rate of growth of the sum of the interaction effects equals −0.29 percent over the full 1948 to 1973 period. Had these effects not been considered, the quality index would have been found to increase at a 1.01 percent annual rate. This compares to 0.72 percent when all main and interaction effects are considered. In brief, failing to consider interaction effects increases greatly the calculated contribution of changing labor quality as a source of economic growth. Relative to the 1.73 percent average annual rate of growth in labor's total contribution to economic growth, neglecting interaction effects would upward bias the calculated contribution by 17 percent. To identify the sources of economic growth, the interaction effects among demographic and occupational characteristics must be explicitly incorporated in the analysis.

While second- and higher-order effects are quantitatively significant, their inclusion does not qualitatively affect the interpretation of the source characteristics of economic growth. The sex and age factors are still the dominant causes of the decline in the growth of the quality index. The interaction effects of age and sex with each other and other factors are generally positive and consequently reduce the aggregate negative effect of -0.22 percent that would be inferred by simply summing the main effects of sex and age, -0.17 percent and -0.05 percent, respectively. The positive interaction between sex and occupation, for example, suggests that women are increasingly entering high-paying occupation groups. Yet even when all interaction effects are taken into account, the conclusion remains that the changing sex/age composition of the aggregate employed labor force has had a negative impact on labor input per hour worked. The combined sex/age contribution to the total quality index is -0.10 percent per year over 1948 to 1973. The increasing entry of women and young workers into low-paying jobs increases hours worked proportionately more than it increases labor input. While the main effect of education is 0.67 percent, the effect of education net of second-and higher-order effects is 0.36 percent. Even when all interaction effects are taken into account, the contribution of education is very substantial, accounting for about half of the increase in the quality of labor input over the period 1948 to 1973.

INVESTMENT IN EDUCATION

Our final objective is to present measures of investment in education for the United States for the period 1948 to 1973. For this purpose we construct a new data base for measuring lifetime labor incomes for all individuals in the U.S. population. Our data base includes demographic accounts in each year for the population by each sex, cross-classified by individual year of age and individual year of highest educational attainment. Our demographic accounts include data on the number of individuals enrolled in formal schooling and data on births, deaths, and migration. These demographic accounts are based on annual population data from the U.S. Bureau of the Census. We incorporate more detailed data from the decennial censuses of population to obtain estimates of the population cross-classified by sex, age, and education.

To measure lifetime labor incomes for all individuals in the U.S. population we begin with the data base on labor time devoted to market activities analyzed in the preceding section. We derive estimates of hours worked and labor compensation for each sex by sixty-one age groups and eighteen education groups or a total of 2,196 groups for each year. We impute wage rates for nonmarket activities from wage rates for employed individuals. We allocate the total time available for all individuals in the population among work, schooling, household production and leisure, and maintenance. We exclude maintenance through the satisfaction of physiological needs from our accounts for lifetime labor incomes. We assign the value of time spent in household production and leisure to consumption and time spent in schooling to investment.

Our final step in measuring lifetime labor incomes for all individuals in the U.S. population is to project incomes for future years and to discount incomes for all future years back to the present, weighting income by the probability of survival. We combine estimates of lifetime labor incomes by sex, age, and education with demographic accounts for the numbers of individuals to obtain estimates of investment in education. We present these estimates in current and constant prices for the period 1948 to 1973 for all individuals in the U.S. population. In the next section we compare our estimates of investment in education with those of Kendrick (1976).

In the preceding section we analyzed a data base that includes the number of employed persons for the United States on an annual basis, cross-classified by sex, employment class, age, education, occupation, and industry. We aggregated over employment class, occupation, and industry, and distributed the work force of each sex by individual years of age from fourteen to seventy-four and by individual years of educational attainment from one to eighteen. The data base utilized also includes data on hours worked and labor compensation on the same basis as data on employed persons. We derived annual estimates of hours worked and labor compensation required for measuring incomes from market labor activities by summing over employment class, occupation, and industry, as before. We obtained average hourly labor compensation for individuals classified by the two sexes, sixty-one age groups, and eighteen education groups for a total of 2,196 groups by dividing market labor compensation by hours worked for each group.

Labor input in constant prices is based on data on annual hours worked and labor compensation per hour, cross-classified by sex, age and education. To construct an index of labor input, we assume that labor input can be expressed as a translog function of its 2,196 components. The corresponding index of labor input is a translog quantity index of individual labor inputs where weights are given by average shares of each component in the value of labor outlay. Table 3–8 presents our estimates of the value of market labor activities in current prices, cross-classified by sex and educational attainment, for the U.S. economy from 1948 to 1973. Table 3–9 presents the corresponding estimates in constant prices of 1972.

Table 3–8. Value of Market Labor Activities by Sex and Educational Attainment, 1948–73 (billions of current dollars).

Year	Total	Male			Female		
		Elementary	Secondary	College	Elementary	Secondary	College
1948	178.1	53.5	61.9	31.4	8.3	16.6	6.5
1949	177.5	52.1	61.0	32.2	8.4	16.9	6.9
1950	191.0	55.4	64.8	35.6	8.9	18.2	8.2
1951	215.5	61.1	74.5	40.3	10.1	20.9	8.6
1952	230.2	62.2	80.5	44.9	10.3	22.8	9.5
1953	246.1	64.1	87.4	49.6	10.7	24.3	10.0
1954	245.9	61.2	87.7	51.2	10.3	25.0	10.5
1955	263.5	62.8	95.1	55.4	11.2	27.4	11.6
1956	284.9	65.6	103.9	60.4	11.9	30.5	12.5
1957	299.2	65.6	110.1	65.2	12.1	32.7	13.6
1958	301.4	62.1	110.5	68.4	12.0	33.9	14.6
1959	324.7	64.6	120.6	74.5	12.8	36.4	15.7
1960	339.9	66.5	126.5	84.0	12.1	33.4	17.2
1961	348.8	61.0	128.1	88.3	12.5	39.4	19.5
1962	370.3	59.4	138.5	96.8	12.0	42.2	21.3
1963	387.4	60.8	146.9	99.9	12.6	45.8	21.5
1964	413.6	60.1	159.4	108.1	12.7	49.8	23.5
1965	443.1	62.3	172.4	115.3	12.9	54.8	25.3
1966	484.7	64.0	188.9	128.8	13.4	61.0	28.6
1967	518.6	64.8	198.8	143.6	14.0	66.0	31.6
1968	569.4	66.5	219.0	159.3	14.5	73.7	36.4
1969	626.7	69.0	239.5	178.5	15.1	84.2	40.5
1970	668.1	73.6	251.5	195.8	15.7	85.8	45.8
1971	714.8	68.6	267.8	215.3	15.0	95.6	52.6
1972	783.1	69.7	291.4	239.7	15.1	108.0	59.2
1973	866.1	70.6	321.4	269.9	15.4	120.0	68.8

Table 3-9. Value of Market Labor Activities by Sex and Educational Attainment, 1948–73 (billions of constant 1972 dollars).

Year	Total	Male			Female		
		Elementary	Secondary	College	Elementary	Secondary	College
1948	561.1	162.6	197.1	104.9	24.5	50.0	22.0
1949	543.3	154.7	188.7	103.5	24.3	49.5	22.6
1950	564.5	161.6	193.0	109.3	24.2	51.1	25.4
1951	586.3	161.6	204.3	113.8	26.2	55.7	24.8
1952	598.8	157.8	211.2	120.4	25.3	58.1	25.9
1953	609.4	154.9	218.0	125.8	25.0	59.5	26.1
1954	594.6	145.4	213.3	126.1	23.8	59.7	26.2
1955	610.8	144.1	221.4	129.0	25.1	63.5	27.6
1956	621.4	140.6	227.0	133.1	25.4	66.9	28.4
1957	619.7	133.3	227.9	136.2	24.7	68.4	29.2
1958	605.1	122.9	221.5	138.3	23.9	68.7	29.9
1959	623.9	122.3	230.8	143.9	24.6	71.4	30.9
1960	641.0	126.0	237.8	157.0	22.4	64.6	33.1
1961	636.2	110.2	232.7	161.0	22.7	72.7	36.8
1962	657.0	104.4	244.5	171.4	21.3	76.0	39.4
1963	663.2	102.8	249.6	172.0	21.6	79.0	38.3
1964	677.9	97.4	259.1	177.9	20.8	82.7	39.9
1965	699.4	96.3	268.9	184.7	20.4	87.3	41.9
1966	721.7	94.3	278.8	192.3	19.5	92.2	44.5
1967	732.6	90.5	279.3	203.0	19.5	94.2	46.1
1968	746.9	86.3	285.1	209.9	18.5	97.6	49.4
1969	765.2	82.9	290.6	219.0	17.9	103.7	51.1
1970	765.6	84.1	288.8	224.3	17.7	98.0	52.8
1971	763.1	72.8	285.7	230.0	15.7	102.6	56.4
1972	783.1	69.7	291.4	239.7	15.1	108.0	59.2
1973	815.2	65.2	302.4	256.5	14.3	112.2	64.6

Table 3–10. Employment by Sex and Educational Attainment, 1948–73 (thousands).

Year	Total	Male			Female		
		Elementary	Secondary	College	Elementary	Secondary	College
1948	61,342	19,687	17,935	6,038	5,878	9,124	2,679
1949	59,812	18,901	17,254	5,998	5,858	9,044	2,759
1950	61,336	19,534	17,432	6,295	5,777	9,217	3,081
1951	63,946	19,556	18,442	6,489	6,298	10,147	3,015
1952	64,694	19,046	18,889	6,823	6,169	10,620	3,147
1953	65,666	18,866	19,583	7,186	6,114	10,773	3,146
1954	64,192	17,824	19,223	7,225	5,868	10,857	3,195
1955	65,881	17,549	19,956	7,415	6,157	11,460	3,344
1956	67,486	17,248	20,667	7,728	6,289	12,115	3,440
1957	67,692	16,564	20,969	8,005	6,145	12,448	3,561
1958	66,113	15,394	20,470	8,187	5,949	12,475	3,637
1959	67,834	15,248	21,353	8,550	6,032	12,940	3,711
1960	68,535	15,048	21,187	9,044	6,013	12,865	4,379
1961	68,632	13,784	21,624	9,623	5,764	13,384	4,454
1962	69,924	13,054	22,531	10,226	5,479	13,913	4,722
1963	70,633	12,774	23,047	10,201	5,519	14,483	4,609
1964	72,133	12,164	24,056	10,590	5,356	15,179	4,789
1965	74,460	12,014	25,062	10,960	5,273	16,074	5,078
1966	77,516	11,791	26,106	11,558	5,235	17,311	5,517
1967	78,933	11,393	26,262	12,356	5,234	17,833	5,855
1968	80,865	10,955	27,005	12,893	5,096	18,545	6,372
1969	83,031	10,554	27,665	13,493	4,946	19,714	6,659
1970	83,046	10,583	27,113	13,917	4,846	19,364	7,224
1971	83,340	9,443	27,484	14,613	4,443	19,831	7,526
1972	85,776	9,071	28,148	15,452	4,252	20,914	7,939
1973	89,178	8,560	29,448	16,605	4,038	21,844	8,683

The value of market labor compensation in current prices has increased by 411.6 percent over the postwar period. The proportional increases were greatest for college-trained workers—811.8 percent for males and 1,046.7 percent for females. By contrast compensation for workers with only elementary education has increased by 37.9 percent for males and 97.4 percent for females. Compensation for workers with secondary education has increased by 446.6 percent for males and 659.5 percent for females. For all levels of educational attainment the proportional increase for females has exceeded that for males. The corresponding patterns for market labor compensation in constant prices are very similar. Labor compensation in constant prices represents a quantity index of labor input. The quantity of labor input for the economy as a whole has increased by 46.4 percent over the postwar period. The quantity of labor input for workers with only elementary education has fallen 60.2 percent for males and 40.7 percent for females. By contrast the quantity of labor input for college trained workers has increased by 150.2 percent for males and 203.3 percent for females.

We next analyze the sources of growth in labor input in more detail. For each of the 2,196 components of the labor force incorporated into our data base, labor input is the product of the number of persons employed and annual hours worked per person. We present estimates of the number of persons employed, cross-classified by sex and educational attainment, in Table 3-10. We present the corresponding estimates of annual hours worked per person, also cross-classified by sex and educational attainment, in Table 3-11. Finally, we define the quality of hours worked as the ratio of the translog index of labor input from Table 3-9 to the number of hours worked by the corresponding component of the work force. Labor input then becomes the product of the number of persons employed, annual hours worked per person, and the quality of hours worked. We present indexes of labor quality by sex and educational attainment in Table 3-12. Employment declines for both male and female workers with elementary education, increases substantially for workers with secondary education, and increases very rapidly for college-trained workers. By contrast hours worked per person decline for workers of both sexes at all three levels of educational attainment. Changes in the quality of hours worked within each category are relatively small.

Finally, we analyze changes in the structure of labor input for the U.S. economy over the period 1948 to 1973. For this purpose we present growth rates of the value of market labor activities in current and constant prices, the quantity of labor input per worker, and the price of labor input for the period as a whole and for six subperiods in Table 3-13. The annual growth rates for market labor compensation in current and constant prices for the postwar period as a whole reflect the trends we have already analyzed in Tables 3-8 and 3-9. For both males and females the price of labor input

Table 3-11.   Annual Hours per Person by Sex and Educational Attainment, 1948-73.

Year	Total	Male			Female		
		Elementary	Secondary	College	Elementary	Secondary	College
1948	2,048	2,125	2,135	2,184	1,823	1,813	1,892
1949	2,026	2,103	2,113	2,161	1,809	1,799	1,873
1950	2,028	2,106	2,117	2,157	1,812	1,801	1,859
1951	2,027	2,111	2,119	2,168	1,805	1,792	1,862
1952	2,016	2,106	2,112	2,159	1,788	1,777	1,842
1953	2,005	2,086	2,091	2,130	1,794	1,790	1,845
1954	1,983	2,065	2,068	2,108	1,777	1,773	1,823
1955	1,988	2,072	2,071	2,113	1,788	1,784	1,830
1956	1,973	2,057	2,052	2,097	1,781	1,779	1,822
1957	1,947	2,026	2,026	2,071	1,760	1,764	1,808
1958	1,932	2,001	2,010	2,055	1,751	1,760	1,804
1959	1,938	2,005	2,014	2,062	1,768	1,766	1,812
1960	1,928	2,063	2,076	2,158	1,618	1,595	1,681
1961	1,915	1,995	1,999	2,044	1,722	1,734	1,770
1962	1,915	1,993	2,005	2,050	1,705	1,728	1,771
1963	1,913	1,995	2,008	2,049	1,703	1,723	1,766
1964	1,905	1,980	1,999	2,043	1,692	1,719	1,765
1965	1,904	1,985	2,001	2,045	1,681	1,718	1,752
1966	1,884	1,977	1,990	2,035	1,639	1,684	1,730
1967	1,868	1,962	1,971	2,022	1,618	1,673	1,715
1968	1,854	1,949	1,957	2,006	1,603	1,662	1,705
1969	1,849	1,949	1,953	2,004	1,603	1,659	1,699
1970	1,824	1,953	1,947	2,019	1,585	1,574	1,633
1971	1,819	1,915	1,927	1,974	1,567	1,623	1,666
1972	1,820	1,907	1,932	1,981	1,559	1,625	1,665
1973	1,817	1,898	1,930	1,982	1,545	1,621	1,663

Table 3-12. Quality of Labor Input by Sex and Educational Attainment, 1948–73 (1972 = 1.000).

Year	Total	Male			Female		
		Elementary	Secondary	College	Elementary	Secondary	College
1948	0.895	0.964	0.961	1.016	1.005	0.952	0.971
1949	0.898	0.965	0.966	1.020	1.007	0.958	0.979
1950	0.909	0.974	0.976	1.029	1.015	0.968	0.989
1951	0.906	0.971	0.976	1.033	1.012	0.963	0.985
1952	0.919	0.976	0.988	1.044	1.009	0.969	0.998
1953	0.926	0.977	0.994	1.050	1.004	0.971	1.003
1954	0.934	0.980	1.001	1.058	1.004	0.976	1.006
1955	0.933	0.983	1.000	1.052	1.003	0.978	1.009
1956	0.933	0.983	0.999	1.049	0.998	0.977	1.010
1957	0.939	0.986	1.001	1.049	1.004	0.980	1.013
1958	0.946	0.989	1.005	1.050	1.007	0.984	1.017
1959	0.948	0.992	1.002	1.043	1.013	0.984	1.026
1960	0.969	1.007	1.009	1.027	1.013	0.991	1.006
1961	0.967	0.994	1.005	1.045	1.005	0.986	1.044
1962	0.980	0.995	1.010	1.045	1.002	0.995	1.052
1963	0.980	1.000	1.007	1.051	1.010	0.996	1.050
1964	0.985	1.003	1.006	1.050	1.009	0.997	1.055
1965	0.985	1.002	1.000	1.052	1.011	0.995	1.053
1966	0.986	1.004	1.001	1.045	1.000	0.995	1.042
1967	0.991	1.005	1.007	1.038	1.014	0.993	1.025
1968	0.994	1.002	1.007	1.037	0.997	0.997	1.017
1969	0.994	1.000	1.004	1.035	0.991	0.998	1.009
1970	1.008	1.009	1.021	1.020	1.014	1.012	0.999
1971	1.004	0.999	1.007	1.018	0.993	1.003	1.004
1972	1.000	1.000	1.000	1.000	1.000	1.000	1.000
1973	1.003	0.996	0.993	0.995	1.005	0.998	0.999

Table 3-13. Value of Market Labor Activities by Educational Attainment and Sex, Rates of Growth, 1948–73.

	1948–73	1948–53	1953–57	1957–60	1960–66	1966–69	1969–73
Elementary							
Male							
Value (current)	1.12	3.69	0.60	0.43	−0.63	2.54	0.57
Value (constant)	−3.59	−0.96	−3.68	−1.87	−4.71	−4.20	−5.83
Per capita (constant)	−0.32	−0.11	−0.50	1.32	−0.76	−0.59	−0.77
Price index	4.88	4.69	4.44	2.35	4.28	7.03	6.80
Female							
Value (current)	2.47	5.15	3.02	0.21	1.61	4.14	0.42
Value (constant)	−2.14	0.44	−0.36	−3.15	−2.29	−2.90	−5.50
Per capita (constant)	−0.66	−0.35	−0.49	−2.44	−0.00	−1.04	−0.58
Price index	4.72	4.68	3.40	3.46	3.99	7.25	6.27
Secondary							
Male							
Value (current)	6.81	7.16	5.92	4.76	6.90	8.24	7.62
Value (constant)	1.73	2.04	1.11	1.42	2.69	1.39	1.00
Per capita (constant)	−0.27	0.26	−0.60	1.07	−0.82	−0.55	−0.56
Price index	5.00	5.02	4.76	3.29	4.11	6.76	6.56
Female							
Value (current)	8.24	7.94	7.68	0.77	10.55	11.33	9.27
Value (constant)	3.29	3.52	3.56	−1.86	6.10	4.01	1.99
Per capita (constant)	−0.26	0.14	−0.12	−2.94	0.97	−0.40	−0.59
Price index	4.80	4.27	3.97	2.68	4.20	7.04	7.14

College

Male

Value (current)	8.98	9.54	7.08	8.84	7.37	11.48	10.90
Value (constant)	3.64	3.70	2.00	4.85	3.44	4.42	4.03
Per capita (constant)	-0.47	0.15	-0.72	0.67	-0.70	-0.83	-1.23
Price index	5.15	5.63	4.98	3.81	3.80	6.76	6.60

Female

Value (current)	9.93	9.15	8.01	8.23	8.81	12.25	14.18
Value (constant)	4.40	3.42	2.89	4.30	5.04	4.72	6.01
Per capita (constant)	-0.40	0.15	-0.25	-2.65	1.08	-1.65	-0.79
Price index	5.30	5.54	4.98	3.77	3.58	7.20	7.70

increases most rapidly for college trained workers, next most rapidly for workers with secondary education, and least rapidly for workers with elementary education. The patterns are positively correlated with the growth of labor input within these categories—higher rates of price increase are associated with higher rates of growth of labor input.

We have now completed the presentation of the utilization of human resources in the labor market. Our next objective is to evaluate the time spent on nonmarket activities, considering both consumption and investment activities. The importance of the valuation of nonmarket activities is widely recognized. Nordhaus and Tobin (1972) have incorporated nonmarket activities into their measure of economic welfare. Kendrick (1976) and Eisner (1978) have extended the national income and product accounts by imputing value to time spent outside the labor market.[9] Unfortunately, there is no clear agreement on what types of activities should be included or on methods appropriate for valuation of nonmarket activities.

To account for nonmarket labor activities in a complete accounting system, we consider only contributions to final product and deduct all uses of time that are instrumental to the production of goods. Six types of nonmarket activities are commonly distinguished in studies of time allocation—production of goods and services within the household unit, volunteer work outside the household unit, commuting to work, formal education, leisure, and the satisfaction of physiological needs such as eating and sleeping.[10] We classify time spent satisfying physiological needs as maintenance and exclude this time from our measure of time spent in nonmarket activities. We assume that the time available for all market and nonmarket activities has been constant over time and is equal to fourteen hours per day for all individuals.

We allocate the annual time available for all individuals in the population among work, schooling, household production and leisure, and maintenance. Our system of demographic accounts includes the enrollment status for individuals of each sex between five and thirty-four years of age. We estimate the time spent in formal schooling for all individuals by assigning 1,300 hours per year to each person enrolled in school.[11] We allocate time spent in schooling to investment. Similarly, our demographic accounts include employment status for individuals of each sex between fourteen and seventy-four years of age. Hours worked for all employed individuals, classified by sex, age, and education, are included in our data base for market labor activities. We allocate time that is not spent working or in formal schooling directly to consumption. For all individuals this time is equal to the difference between fourteen hours per day and time spent working or in school.

The final step in the measurement of lifetime labor incomes is to impute the value of labor compensation for nonmarket activities.[12] For this purpose we first obtain average hourly labor compensation for all employed persons, cross-classified by sex, age, and education, from our data base for market labor activities. Second, we estimate marginal tax rates for all employed persons, again cross-classified by sex, age, and education.[13] We multiply compensation per hour by one minus the marginal tax rate to obtain imputed hourly labor compensation for nonmarket activities other than formal schooling. Since individuals under fourteen years of age do not participate in the labor force, their imputed hourly labor compensation is set equal to zero. Individuals over seventy-four years of age are also assigned zero as their hourly labor compensation.

We multiply compensation per hour by one minus the marginal tax rate to obtain the value of compensation per hour for nonmarket activities. Hours used in nonmarket activities are obtained by subtracting hours spent on the market and hours spent in formal education from the total time available. Table 3–14 presents our estimates of the value of leisure and nonmarket labor activities other than formal education in current prices, cross-classified by sex and educational attainment, for the U.S. economy from 1948 to 1973. Table 3–15 presents the corresponding estimates in constant prices of 1972.

The value of nonmarket activities in current prices has increased by 421.2 percent over the postwar period by comparison with the 411.6 percent increase in the value of market labor activities. Similarly, the value of nonmarket activities in constant prices, a quantity index of labor time devoted to these activities in constant prices, has increased by 50.9 percent by comparison with an increase in the quantity of market labor activities of 46.4 percent. Proportional increases in the value of nonmarket labor activities in both current and constant prices were largest for workers with college education, next largest for those with secondary education, and smallest for those with elementary education. This pattern coincides with that for increases in the value of market labor activities. Proportional increases for the nonmarket labor activities were largest for male workers, the reverse of the pattern for market labor activities, where proportional increases were largest for female workers.

Finally, we analyze changes in the structure of nonmarket labor activities for the U.S. economy over the period 1948 to 1973. For this purpose we present growth rates of the value of nonmarket labor activities in current and constant prices, the quantity of nonmarket activity per worker, and the price of labor utilized in nonmarket activities for the period as a whole and for six subperiods in Table 3–16. The annual growth rates for nonmarket labor compensation in current and constant prices for the postwar period as a whole reflect the trends we have analyzed in Tables 3–14 and 3–15. For both males and females the price of labor utilized in nonmarket activities increased most rapidly for college trained workers, next most rapidly

Table 3–14. Value of Nonmarket Labor Activities by Sex and Educational Attainment, 1948–73 (billions of current dollars).

Year	Total	Male			Female		
		Elementary	Secondary	College	Elementary	Secondary	College
1948	405.7	88.3	82.2	38.5	73.2	93.4	30.0
1949	429.5	91.5	89.3	42.8	73.8	99.5	32.6
1950	446.2	90.7	93.6	45.9	76.1	105.0	34.8
1951	467.7	95.5	99.6	49.1	76.0	110.3	37.1
1952	488.1	97.2	104.7	52.3	78.2	116.3	39.4
1953	518.9	101.3	113.0	57.3	81.1	124.1	42.1
1954	555.2	105.8	124.0	63.8	81.9	133.5	46.3
1955	580.2	108.7	131.9	69.0	81.9	139.6	49.1
1956	621.2	114.7	143.9	75.4	84.3	150.1	52.7
1957	666.5	121.3	157.2	83.0	86.8	161.0	57.3
1958	704.1	124.7	169.3	90.1	87.2	170.8	61.9
1959	733.9	127.8	179.9	96.4	85.3	178.8	65.8
1960	762.2	124.6	185.6	101.1	90.8	189.7	70.5
1961	809.4	130.2	200.3	113.3	89.3	201.6	74.7
1962	844.2	131.3	211.2	121.0	89.8	211.7	79.1
1963	886.6	132.3	223.5	128.8	90.5	226.4	85.1
1964	956.4	136.9	243.4	142.9	95.7	243.6	93.9
1965	1016.6	139.2	261.9	153.5	98.3	262.9	100.8
1966	1096.3	144.4	281.1	171.4	104.3	283.0	111.9
1967	1171.2	147.8	303.2	187.1	102.9	306.1	124.0
1968	1269.7	151.0	331.0	207.1	112.1	332.5	136.0
1969	1379.5	155.7	360.3	230.1	119.1	362.3	152.1
1970	1540.8	160.1	403.7	266.6	120.8	410.3	179.2
1971	1711.0	181.5	453.2	297.4	135.7	447.3	195.9
1972	1819.2	189.5	485.3	315.6	136.5	481.3	211.0
1973	1960.0	211.3	518.2	336.2	149.4	518.3	226.8

Table 3-15. Value of Nonmarket Labor Activities by Sex and Educational Attainment, 1948–73 (billions of constant 1972 dollars).

Year	Total	Male			Female		
		Elementary	Secondary	College	Elementary	Secondary	College
1948	1243.8	278.0	269.3	131.8	206.3	262.2	96.1
1949	1264.1	274.9	277.5	137.5	203.8	270.4	99.9
1950	1282.1	271.3	285.1	143.2	200.9	278.0	103.5
1951	1298.3	268.9	291.9	148.0	198.4	285.5	105.7
1952	1314.8	266.3	298.7	153.0	195.8	292.9	108.1
1953	1330.4	263.2	305.5	158.0	193.0	300.1	110.6
1954	1347.7	260.3	312.8	163.6	190.2	307.5	113.4
1955	1365.1	257.2	320.0	169.4	187.4	314.8	116.3
1956	1384.0	254.2	327.7	175.5	184.6	322.5	119.5
1957	1404.1	251.4	335.6	181.8	182.1	330.3	122.9
1958	1422.4	247.3	343.6	188.2	178.7	338.2	126.4
1959	1441.2	242.9	352.1	195.0	174.7	346.4	130.2
1960	1487.2	239.2	362.6	203.0	171.2	356.4	134.9
1961	1494.5	237.4	371.9	210.6	169.6	365.6	139.4
1962	1519.9	232.9	381.9	218.9	166.1	375.5	144.6
1963	1543.7	227.3	391.7	227.4	162.1	385.4	150.0
1964	1568.5	221.4	401.6	236.3	158.0	395.6	155.7
1965	1597.4	215.9	412.8	245.7	154.2	407.0	161.8
1966	1628.7	210.3	424.1	256.5	150.3	418.4	169.1
1967	1660.6	204.4	435.0	268.0	146.3	429.8	177.0
1968	1693.6	198.2	446.2	280.1	142.2	441.5	185.4
1969	1727.3	191.6	457.7	292.8	137.6	453.3	194.2
1970	1763.4	184.5	470.1	306.6	132.6	465.7	203.8
1971	1791.2	187.3	477.6	310.9	134.7	473.6	207.2
1972	1819.2	189.5	485.3	315.6	136.5	481.3	211.0
1973	1847.6	191.7	493.3	320.5	138.3	489.2	214.7

Table 3-16. Value of Nonmarket Labor Activities by Educational Attainment and Sex, Rates of Growth, 1948-73.

	1948-73	1948-53	1953-57	1957-60	1960-66	1966-69	1969-73
Elementary							
Male							
Value (current)	3.55	2.77	4.60	0.92	2.49	2.53	7.94
Value (constant)	-1.48	-1.09	-1.14	-1.65	-2.12	-3.06	0.01
Per capita (constant)	-1.55	-2.08	-2.20	-2.36	-1.75	-1.53	0.70
Price index	5.10	3.91	5.80	2.61	4.71	5.76	7.92
Female							
Value (current)	2.89	2.06	1.71	1.50	2.35	4.50	5.83
Value (constant)	-1.59	-1.32	-1.44	-2.05	-2.15	-2.89	0.11
Per capita (constant)	-1.77	-2.45	-2.62	-2.89	-1.89	-1.46	0.78
Price index	4.55	3.42	3.19	3.62	4.60	7.61	5.71
Secondary							
Male							
Value (current)	7.64	6.58	8.59	5.69	7.17	8.62	9.51
Value (constant)	2.45	2.55	2.38	2.62	2.64	2.58	1.89
Per capita (constant)	0.01	0.45	0.07	-0.21	-0.24	0.03	-0.10
Price index	5.07	3.93	6.07	2.99	4.41	5.90	7.48
Female							
Value (current)	7.09	5.84	6.73	5.62	6.90	8.58	9.36
Value (constant)	2.53	2.74	2.42	2.57	2.71	2.71	1.92
Per capita (constant)	0.02	0.35	-0.02	-0.21	-0.14	0.10	-0.01
Price index	4.46	3.02	4.21	2.97	4.08	5.71	7.30

College

Male							
Value (current)	9.05	8.28	9.70	6.80	9.20	10.31	9.94
Value (constant)	3.62	3.70	3.57	3.74	3.98	4.51	2.29
Per capita (constant)	-0.10	0.38	0.31	0.03	-0.37	-0.65	-0.39
Price index	5.25	4.42	5.92	2.95	5.02	5.56	7.49
Female							
Value (current)	8.42	6.99	8.01	7.17	8.00	10.75	10.51
Value (constant)	3.27	2.84	2.66	3.15	3.85	4.72	2.54
Per capita (constant)	-0.12	0.32	0.08	-0.14	-0.40	-0.46	-0.17
Price index	4.99	4.03	5.22	3.89	4.00	5.76	7.77

for workers with elementary education and least rapidly for workers with secondary education. For the price of labor utilized in market labor activities the increases were greatest for college trained workers and least for workers with elementary education.

The measurement of human capital is a very active area of research. Investment in formal education has been measured by Schultz (1961), Machlup (1962), Kendrick (1976), and many others.[14] To estimate lifetime labor incomes for all individuals in the U.S. population we distinguish among three stages in the life cycle. In the first stage individuals may participate in formal schooling but not in the labor market. In the second stage individuals may enroll in school and also work. In the third stage individuals may participate in the labor market but not in formal schooling. For individuals in the third stage of the life cycle total labor compensation is the sum of compensation for market labor activities after taxes and imputed compensation for nonmarket labor activities. For individuals in the second stage of the life cycle total labor compensation also includes imputed labor compensation for schooling. For individuals in the first stage of the life cycle labor compensation includes only the imputed value of time spent in schooling.

For an individual in the third stage of the life cycle, we assume that expected incomes in future time periods are equal to the incomes of individuals of the same sex and education, but with the age that the individual will have in the future time period, adjusted for increases in real income. We assume that real incomes rise over time at the rate of Harrod-neutral technical change, which we estimate at 2 percent per year. We weight income for each future year by the probability of survival, given the initial age of the individual. We obtain these probabilities by sex from publications of the National Center for Health Statistics. Where necessary, these survival functions, giving probability of survival by age and sex, are interpolated by means of standard demographic techniques. Finally, we discount expected future incomes at a real rate of return of 4 percent per year to obtain the lifetime labor income of an individual of a given sex, age, and education.

For an individual at the second stage of the life cycle, combining formal schooling with the possibility of participation in the labor market, we impute the value of time spent in schooling through its impact on lifetime labor income. For an individual of a given sex and age who is completing the highest level of schooling, grade eighteen, lifetime labor income is the discounted value of expected future labor incomes for a person of that sex and age and eighteen years of schooling. The imputed labor compensation for the time spent in formal schooling is equal to the difference between the lifetime labor incomes of an individual with eighteen years of education and an individual with the same sex and age and one less year of education, less tuition and fees for that grade of schooling. Total labor compensation is equal to the value of time spent in formal schooling plus labor compensation for market and nonmarket activities other than formal schooling.

For an individual completing grade seventeen, lifetime labor income is equal to the lifetime labor income of an individual of the same sex and education, but one year older, plus expected labor compensation for one year, discounted back to the present and multiplied by the probability of survival for one year. Expected labor compensation is equal to the probability of enrollment in grade eighteen, multiplied by market and nonmarket labor compensation for a person enrolled in that grade, and one minus the probability of enrollment, multiplied by market and nonlabor compensation for a person with seventeen years of education, not enrolled in school. As before, the imputed labor compensation for the time spent in formal schooling is equal to the difference between the lifetime incomes of an individual with seventeen years of education and an individual with the same sex and age and one less year of education, less tuition and fees. Using the same approach to defining lifetime labor incomes for individuals completing earlier grades, lifetime incomes and imputed labor compensation for the time spent in formal schooling can be determined for individuals completing sixteen years of education, fifteen years of education, and so on.

For an individual in the first stage of the life cycle, where participation in the labor market is ruled out, the value of labor compensation is limited to the imputed value of schooling. Lifetime incomes for individuals at this stage of the life cycle can be determined for individuals completing one year of education, two years of education, and so on, working back from higher levels of education as outlined above. For individuals too young to be enrolled in school, imputed labor compensation is zero, but lifetime labor incomes are well-defined. The value of a newborn entrant into the population is equal to the lifetime labor income of the individual at age zero.

To estimate investment in human capital through education we employ data on lifetime labor incomes, cross-classified by single year of age and single grade of highest educational attainment. We use the increments in lifetime labor incomes and the number of individuals enrolled in school to estimate the value of investment in education. In Table 3–17 we present our estimates of the investment in formal education in current dollars. The most striking feature of our estimates is the high values we obtain. In 1948 investment through formal education is 2.8 times the value of market labor input presented in Table 3–8. The rate of growth of the value of investment in education, 10.8 percent per year, is considerably higher than the rate of growth of the value of labor input, 6.5 percent per year. Investment is highest for elementary education, second highest for secondary education, and lowest for higher education. Considering shares in investment by sex, we see that the male share has decreased throughout the postwar period.

Table 3–18 presents our estimates of investment in formal education in

Table 3–17. Investment in Formal Education by Sex and Educational Attainment, 1948–73 (billions of current dollars).

Year	Total	Male			Female		
		Elementary	Secondary	College	Elementary	Secondary	College
1948	498.7	246.1	73.4	16.9	125.0	29.7	7.7
1949	554.6	273.5	78.3	18.7	143.2	32.5	8.5
1950	600.9	302.1	82.0	20.6	152.4	34.4	9.6
1951	660.0	322.5	88.2	22.5	175.1	40.5	11.1
1952	721.5	351.2	95.9	24.2	192.0	45.8	12.4
1953	814.1	398.2	106.7	26.1	218.2	51.6	13.3
1954	961.2	465.4	122.3	28.6	266.4	62.6	15.8
1955	1,098.7	530.1	138.4	31.4	307.5	73.3	18.0
1956	1,214.6	584.5	152.5	33.7	342.7	81.5	19.7
1957	1,384.9	656.9	173.9	37.0	397.0	97.3	22.8
1958	1,549.1	717.3	197.4	39.6	451.4	117.4	26.1
1959	1,721.6	780.9	221.7	42.6	508.5	138.2	29.6
1960	1,900.0	880.2	251.7	47.0	533.7	152.6	34.8
1961	2,159.5	1,002.1	287.4	50.7	615.4	168.5	35.4
1962	2,362.7	1,090.4	329.7	57.9	654.5	190.0	40.2
1963	2,535.0	1,141.6	365.5	63.9	703.6	215.4	45.1
1964	2,887.0	1,282.1	430.4	73.4	788.7	258.7	53.6
1965	3,059.1	1,347.2	467.6	79.2	826.2	280.9	58.2
1966	3,434.1	1,520.1	536.4	91.7	899.7	315.1	71.1
1967	3,830.7	1,676.7	602.6	108.6	998.4	358.8	85.6
1968	4,087.1	1,762.9	643.8	118.7	1,071.3	394.2	96.2
1969	4,099.8	1,920.2	727.0	135.3	1,171.9	440.7	104.6
1970	5,576.1	2,344.0	931.3	169.8	1,436.7	562.6	131.7
1971	6,081.2	2,543.8	1,026.2	186.9	1,549.4	627.2	147.6
1972	6,263.1	2,542.9	1,057.7	201.7	1,618.7	677.7	164.4
1973	6,520.1	2,599.4	1,125.5	224.3	1,671.3	723.7	175.9

Table 3-18. Investment in Formal Education by Sex and Educational Attainment, 1948–73 (billions of constant 1972 dollars).

Year	Total	Male			Female		
		Elementary	Secondary	College	Elementary	Secondary	College
1948	2,927.1	1,275.7	424.2	74.7	809.2	292.8	50.5
1949	3,013.6	1,328.1	422.8	77.2	844.2	289.7	51.9
1950	3,108.8	1,390.5	417.2	79.7	881.7	286.8	52.9
1951	3,195.5	1,433.7	424.5	80.4	912.2	291.8	52.9
1952	3,285.4	1,476.5	433.8	81.0	942.7	298.5	52.9
1953	3,438.1	1,551.6	447.4	81.6	996.3	308.2	53.1
1954	3,613.6	1,639.7	463.6	83.0	1,054.4	318.6	54.3
1955	3,776.7	1,719.4	479.3	84.6	1,108.4	329.2	55.8
1956	3,941.4	1,795.6	499.7	86.2	1,159.4	343.0	57.5
1957	4,109.8	1,867.6	526.0	88.3	1,207.4	360.7	59.8
1958	4,284.1	1,931.4	563.6	90.9	1,248.8	387.0	62.4
1959	4,462.3	1,994.9	603.5	93.7	1,293.2	411.8	65.3
1960	4,664.6	2,078.7	637.3	97.9	1,350.8	430.5	69.4
1961	4,847.5	2,161.6	659.6	102.9	1,406.0	442.2	74.9
1962	5,029.5	2,223.6	702.0	109.7	1,438.7	472.6	82.8
1963	5,213.2	2,269.9	759.6	116.8	1,468.2	509.4	89.2
1964	5,397.6	2,323.2	813.1	122.9	1,501.6	542.5	94.3
1965	5,572.6	2,377.0	861.6	129.0	1,535.2	570.7	99.1
1966	5,725.6	2,429.2	893.8	140.3	1,566.3	582.8	113.3
1967	5,862.1	2,477.6	914.3	155.0	1,594.4	594.0	126.8
1968	5,992.2	2,518.7	942.5	166.8	1,617.0	610.3	137.0
1969	6,110.7	2,549.4	976.6	177.5	1,631.8	629.7	145.7
1970	6,215.5	2,569.4	1,012.8	189.5	1,638.6	649.2	156.0
1971	6,255.8	2,566.3	1,035.3	195.6	1,635.4	663.3	160.1
1972	6,263.1	2,542.9	1,057.7	201.7	1,618.7	677.7	164.4
1973	6,244.9	2,505.2	1,079.4	207.7	1,593.3	690.4	168.8

Table 3–19. Investment per Student by Sex and Educational Attainment, Market and Nonmarket Labor Activities, 1948–73 (thousands of current dollars).

Year	Total	Male			Female		
		Elementary	Secondary	College	Elementary	Secondary	College
1948	17.7	22.9	21.3	10.5	13.5	9.0	10.2
1949	19.2	26.8	22.9	11.4	15.0	9.9	11.3
1950	20.3	28.5	24.2	12.4	15.4	10.5	12.6
1951	21.8	29.7	25.6	14.0	17.2	12.1	14.6
1952	23.3	31.5	27.1	15.4	18.3	13.3	16.1
1953	23.3	34.0	29.3	16.9	19.8	14.6	16.8
1954	28.6	37.9	32.6	18.5	23.0	17.1	19.2
1955	31.4	41.4	35.6	20.2	25.5	19.3	21.1
1956	33.5	44.1	37.6	21.3	27.4	20.5	21.8
1957	36.8	48.2	40.3	22.7	30.8	22.9	23.9
1958	39.7	51.2	43.1	23.5	34.0	26.1	25.8
1959	42.5	54.0	46.4	24.2	37.7	29.5	27.4
1960	45.2	58.7	50.9	24.9	37.4	31.6	29.5
1961	49.6	65.5	54.9	24.7	42.4	32.9	27.0
1962	52.5	70.1	58.9	26.1	44.4	34.7	28.1
1963	54.4	72.1	61.3	26.8	46.8	37.0	29.3
1964	60.0	79.4	68.5	28.8	51.5	42.3	32.3
1965	61.9	82.1	72.4	28.0	53.0	45.0	31.1
1966	67.8	91.4	81.3	29.1	56.9	49.5	34.1
1967	73.9	99.6	89.2	31.4	62.5	55.1	37.3
1968	77.1	103.9	92.7	31.4	66.5	58.8	38.5
1969	83.3	112.8	101.8	33.0	72.5	64.0	38.8
1970	101.6	137.8	127.1	38.2	89.1	79.7	45.1
1971	110.1	150.3	137.0	40.9	96.6	86.9	49.3
1972	113.3	152.2	138.5	42.9	102.3	92.2	53.5
1973	118.3	158.3	145.2	46.5	107.6	97.1	55.9

constant dollars. We observe the same striking features: Investment in education is very large by comparison with market labor input, amounting to 7.7 times labor input in 1973; the rate of growth is higher than the rate of growth in labor input—3.0 percent per year for investment in education versus 1.5 percent per year for labor input. Investment is highest for elementary education, next to highest for secondary education, and lowest for higher education. While investment in current prices increases throughout the postwar period, investment in constant prices peaks in 1972 and begins to decline. Investment in constant prices for elementary education peaks for both males and females in 1970. Investment in constant prices for higher education increases throughout the postwar period for both sexes.

In Table 3–19 we present the investment in formal education per student in current dollars. We present the corresponding estimates in constant prices of 1972 in Table 3–20. The estimates of investment per student are very high, considerably in excess of per capita earnings. Second, the highest levels of investment per student correspond to elementary education. Third, investment per student at the college level is higher for females than for males. Fourth, while the value of investment per student in constant prices rises during most or all of this period for males and females with elementary and secondary education, this value peaks for college-trained males in 1955 and for college-trained females in 1950. These results are very different from the usual findings on investment in education. In interpreting our estimates it is important to recall that we include the value of leisure and nonmarket activities in lifetime labor incomes, producing very large values for investment in education and reducing the difference between males and females. We measure expected lifetime labor income of a person with one additional year of education from lifetime labor incomes of persons with all higher educational attainment levels by means of the nested procedure described above.

Table 3–21 presents rates of growth of investment value in formal education by period. For each of the three educational levels and the two sexes, four sets of numbers are presented. The first set is the value measured in current prices; the second is the value measured in constant prices of 1972; the third is the value per student in constant dollars; and the fourth is the price deflator of investment in formal education. Considering the current dollar values we observe that average annual rates of growth for females over the period 1948 to 1973 exceed the average annual rates of growth for males for elementary, secondary, and higher education. In this period the highest rate of growth for both males and females occurs for secondary education. Growth rates for the six subperiods presented in Table 3–21 are similar but not identical to those for the period as a whole.

Considering the constant dollar values presented in Table 3–21 we find that average annual growth rates for the period as a whole are very similar for males and females at the elementary level, are higher for males at the

Table 3–20. Investment per Student by Sex and Educational Attainment, Market and Nonmarket Labor Activities, 1948–73 (thousands of constant 1972 dollars).

Year	Total	Male			Female		
		Elementary	Secondary	College	Elementary	Secondary	College
1948	104.1	129.3	123.5	46.6	88.0	89.1	67.7
1949	104.7	130.2	124.1	47.3	88.6	89.0	68.9
1950	105.4	131.4	123.5	48.3	89.2	88.4	70.0
1951	106.0	132.1	123.2	50.1	89.8	87.8	69.7
1952	106.4	132.5	122.7	51.7	90.2	87.2	68.8
1953	106.9	132.8	123.1	52.8	90.8	87.3	67.3
1954	107.6	133.6	123.8	53.8	91.3	87.4	66.4
1955	108.2	134.5	123.6	54.6	92.0	86.9	65.4
1956	108.8	135.7	123.2	54.6	92.8	86.3	63.9
1957	109.3	137.1	122.0	54.4	93.9	85.1	62.9
1958	109.8	137.9	123.3	54.1	94.3	86.2	61.9
1959	110.4	138.1	126.4	53.2	94.5	88.1	60.5
1960	111.0	138.7	129.0	51.9	94.9	89.4	58.9
1961	111.4	141.3	126.1	50.3	97.0	86.4	57.3
1962	111.8	143.0	125.4	49.5	97.7	86.4	57.9
1963	112.1	143.4	127.6	49.1	97.8	87.7	58.0
1964	112.4	144.0	129.4	48.2	98.1	88.8	57.0
1965	112.9	145.0	133.5	45.6	98.6	91.5	53.2
1966	113.2	146.1	135.6	44.6	99.2	91.7	54.4
1967	113.2	147.3	135.5	44.8	99.8	91.2	55.3
1968	113.1	148.5	135.8	44.2	100.4	91.1	54.8
1969	113.2	149.8	136.8	43.4	101.0	91.5	54.1
1970	113.3	151.1	138.3	42.7	101.6	92.1	53.5
1971	113.3	151.7	138.3	42.9	102.0	92.0	53.6
1972	113.3	152.3	138.5	43.0	102.3	92.2	53.6
1973	113.3	152.7	139.3	43.1	102.6	92.7	53.6

Table 3-21. Investment in Formal Education by Sex and Educational Attainment, 1948–73 (rates of growth).

	1948–73	1948–53	1953–57	1957–60	1960–66	1966–69	1969–73
Elementary							
Male							
Value (current)	9.89	10.10	13.33	10.25	9.53	8.10	7.87
Value (constant)	2.74	3.99	4.74	3.63	2.63	1.62	−0.44
Per capita (constant)	0.67	0.53	0.80	0.39	0.87	0.84	0.47
Price index	6.96	5.88	8.20	6.38	6.72	6.37	8.34
Female							
Value (current)	10.93	11.79	16.14	10.36	9.09	9.21	9.28
Value (constant)	2.75	4.25	4.92	3.81	2.50	1.38	−0.60
Per capita (constant)	0.62	0.62	0.85	0.35	0.75	0.60	0.38
Price index	7.96	7.24	10.69	6.31	6.44	7.73	9.93
Secondary							
Male							
Value (current)	11.54	7.77	12.99	13.13	13.44	10.67	11.55
Value (constant)	3.81	1.07	4.13	6.61	5.80	3.00	2.54
Per capita (constant)	0.48	−0.07	−0.23	1.88	0.84	0.28	0.47
Price index	7.45	6.63	8.51	6.11	7.22	7.45	8.79
Female							
Value (current)	13.63	11.67	17.22	16.15	12.85	11.83	13.20
Value (constant)	3.49	1.03	4.01	6.07	5.18	2.61	2.33
Per capita (constant)	0.16	−0.40	−0.65	1.68	0.42	−0.07	0.32
Price index	9.80	10.54	12.70	9.50	7.30	8.98	10.62

Table 3-21. (Continued).

	1948-73	1948-53	1953-57	1957-60	1960-66	1966-69	1969-73
College							
Male							
Value (current)	10.89	9.10	9.06	8.35	11.76	13.86	13.46
Value (constant)	4.17	1.79	1.97	3.51	6.19	8.15	4.01
Per capita (constant)	-0.31	2.54	0.76	-1.54	-2.50	-0.93	-0.17
Price index	6.45	7.18	6.95	4.68	5.25	5.28	9.09
Female							
Value (current)	13.36	11.73	14.35	15.13	12.68	13.72	13.87
Value (constant)	4.94	0.99	3.02	5.12	8.50	8.75	3.75
Per capita (constant)	-0.93	-0.13	-1.68	-2.14	-1.33	-0.20	-0.19
Price index	8.02	10.64	11.00	9.52	3.85	4.57	9.76

secondary level, and are higher for females in higher education. For subperiods we can observe a displacement of the maximum rate of growth by educational level that reflects the displacement of the "baby-boom" group through the educational sector. For the 1953 to 1957 period the highest rate of growth corresponds to elementary education; for the 1957 to 1960 period the highest rate of growth corresponds to secondary education; for the last two subperiods, the highest rate of growth corresponds to higher education.

To eliminate the effect of the size of a given age cohort we present investment in education in constant prices per student in Table 3–21. For the postwar period as a whole the growth of investment per student at the elementary level is positive for both males and females and similar in magnitude. Growth of investment per student at the secondary level is positive for both sexes, but the average annual growth rate for males exceeds that for females. Investment per student in constant prices in higher education is negative for the postwar period as a whole and is more negative for females than for males. Rapid gains in enrollment rather than increases in investment per student account for the increase in investment in constant prices for both sexes over the postwar period.

To bring out the implications of our methodology for measuring lifetime labor incomes, we have estimated investment in formal education by conventional methods. For this purpose we have restricted the returns to market labor earnings and considered only the earnings of persons with one additional year of schooling. We have used the same rate of return and rate of increase in wages as in estimates that include the value of nonmarket labor activities. In Table 3–22 we present the resulting estimates of investment in education in current dollars. We can observe that the use of more conventional methodology reduces the value of investment in education, that the greatest reduction occurs at the elementary level, and that returns to investment in education for females are reduced more than the returns to investment for males.

Table 3–23 presents a comparison in constant dollars of the results of our two different methods for estimating investment in education. The share of market returns is given by the percentage of the value obtained using market returns in the value obtained using the nested procedure with both market and nonmarket returns. We observe that the estimate using the more restricted definition of labor incomes is only 8 to 9 percent of the estimate derived using the more comprehensive definition. The lowest percentage in the table corresponds to females enrolled in elementary school; the estimate of investment in education using the restricted definition of labor incomes is a little more than 1 percent of investment using the comprehensive definition. The highest percentage corresponds to males enrolled in college with the restricted definition of returns ranging from 64 to 69 percent of the comprehensive definition.

Table 3–22. Investment per Student by Sex and Educational Attainment, Market Labor Activities Only, 1948–73 (thousands of current dollars).

Year	Total	Male			Female		
		Elementary	Secondary	College	Elementary	Secondary	College
1948	3.1	4.4	4.8	9.3	0.5	2.1	2.6
1949	3.1	4.4	4.9	9.6	0.5	2.2	2.9
1950	3.5	5.1	5.0	10.3	0.4	2.3	3.3
1951	3.7	5.4	5.3	11.2	0.5	2.5	3.7
1952	3.8	5.7	5.6	12.0	0.5	2.5	4.1
1953	4.0	6.0	5.8	12.7	0.5	2.6	4.1
1954	4.2	6.3	6.1	13.2	0.5	2.7	4.4
1955	4.5	6.9	6.5	14.2	0.6	2.9	4.9
1956	4.8	7.4	6.8	14.8	0.6	3.1	5.1
1957	5.0	7.7	7.0	15.3	0.7	3.2	5.4
1958	5.1	7.8	7.2	15.4	0.7	3.3	5.7
1959	5.4	8.3	8.0	15.9	0.7	3.6	6.3
1960	5.5	8.2	8.8	16.6	0.7	3.0	5.8
1961	5.1	7.0	8.1	16.8	0.5	3.6	9.1
1962	5.3	7.0	8.6	17.8	0.5	3.7	9.4
1963	5.6	7.4	9.0	18.2	0.6	3.9	9.7
1964	6.1	7.8	9.9	19.5	0.8	4.2	10.6
1965	6.3	7.8	10.5	19.0	0.9	4.6	10.7
1966	6.9	8.2	11.0	20.0	1.8	5.1	9.5
1967	7.0	8.1	11.5	21.9	0.9	5.1	10.4
1968	7.6	8.5	12.1	22.4	1.4	5.8	11.3
1969	7.5	7.4	12.8	23.7	0.7	6.8	11.8
1970	9.1	9.7	13.3	28.7	1.3	7.2	12.7
1971	9.8	9.1	16.5	30.4	1.5	8.3	14.3
1972	10.4	10.5	16.9	29.4	1.4	8.8	15.1
1973	11.0	9.9	18.3	31.1	1.9	9.9	15.8

Table 3-23. Percentage of Investment Based on Market Labor Activities to Total Educational Investment, 1948–73.

Year	Total	Male			Female		
		Elementary	Secondary	College	Elementary	Secondary	College
1948	9.1	8.2	12.9	65.2	1.5	10.0	32.7
1949	8.9	8.1	12.8	65.0	1.4	9.9	32.6
1950	8.8	8.0	12.7	64.8	1.4	9.9	32.5
1951	8.7	7.9	12.8	64.5	1.4	9.9	32.2
1952	8.6	7.8	12.9	64.3	1.3	9.9	32.1
1953	8.5	7.8	12.9	64.2	1.3	9.9	31.8
1954	8.3	7.7	12.9	64.0	1.3	9.9	31.3
1955	8.3	7.6	12.9	63.9	1.3	9.9	30.8
1956	8.2	7.6	12.9	64.0	1.3	9.9	30.5
1957	8.1	7.5	12.9	64.2	1.3	9.8	30.1
1958	8.1	7.5	13.0	64.4	1.3	9.8	29.8
1959	8.2	7.5	13.0	64.7	1.3	9.9	29.6
1960	8.2	7.4	12.9	65.1	1.4	10.0	29.3
1961	8.1	7.3	12.8	65.5	1.4	9.9	28.8
1962	8.2	7.3	12.7	65.9	1.4	9.6	28.1
1963	8.3	7.2	12.7	66.4	1.4	9.6	28.1
1964	8.5	7.2	12.9	67.1	1.4	10.0	28.6
1965	8.5	7.2	12.7	67.6	1.4	9.8	28.9
1966	8.5	7.1	12.4	67.6	1.4	9.7	27.4
1967	8.6	7.1	12.4	67.4	1.4	9.7	27.0
1968	8.8	7.0	12.4	68.3	1.4	9.7	27.7
1969	8.9	7.0	12.3	68.8	1.4	9.7	28.1
1970	9.1	7.0	12.3	68.9	1.4	9.6	28.2
1971	9.1	7.0	12.2	68.7	1.4	9.7	28.2
1972	9.3	6.9	12.2	68.5	1.5	9.6	28.2
1973	9.4	6.9	12.2	68.4	1.5	9.6	28.2

ALTERNATIVE APPROACHES

Useful additional perspectives on our measures of aggregate productivity and investment in education can be discovered by comparing our sources, methods, and results with those of other studies. Our measures of the quantity of aggregate output are based on quantities of value added in each producing sector. Our measures of the quantities of aggregate primary factor inputs are based on all types of primary factor inputs. Finally, our measure of aggregate productivity is an index number constructed from data on prices and quantities of value added in all sectors, all types of capital input, and all types of labor input. This measure of productivity is based on a model of production and technical change for the economy as a whole with the quantity of value added represented as a function of capital input, labor input, and time.

For the U.S. economy as a whole, Christensen and Jorgenson (1969, 1970, 1973a, 1973b) have employed an approach to productivity measurement that is broadly similar to ours. Their study of aggregate productivity covers the period 1929 to 1969 for the private sector of the U.S. economy. Christensen, Cummings, and Jorgenson (1978, 1980, 1981) have extended the estimates of Christensen and Jorgenson through 1973. As in our study, aggregate value added is defined from the producers' point of view, excluding the value of sales and excise taxes and including the value of subsidies. However, the quantity of value added is measured as an index of deliveries to final demand rather than the sum of quantities of value added over industrial sectors. The quantity of capital input is divided among categories of the labor force broken down by educational attainment, but not by sex, age, employment class, or occupation.

The empirical results of Christensen, Cummings, and Jorgenson (1980) for the period 1948 to 1973 are very similar to ours. For this period their estimate of the average rate of growth of value added for the private domestic sector of the U.S. economy is 3.95 percent per year; by comparison our estimate of the rate of growth for the civilian sector of the U.S. economy is 3.85 percent per year. The two estimates are not precisely comparable since Christensen, Cummings, and Jorgenson do not include government sectors in their measure of value added. They estimate the average rate of growth of capital input at 4.16 percent per year for the period 1948 to 1973; our estimate for this period is 4.18 percent per year. These estimates are for the same sectors of the U.S. economy, since neither set of estimates includes capital input for the government sectors. Christensen, Cummings, and Jorgenson estimate the average rate of growth of labor input at 1.61 percent per year, while our estimate is 1.73 percent per year. Finally their estimate of the average rate of technical change is 1.33 percent per year, while our estimate is 1.25 percent per year. Again, the two estimates for labor input and the rate of technical change are not precisely comparable since we include labor input for the government sectors and they do not.

Christensen, Cummings, and Jorgenson (1978, 1980, 1981) have presented estimates of aggregate productivity for Canada, France, Germany, Italy, Japan, Korea, the Netherlands, and the United Kingdom as well as for the United States. Their estimates cover various periods beginning after 1947 and ending in 1973; the estimates cover the period 1960 to 1973 for all countries. Groes and Bjerregaard (1978) have developed comparable data for Denmark for the period 1950 to 1972. On the basis of the close correspondence between our results for the U.S. economy as a whole and those of Christensen, Cummings, and Jorgenson, we conclude that it is appropriate to compare our aggregate results with those for the other countries presented in their study.

Denison (1979) has provided estimates of aggregate productivity for the U.S. economy as a whole covering the period 1929 to 1976. Earlier, Denison (1967) presented comparable estimates at the aggregate level for Belgium, Denmark, France, Germany, the Netherlands, Norway, the United Kingdom, and the United States for the period 1950 to 1962. Walters (1968, 1970) has given estimates for Canada for the period 1950 to 1967 and Denison and Chung (1976) have given estimates for Japan for the period 1952 to 1971 that are closely comparable to Denison's estimates for the United States. A detailed comparison of the results of Christensen and Jorgenson (1969, 1970, 1973a, 1973b) and those of Denison (1967) is given by Jorgenson and Griliches (1972a, 1972b).

For the U.S. economy as a whole Kendrick (1961, 1973) has employed an approach to the measurement of value added through summation over the quantities of value added in all sectors with weights that change periodically. Similarly, his estimates of capital and labor inputs are constructed by summing the corresponding quantities over all sectors with periodically changing weights. He also presents estimates of capital and labor inputs based on unweighted sums of the quantities for all industrial sectors. Kendrick employs unweighted sums as a variant of his principal estimates, which are based on weighted sums with weights that depend on property and labor compensation by sector. Christensen and Jorgenson and Denison disaggregate capital and labor inputs for the economy as a whole by categories of capital stock and hours worked, but not by sector.

There are no other estimates of investment in education on the basis of lifetime labor incomes to compare with our results. However, we can compare our estimates with estimates based on the cost of education. In Table 3–24 we present a comparison of our estimates with those of Kendrick (1976).[15] Kendrick's estimates of the value of investment are only 4 to 6

Table 3-24. Investment in Education Based on Costs and on Lifetime Labor Incomes, 1948–69.

Year	Billions of Current Dollars			Billions of 1958 Dollars		
	Income Based	Kendrick Cost Based	Ratio	Income Based	Kendrick Cost Based	Ratio
1948	498.7	30.7	16.20	1,058.4	44.5	23.80
1949	554.6	30.4	18.22	1,089.8	43.0	25.34
1950	600.9	33.6	17.88	1,124.1	45.9	24.46
1951	660.0	38.8	17.00	1,155.1	49.9	23.12
1952	721.5	42.5	16.95	1,188.0	52.2	22.75
1953	814.1	45.9	17.72	1,243.2	54.6	22.76
1954	961.2	44.9	21.39	1,306.7	52.4	24.94
1955	1,098.7	50.8	21.59	1,365.6	57.4	23.76
1956	1,214.6	56.2	21.60	1,425.2	60.5	23.54
1957	1,384.9	61.3	22.57	1,486.1	63.2	23.49
1958	1,549.1	63.7	24.30	1,549.1	63.7	24.30
1959	1,721.6	71.4	24.10	1,613.5	68.8	23.43
1960	1,900.0	75.2	25.24	1,686.7	70.6	23.88
1961	2,159.5	79.8	27.03	1,752.8	73.2	23.92
1962	2,362.7	88.2	26.76	1,818.6	78.7	23.08
1963	2,535.0	95.8	26.44	1,885.1	83.2	22.66
1964	2,887.0	106.1	27.19	1,951.7	89.1	21.90
1965	3,059.1	118.4	28.84	2,015.0	96.4	20.89
1966	3,434.1	137.4	24.99	2,070.7	107.6	19.24
1967	3,830.7	148.6	25.76	2,119.7	112.0	18.92
1968	4,087.1	170.4	23.99	2,166.7	121.8	17.78
1969	4,499.8	192.3	23.39	2,209.6	129.9	17.00

percent of our estimates. As indicated in Table 3–23, the traditional method of imputing investment in education from lifetime earnings results in estimates between 8 and 9 percent of our estimates, implying that the traditional method of imputing lifetime earnings leads to estimates that are roughly twice as large as those based on costs of education. Our overall conclusion is that the most important innovation we have made is to incorporate both market and nonmarket activities into our measures of lifetime labor incomes.

APPENDIX TABLES

(Appendix tables commence on page 150)

Appendix Table 3-1. Translog Indexes of Labor Input.

Year	Hours	S	C	A	E	O	SC	SA
1948	0.807	0.844	0.776	0.816	0.692	0.737	0.805	0.850
1949	0.779	0.813	0.748	0.791	0.670	0.712	0.773	0.820
1950	0.799	0.834	0.772	0.820	0.692	0.739	0.798	0.850
1951	0.832	0.866	0.807	0.850	0.720	0.774	0.833	0.879
1952	0.837	0.870	0.813	0.860	0.729	0.787	0.838	0.889
1953	0.845	0.878	0.822	0.870	0.739	0.795	0.848	0.898
1954	0.817	0.847	0.794	0.843	0.719	0.768	0.816	0.869
1955	0.841	0.868	0.820	0.867	0.742	0.792	0.840	0.890
1956	0.854	0.880	0.836	0.880	0.758	0.810	0.855	0.900
1957	0.846	0.869	0.829	0.872	0.756	0.807	0.846	0.890
1958	0.819	0.839	0.803	0.845	0.739	0.785	0.817	0.860
1959	0.842	0.862	0.829	0.869	0.763	0.810	0.843	0.882
1960	0.847	0.872	0.832	0.879	0.771	0.819	0.855	0.900
1961	0.842	0.857	0.828	0.864	0.776	0.812	0.840	0.876
1962	0.858	0.873	0.846	0.881	0.802	0.832	0.859	0.893
1963	0.866	0.880	0.856	0.888	0.808	0.841	0.868	0.899
1964	0.881	0.893	0.872	0.900	0.829	0.860	0.883	0.910
1965	0.908	0.920	0.901	0.925	0.859	0.888	0.912	0.934
1966	0.936	0.946	0.932	0.951	0.893	0.928	0.941	0.960
1967	0.944	0.953	0.941	0.959	0.906	0.939	0.949	0.967
1968	0.960	0.966	0.958	0.973	0.929	0.959	0.964	0.980
1969	0.984	0.987	0.983	0.993	0.957	0.985	0.986	0.997
1970	0.970	0.977	0.969	0.993	0.948	0.971	0.976	0.999
1971	0.971	0.973	0.970	0.976	0.963	0.979	0.971	0.978
1972	1.000	1.000	1.000	1.000	1.000	1.000	1.000	1.000
1973	1.038	1.037	1.039	1.033	1.048	1.042	1.038	1.032
Average annual rate of growth	0.0101	0.0082	0.0116	0.0094	0.0166	0.0138	0.0102	0.0078

Appendix Table 3-1.   Translog Indexes of Labor Input (continued).

Year	SE	SO	CA	CE	CO	AE	AO	EO
1948	0.712	0.753	0.778	0.669	0.714	0.697	0.744	0.680
1949	0.688	0.726	0.752	0.647	0.689	0.678	0.720	0.657
1950	0.709	0.751	0.785	0.671	0.714	0.705	0.753	0.682
1951	0.737	0.786	0.818	0.701	0.752	0.732	0.786	0.715
1952	0.746	0.798	0.830	0.711	0.765	0.747	0.804	0.728
1953	0.757	0.808	0.841	0.722	0.774	0.759	0.814	0.737
1954	0.735	0.781	0.815	0.701	0.747	0.741	0.789	0.714
1955	0.756	0.803	0.841	0.726	0.772	0.764	0.812	0.737
1956	0.771	0.821	0.856	0.743	0.790	0.779	0.829	0.755
1957	0.768	0.818	0.851	0.743	0.788	0.778	0.827	0.754
1958	0.749	0.794	0.825	0.726	0.766	0.761	0.804	0.734
1959	0.773	0.819	0.851	0.751	0.794	0.786	0.829	0.760
1960	0.789	0.837	0.863	0.761	0.805	0.800	0.843	0.770
1961	0.785	0.822	0.849	0.766	0.798	0.798	0.831	0.771
1962	0.812	0.843	0.868	0.793	0.821	0.825	0.851	0.798
1963	0.817	0.850	0.878	0.801	0.831	0.831	0.860	0.805
1964	0.838	0.869	0.892	0.824	0.852	0.851	0.877	0.829
1965	0.868	0.896	0.918	0.855	0.881	0.879	0.903	0.859
1966	0.901	0.934	0.947	0.891	0.923	0.910	0.938	0.900
1967	0.913	0.946	0.957	0.905	0.936	0.923	0.950	0.912
1968	0.933	0.965	0.972	0.928	0.957	0.944	0.969	0.935
1969	0.960	0.989	0.993	0.957	0.984	0.969	0.993	0.965
1970	0.953	0.978	0.992	0.948	0.969	0.967	0.987	0.952
1971	0.965	0.981	0.975	0.962	0.979	0.971	0.983	0.970
1972	1.000	1.000	1.000	1.000	1.000	1.000	1.000	1.000
1973	1.048	1.039	1.033	1.048	1.043	1.043	1.037	1.050
Average annual rate of growth	0.0154	0.0129	0.0114	0.0180	0.0152	0.0161	0.0133	0.0173

Appendix Table 3-1.   Translog Indexes of Labor Input (continued).

Year	SCA	SCE	SCO	SAE	SAO	SEO	CAE	CAO
1948	0.807	0.685	0.729	0.717	0.761	0.694	0.665	0.720
1949	0.777	0.661	0.703	0.695	0.736	0.670	0.646	0.696
1950	0.810	0.684	0.725	0.722	0.767	0.693	0.676	0.727
1951	0.843	0.715	0.764	0.749	0.800	0.726	0.706	0.764
1952	0.855	0.725	0.777	0.763	0.817	0.739	0.722	0.782
1953	0.866	0.736	0.787	0.776	0.828	0.750	0.735	0.792
1954	0.836	0.714	0.759	0.756	0.803	0.726	0.717	0.768
1955	0.860	0.737	0.783	0.777	0.824	0.748	0.742	0.792
1956	0.873	0.753	0.801	0.790	0.839	0.766	0.759	0.809
1957	0.866	0.752	0.799	0.788	0.837	0.765	0.760	0.808
1958	0.836	0.733	0.775	0.769	0.813	0.744	0.744	0.785
1959	0.861	0.759	0.803	0.792	0.836	0.769	0.770	0.814
1960	0.882	0.777	0.822	0.813	0.859	0.787	0.786	0.829
1961	0.859	0.773	0.808	0.804	0.841	0.781	0.785	0.818
1962	0.878	0.802	0.832	0.831	0.861	0.809	0.814	0.841
1963	0.887	0.809	0.840	0.837	0.869	0.816	0.822	0.851
1964	0.900	0.832	0.860	0.857	0.885	0.838	0.844	0.870
1965	0.926	0.863	0.889	0.884	0.910	0.868	0.873	0.896
1966	0.956	0.899	0.930	0.916	0.944	0.907	0.907	0.935
1967	0.965	0.912	0.943	0.929	0.957	0.920	0.922	0.947
1968	0.978	0.932	0.963	0.949	0.975	0.942	0.943	0.968
1969	0.997	0.959	0.987	0.973	0.996	0.969	0.969	0.992
1970	0.999	0.953	0.976	0.972	0.995	0.960	0.968	0.985
1971	0.977	0.963	0.981	0.972	0.985	0.972	0.970	0.984
1972	1.000	1.000	1.000	1.000	1.000	1.000	1.000	1.000
1973	1.033	1.048	1.041	1.043	1.035	1.047	1.044	1.038
Average annual rate of growth	0.0099	0.0170	0.0142	0.0150	0.0123	0.0164	0.0180	0.0147

Appendix Table 3-1.   Translog Indexes of Labor Input (continued).

Year	CEO	AEO	SCAE	SCAO	SCEO	SAEO	CAEO	SCAEO
1948	0.663	0.683	0.681	0.736	0.676	0.698	0.662	0.677
1949	0.640	0.661	0.659	0.711	0.652	0.674	0.641	0.654
1950	0.662	0.691	0.688	0.739	0.673	0.703	0.669	0.680
1951	0.699	0.724	0.719	0.777	0.709	0.735	0.705	0.716
1952	0.712	0.742	0.735	0.794	0.723	0.753	0.724	0.735
1953	0.722	0.753	0.749	0.806	0.734	0.766	0.736	0.748
1954	0.698	0.732	0.729	0.781	0.710	0.745	0.715	0.727
1955	0.723	0.755	0.751	0.803	0.733	0.766	0.740	0.750
1956	0.741	0.773	0.767	0.819	0.751	0.783	0.757	0.766
1957	0.740	0.773	0.767	0.818	0.751	0.783	0.757	0.767
1958	0.721	0.753	0.748	0.793	0.731	0.762	0.738	0.746
1959	0.749	0.779	0.773	0.820	0.758	0.786	0.767	0.773
1960	0.761	0.793	0.797	0.843	0.777	0.808	0.782	0.795
1961	0.762	0.790	0.788	0.826	0.771	0.798	0.780	0.787
1962	0.791	0.817	0.818	0.850	0.801	0.825	0.809	0.817
1963	0.799	0.825	0.827	0.859	0.809	0.833	0.818	0.826
1964	0.824	0.847	0.848	0.877	0.833	0.854	0.841	0.848
1965	0.855	0.876	0.878	0.903	0.864	0.883	0.871	0.878
1966	0.898	0.912	0.913	0.941	0.905	0.918	0.911	0.916
1967	0.911	0.925	0.927	0.955	0.919	0.932	0.924	0.931
1968	0.935	0.947	0.948	0.974	0.942	0.953	0.948	0.953
1969	0.965	0.974	0.972	0.995	0.969	0.978	0.974	0.978
1970	0.952	0.967	0.972	0.993	0.959	0.975	0.967	0.974
1971	0.970	0.975	0.971	0.985	0.972	0.976	0.975	0.977
1972	1.000	1.000	1.000	1.000	1.000	1.000	1.000	1.000
1973	1.051	1.045	1.043	1.036	1.048	1.043	1.046	1.043
Average annual rate of growth	0.0184	0.0170	0.0170	0.0137	0.0175	0.0161	0.0183	0.0173

Appendix Table 3–2. Decomposition of Labor Quality.

Year	Quality	S	C	A	E	O	SC	SA
1948	0.839	1.042	0.958	1.008	0.854	0.910	0.995	0.998
1949	0.840	1.039	0.956	1.011	0.857	0.910	0.994	0.998
1950	0.850	1.039	0.962	1.021	0.861	0.921	0.994	0.997
1951	0.861	1.036	0.966	1.017	0.861	0.926	0.995	0.997
1952	0.878	1.035	0.967	1.023	0.867	0.936	0.995	0.997
1953	0.885	1.035	0.969	1.025	0.871	0.936	0.996	0.997
1954	0.890	1.032	0.967	1.028	0.877	0.936	0.995	0.997
1955	0.892	1.029	0.971	1.027	0.879	0.938	0.996	0.997
1956	0.897	1.026	0.974	1.025	0.883	0.944	0.996	0.996
1957	0.907	1.024	0.976	1.027	0.890	0.951	0.996	0.996
1958	0.911	1.020	0.977	1.028	0.899	0.954	0.996	0.996
1959	0.918	1.020	0.980	1.027	0.902	0.958	0.997	0.995
1960	0.940	1.030	0.982	1.037	0.910	0.967	0.997	0.994
1961	0.935	1.016	0.983	1.025	0.921	0.963	0.997	0.996
1962	0.951	1.017	0.985	1.025	0.934	0.969	0.997	0.996
1963	0.954	1.015	0.988	1.025	0.932	0.970	0.998	0.996
1964	0.963	1.014	0.990	1.022	0.941	0.976	0.998	0.996
1965	0.966	1.012	0.992	1.018	0.946	0.977	0.998	0.997
1966	0.979	1.010	0.995	1.016	0.954	0.991	0.999	0.998
1967	0.986	1.008	0.996	1.015	0.959	0.993	0.999	0.999
1968	0.993	1.006	0.997	1.013	0.967	0.998	0.999	0.999
1969	0.994	1.003	0.998	1.009	0.972	1.001	0.999	1.000
1970	1.004	1.007	0.999	1.023	0.976	1.000	0.999	1.000
1971	1.006	1.001	0.998	1.005	0.992	1.008	0.999	0.999
1972	1.000	1.000	1.000	1.000	1.000	1.000	1.000	1.000
1973	1.005	0.999	1.000	0.995	1.009	1.003	1.000	1.000
Average annual rate of growth	0.0072	−0.0017	0.0017	−0.0005	0.0067	0.0039	0.0002	0.0001

Appendix Table 3-2. Decomposition of Labor Quality (continued).

Year	SE	SO	CA	CE	CO	AE	AO	EO
1948	0.987	0.979	0.994	1.009	1.010	0.999	1.001	1.080
1949	0.987	0.981	0.994	1.009	1.011	0.999	1.000	1.075
1950	0.986	0.978	0.995	1.008	1.003	0.997	0.997	1.070
1951	0.987	0.979	0.996	1.008	1.005	0.999	0.998	1.072
1952	0.988	0.980	0.997	1.007	1.005	1.000	0.998	1.067
1953	0.989	0.982	0.997	1.007	1.004	1.001	0.999	1.064
1954	0.989	0.984	0.998	1.007	1.005	1.002	0.999	1.059
1955	0.990	0.985	0.998	1.006	1.003	1.002	0.997	1.058
1956	0.991	0.987	0.998	1.006	1.001	1.002	0.997	1.055
1957	0.992	0.989	0.999	1.005	0.999	1.002	0.997	1.048
1958	0.992	0.991	0.999	1.005	0.999	1.002	0.996	1.041
1959	0.993	0.990	0.999	1.004	1.000	1.002	0.996	1.039
1960	0.993	0.991	0.999	1.004	0.999	0.999	0.991	1.032
1961	0.994	0.995	0.999	1.003	0.999	1.003	0.998	1.030
1962	0.995	0.996	1.000	1.003	1.000	1.002	0.997	1.026
1963	0.996	0.996	1.000	1.003	0.999	1.003	0.997	1.027
1964	0.996	0.996	1.000	1.002	1.000	1.004	0.997	1.023
1965	0.997	0.996	1.000	1.002	0.999	1.003	0.998	1.022
1966	0.997	0.996	1.000	1.002	0.999	1.003	0.995	1.016
1967	0.998	0.999	1.000	1.001	0.999	1.003	0.996	1.012
1968	0.998	0.999	1.001	1.001	1.000	1.002	0.997	1.008
1969	0.999	1.000	1.000	1.001	1.000	1.003	0.998	1.006
1970	0.998	0.999	1.001	1.001	0.999	0.997	0.993	1.004
1971	0.999	0.999	1.000	1.000	1.001	1.001	0.998	0.998
1972	1.000	1.000	1.000	1.000	1.000	1.000	1.000	1.000
1973	1.000	0.998	0.999	0.999	1.000	1.000	1.001	0.998
Average annual rate of growth	0.0005	0.0008	0.0002	−0.0004	−0.0004	0.0001	−0.0000	−0.0032

Appendix Table 3-2. Decomposition of Labor Quality (continued).

Year	SCA	SCE	SCO	SAE	SAO	SEO	CAE	CAO
1948	1.001	1.000	1.005	1.001	1.003	1.012	0.993	1.004
1949	1.001	1.000	1.005	1.001	1.003	1.012	0.993	1.004
1950	1.000	1.000	1.005	1.001	1.004	1.013	0.993	1.004
1951	1.001	1.000	1.004	1.001	1.004	1.012	0.993	1.003
1952	1.001	1.000	1.004	1.000	1.003	1.012	0.994	1.003
1953	1.001	1.000	1.004	1.000	1.003	1.011	0.994	1.002
1954	1.000	1.000	1.004	1.000	1.003	1.011	0.994	1.002
1955	1.000	1.000	1.004	1.000	1.003	1.010	0.995	1.002
1956	1.000	1.000	1.003	1.000	1.003	1.010	0.995	1.001
1957	1.000	1.000	1.003	1.000	1.002	1.009	0.995	1.001
1958	1.000	1.000	1.003	0.999	1.002	1.009	0.995	1.001
1959	1.000	1.000	1.002	0.999	1.002	1.008	0.996	1.001
1960	0.999	1.000	1.001	0.999	1.003	1.007	0.996	1.001
1961	1.000	1.000	1.002	0.999	1.002	1.006	0.996	1.001
1962	1.000	1.000	1.001	0.999	1.002	1.005	0.997	1.001
1963	1.000	1.000	1.001	0.999	1.002	1.005	0.997	1.000
1964	1.000	1.000	1.001	0.999	1.002	1.004	0.998	1.000
1965	1.000	1.000	1.000	0.999	1.001	1.004	0.998	1.000
1966	1.000	1.000	1.000	0.999	1.000	1.003	0.998	1.000
1967	1.000	1.000	1.000	0.999	0.999	1.002	0.998	1.000
1968	1.000	1.000	1.000	0.999	0.999	1.002	0.999	1.000
1969	1.000	1.000	1.000	0.999	0.999	1.001	0.999	1.000
1970	1.000	1.000	1.000	1.000	1.001	1.002	0.999	0.999
1971	1.000	1.000	1.000	1.000	1.000	1.000	0.999	0.999
1972	1.000	1.000	1.000	1.000	1.000	1.000	1.000	1.000
1973	0.999	1.000	0.999	1.000	1.000	0.999	1.000	1.000
Average annual rate of growth	−0.0001	−0.0000	−0.0002	−0.0001	−0.0001	−0.0005	0.0003	−0.0002

Appendix Table 3–2. Decomposition of Labor Quality (continued).

Year	CEO	AEO	SCAE	SCAO	SCEO	SAEO	CAEO	SCAEO
1948	0.996	0.995	0.998	0.998	0.999	0.997	1.004	1.001
1949	0.996	0.995	0.998	0.998	0.999	0.997	1.004	1.001
1950	0.997	0.996	0.998	0.998	0.999	0.998	1.003	1.001
1951	0.997	0.996	0.998	0.998	0.999	0.997	1.003	1.001
1952	0.998	0.996	0.998	0.998	0.999	0.998	1.003	1.001
1953	0.998	0.996	0.999	0.998	0.999	0.998	1.003	1.001
1954	0.998	0.996	0.998	0.998	0.999	0.998	1.003	1.001
1955	0.999	0.997	0.998	0.999	0.999	0.998	1.003	1.001
1956	0.999	0.998	0.998	0.999	0.999	0.998	1.002	1.001
1957	0.999	0.998	0.998	0.999	0.999	0.998	1.002	1.001
1958	1.000	0.999	0.998	0.999	0.999	0.998	1.002	1.001
1959	1.000	0.999	0.999	0.999	0.999	0.999	1.002	1.001
1960	1.000	1.000	0.999	0.999	0.999	0.999	1.001	1.001
1961	1.001	0.997	0.999	0.999	0.999	0.999	1.001	1.001
1962	1.001	0.998	0.999	0.999	0.999	0.999	1.001	1.001
1963	1.001	0.998	0.999	0.999	0.999	0.999	1.000	1.000
1964	1.001	0.997	0.999	0.999	0.999	0.999	1.000	1.000
1965	1.001	0.998	0.999	0.999	0.999	0.999	1.000	1.000
1966	1.000	0.999	0.999	0.999	0.999	0.999	1.000	1.000
1967	1.000	0.999	0.999	0.999	0.999	1.000	1.000	1.000
1968	1.000	0.999	0.999	0.999	0.999	0.999	1.000	1.000
1969	1.000	0.998	1.000	0.999	1.000	1.000	1.000	1.000
1970	1.000	1.001	0.999	1.000	1.000	1.000	1.000	1.000
1971	1.000	0.999	1.000	0.999	1.000	0.999	1.000	1.000
1972	1.000	1.000	1.000	1.000	1.000	1.000	1.000	1.000
1973	0.999	0.999	1.000	1.000	1.000	1.000	1.000	1.000
Average annual rate of growth	0.0001	0.0002	0.0001	0.0001	0.0000	0.0001	−0.0002	−0.0001

NOTES

1. An aggregate production function was introduced by Cobb and Douglas (1928). References to aggregate production studies based on this approach are given in a survey paper by Douglas (1948). References to more recent studies of production at the aggregate level are given by Kennedy and Thirlwall (1972) and Nadiri (1970). Additional references are given by Takayama (1974).

2. Alternative approaches to generating data and analyzing the sources of U.S. economic growth at the aggregate level are discussed by Christensen and Jorgenson (1969, 1970, 1973a, 1973b), Denison (1962, 1967, 1969, 1972, 1974, 1979), Jorgenson and Griliches (1967, 1972a, 1972b), and Kendrick (1961, 1973).

3. The breakdown of capital input by class of asset and legal form of organization was originated by Christensen and Jorgenson (1969, 1970, 1973a, 1973b). Changes in the structure of capital input for the United States have been discussed by Griliches and Jorgenson (1966) and by Jorgenson and Griliches (1967, 1972a, 1972b). Gollop and Jorgenson (1980) have presented the first results based on this approach at the sectoral level.

4. The breakdown of labor input by demographic characteristics was originated by Griliches (1960) and by Denison (1962, 1967, 1974). Changes in the structure of labor input for the United States have been discussed by Jorgenson and Griliches (1967, 1972a, 1972b). Gollop and Jorgenson (1980) have presented the first results based on this approach at the sectoral level.

5. The translog index of technical change was introduced by Christensen and Jorgenson (1970). It was first derived from the translog production function by Diewert (1980). The translog production function was introduced by Christensen, Jorgenson, and Lau (1971, 1973).

6. The translog index numbers were introduced by Fisher (1922) and have been discussed by Tornquist (1936), Theil (1965) and Kloek (1966). They were first derived from the translog production function by Diewert (1976).

7. The decomposition of growth in labor input between growth in hours worked and growth in labor quality is discussed in greater detail in the next section.

8. Detailed discussions of quality indexes and applications to disaggregated labor data can be found in the doctoral dissertations by Barger (1971) and Chinloy (1974). The initial design of our approach to the measurement of labor input, the collection of data, and much of the required estimation were carried out in collaboration with Chinloy. Chinloy (1980) presents an application to U.S. aggregate data. Extremely valuable assistance in programming the computations was provided by Peter Derksen.

9. Campbell and Peskin (1979) have summarized accounting systems developed by Kendrick (1976, 1979), Ruggles and Ruggles (1970, 1973), and Eisner (1978, 1980). Kendrick's accounting system is also discussed by Engerman and Rosen (1980). We present a comparison between our estimates of investment in education and human wealth and those of Kendrick in the last section of this paper.

10. An economic theory of time allocation is presented by Becker (1965). Detailed references to more recent literature on time allocation are given by Murphy (1980).

Results of a comprehensive empirical study for the United States are presented by Juster, Courant, Duncan, Robinson, and Stafford (1978). Kendrick (1979) summarizes the results of an unpublished paper by Wehle, comparing seventeen studies of time allocation for the United States, covering the period 1924 to 1976.

11. A review of estimates of time spent in formal schooling is given by Parsons (1974).

12. Nineteen empirical studies of the valuation of nonmarket labor activities for the United States are surveyed by Murphy (1980). Kendrick (1979) provides recent estimates covering the period 1929 to 1973.

13. Houthakker (1959) has allocated income taxes to individuals on the basis of demographic characteristics. We control the total taxes paid on labor incomes to estimates for the U.S. economy as a whole based on the methods of Frane and Klein (1953).

14. A complete account for the educational sector is needed to estimate rates of return to educational investment. Estimates of investment in education have been presented by Schultz (1961). Rates of return are given by Becker (1964). Kendrick (1976) provides estimates covering the period 1929 to 1969. Detailed references to recent literature are provided by Campbell and Peskin (1979).

15. Kendrick's estimates of human capital have been compared with estimates based on lifetime labor incomes for males between the ages of fourteen and seventy-four for the United States, excluding the value of nonmarket activities, for the year 1969 by Graham and Webb (1979).

REFERENCES

Barger, William J. 1971. "The Measurement of Labor Input: U.S. Manufacturing Industries, 1948-1966." Ph.D. dissertation, Harvard University.

Becker, Gary S. 1964. 2d ed. 1975. *Human Capital.* New York: Columbia University Press.

———. 1965. "A Theory of the Allocation of Time." *Economic Journal* 75, no. 299 (September): 493-517.

Bureau of Economic Analysis. 1977. *The National Income and Product Accounts of the United States, 1929-1974; Statistical Tables.* Washington, D.C.: U.S. Government Printing Office.

Campbell, Beth, and Janice Peskin. 1979. "Expanding Economic Accounts and Measuring Economic Welfare: A Review of Proposals," Washington, D.C.: Bureau of Economic Analysis, U.S. Department of Commerce.

Chinloy, Peter T. 1974. "Issues in the Measurement of Labor Input." Ph.D. dissertation, Harvard University.

———. 1980. "Sources of Quality Change in Labor Input." *American Economic Review* 70, no. 1 (March): 108-19.

Christensen, Laurits R., and Dale W. Jorgenson. 1969. "The Measurement of U.S. Real Capital Input, 1929-1967." *Review of Income and Wealth,* series 15, no. 4 (December): 293-320.

———. 1970. "U.S. Real Product and Real Factor Input, 1929-1967." *Review of Income and Wealth,* series 16 (March): 19-50.

————. 1973a. "Measuring the Performance of the Private Sector of the U.S. Economy, 1929-1969." In *Measuring Economic and Social Performance,* edited by Milton Moss, pp. 233-238. New York: National Bureau of Economic Research.

————. 1973b. "U.S. Income, Saving, and Wealth, 1929-1969." *Review of Income and Wealth,* series 19, no. 4 (December): 329-62.

Christensen, Laurits R.; Dianne Cummings; and Dale W. Jorgenson. 1978. "Productivity Growth, 1947-1973: An International Comparison." In *The Impact of International Trade and Investment on Employment,* edited by W. Dewald, pp. 211-33. Washington, D.C.: U.S. Government Printing Office.

————. 1980. "Economic Growth, 1947-1973: An International Comparison." In *New Developments in Productivity Measurement,* vol. 41, edited by John W. Kendrick and Beatrice Vaccara, pp. 595-698. Chicago: University of Chicago Press.

————. 1981. "Relative Productivity Levels, 1947-1973: An International Comparison." *European Economic Review* 16, no. 1 (May): 61-94.

Christensen, Laurits R.; Dale W. Jorgenson; and Lawrence J. Lau. 1971. "Congugate Duality and the Transcendental Logarithmic Production Function." *Econometrica* 39, no. 4 (July): 255-56.

————. 1973. "Transcendental Logarithmic Production Frontiers." *Review of Economics and Statistics* 55, no. 1 (February): 28-45.

Cobb, Charles W., and Paul H. Douglas. 1928. "A Theory of Production." *American Economic Review* 18, no. 1 (March): 139-65.

Denison, Edward F. 1962. *Sources of Economic Growth in the United States and the Alternatives before Us.* New York: The Committee for Economic Development.

————. 1967. *Why Growth Rates Differ.* Washington, D.C.: The Brookings Institution.

————. 1969. "Some Major Issues in Productivity Analysis: An Examination of Estimates by Jorgenson and Griliches." *Survey of Current Business* 49, no. 5, pt. 2 (May): 1-27.

————. 1972. "Final Comments." *Survey of Current Business* 52, no. 5, pt. 2 (May): 95-110.

————. 1974. *Accounting for United States Economic Growth, 1929 to 1969.* Washington, D.C.: The Brookings Institution.

————. 1979. *Accounting for Slower Economic Growth: The United States in the 1970's.* Washington, D.C.: The Brookings Institution.

Denison, Edward F., and William K. Chung. 1976. *How Japan's Economy Grew So Fast.* Washington, D.C.: The Brookings Institution.

Diewert, W. Erwin. 1976. "Exact and Superlative Index Numbers." *Journal of Econometrics* 4, no. 2 (May): 115-46.

————. 1980. "Aggregation Problems in the Measurement of Capital." In *The Measurement of Capital,* edited by Dan Usher, pp. 433-528. Chicago: University of Chicago Press.

Douglas, Paul H. 1948. "Are There Laws of Production?" *American Economic Review* 38, no. 1 (March): 1-41.

Eisner, Robert. 1978. "Total Incomes in the United States, 1959 and 1969." *Review of Income and Wealth,* series 24, no. 1 (March): 41-70.

————. 1980. "Capital Gains and Income: Real Changes in the Value of Capital in the United States, 1946–1977." In *The Measurement of Capital,* edited by Dan Usher, pp. 175–342. Chicago: University of Chicago Press.

Engerman, Stanley, and Sherwin Rosen. 1980. "New Books on the Measurement of Capital." In *The Measurement of Capital,* edited by Dan Usher, pp. 153–70. Chicago: University of Chicago Press.

Fisher, I. 1922. *The Making of Index Numbers.* Boston: Houghton Mifflin.

Frane, Lenore, and Lawrence R. Klein. 1953. "The Estimation of Disposable Income by Distributive Shares." *Review of Economics and Statistics* 35, no. 4 (November): 333–37.

Gollop, Frank M., and Dale W. Jorgenson. 1980. "U.S. Productivity Growth by Industry, 1947–1973." In *New Developments in Productivity Measurement,* edited by John W. Kendrick and Beatrice Vaccara, vol. 41, pp. 17–136. Chicago: University of Chicago Press.

Graham, John W., and Roy H. Webb. 1979. "Stocks and Depreciation of Human Capital: New Evidence from a Present-Value Perspective." *Review of Income and Wealth,* series 25, no. 2 (June): 209–24.

Griliches, Zvi. 1960. "Measuring Inputs in Agriculture: A Critical Survey." *Journal of Farm Economics* 42, no. 4 (December): 1411–27.

Griliches, Zvi, and Dale W. Jorgenson. 1966. "Sources of Measured Productivity Change: Capital Input." *American Economic Review* 56, no. 2 (May): 50–61.

Groes, Nils, and Peter Bjerregaard. 1978. *Real Product, Real Factor Input and Productivity in Denmark, 1950–1972.* Copenhagen: Institute of Economics, University of Copenhagen.

Houthakker, Hendrick S. 1959. "Education and Income," *Review of Economics and Statistics* 41, no. 1 (February): 24–28.

Jorgenson, Dale W., and Zvi Griliches. 1967. "The Explanation of Productivity Change." *The Review of Economic Studies* 34(3), no. 99 (July): 249–83.

————. 1972a. "Issues in Growth Accounting: A Reply to Edward F. Denison." *Survey of Current Business* 52, no. 5, pt. 2 (May): 65–94.

————. 1972b. "Issues in Growth Accounting: Final Reply." *Survey of Current Business* 52, no. 5, pt. 2 (May): 111.

Jorgenson, Dale W., and Alvaro Pachon. 1983a. "The Accumulation of Human and Nonhuman Wealth." In *The Determinants of National Saving and Wealth,* edited by R. Hemming and F. Modigliani, pp. 302–50. London: Macmillan.

————. 1983b. "Lifetime, Income and Human Capital." In *Human Resources, Employment, and Development,* edited by P. Streeten and H. Maier, London: Macmillan: 29–90.

Juster, F. Thomas; Paul Courant; Greg J. Duncan; John Robinson; and Frank P. Stafford. 1978. *Time Use in Economic and Social Accounts.* Ann Arbor: Institute for Social Research, University of Michigan.

Kendrick, John W. 1961. *Productivity Trends in the United States.* Princeton, N.J.: Princeton University Press.

————. 1973. *Postwar Productivity Trends in the United States, 1948–1969.* New York: National Bureau of Economic Research.

———. 1976. *The Formation and Stocks of Total Capital.* New York: Columbia University Press.

———. 1979. "Expanding Imputed Values in the National Income and Product Accounts." *Review of Income and Wealth,* series 25, no. 4 (December): 249–364.

Kennedy, Charles, and A.P. Thirlwall. 1972. "Technical Progress: A Survey." *Economic Journal* 82, no. 325 (March): 11–72.

Kloek, T. 1966. *Indexcijfers: Enige Methodologisch Aspecten.* The Hague: Pasmans.

Machlup, Fritz. 1962. *The Production and Distribution of Knowledge in the United States.* Princeton, N.J.: Princeton University Press.

Murphy, Martin. 1980. "The Measurement and Valuation of Household Nonmarket Time." Washington, D.C.: Bureau of Economic Analysis, U.S. Department of Commerce.

Nadiri, Mohammed I. 1970. "Some Approaches to the Theory and Measurement of Total Factor Productivity: A Survey." *Journal of Economic Literature* 8, no. 4 (December): 1137–78.

Nordhaus, William D., and James Tobin. 1972. *Economic Growth.* New York: National Bureau of Economic Research.

Parsons, Donald O. 1974. "The Cost of School Time, Foregone Earnings, and Human Capital Formation." *Journal of Political Economy* 82, no. 2, pt. 1 (March/April): 251–66.

Ruggles, Nancy, and Richard Ruggles. 1970. *The Design of Economic Accounts.* New York: Columbia University Press.

———. 1973. "A Proposal for a System of Economic and Social Accounts." In *The Measurement of Social and Economic Performance,* edited by Milton Moss, pp. 111–145. New York: Columbia University Press.

Schultz, Theodore W. 1961. "Investment in Human Capital." *American Economic Review* 51, no. 1 (March): 1–17.

Takayama, Akira. 1974. "On Biased Technological Progress." *American Economic Review* 64, no. 4 (September): 631–39.

Theil, H. 1965. "The Information Approach to Demand Analysis." *Econometrica* 33, no. 1 (January): 67–87.

Tornquist, Leo. 1936. "The Bank of Finland's Consumption Price Index." *Bank of Finland Monthly Bulletin* 10: 1–8.

Walters, Dorothy. 1968. *Canadian Income Levels and Growth: An International Perspective.* Ottawa: Economic Council of Canada.

———. 1970. *Canadian Growth Revisited, 1950-1967.* Ottawa: Economic Council of Canada.

* *Chapter 4*

Measuring the Impact of Education on Productivity

Mark Plant and Finis Welch

Economies grow by accumulating productive resources and by improving the processes through which resources are transformed into consumable goods and services. The concurrent growth of education and output in most economies has provided an impetus for establishing a causal link from education to productivity. The evaluation of this investment in education as a source of growth has been the task of a host of economic studies, including the human-capital literature and much of the growth-accounting literature. The essential underpinning of this literature is simple: Education is a factor of production. Its primary function may be allocative, as proposed by Nelson and Phelps (1966) and Welch (1970), or it may be physically productive. But in either case, the basic inference drawn from his literature is that education is a form of productive capital.

Our purpose in this paper is to step back from the myriad of technical questions surrounding the complex growth-accounting formulas used to dissect growth into its components and to consider the underlying models in a simple, unadorned framework. Specifically, we argue that the questions asked by the current growth-accounting literature are less fundamental than they appear to be at first blush and are poorly formed in the sense that they do not actually measure the contribution of education to growth in output. We contend that standard methods of growth accounting are a reasonable convention for simple measurement of factor contributions where outputs

The authors thank H. Levin, M. Murray and R. Nelson for constructive comments. Support for this work was provided by the National Institute of Education.

are well-measured and when factor growth is exogenous. For education and other forms of producer capital that are legitimately viewed as intermediate products, the standard techniques seem less desirable. We propose an alternative measure that we consider more amenable to measuring the contribution of an intermediate input such as education. This measure is derived using tools similar to those used to analyze consumer's surplus. A direct analogy with the consumer's case is given, and the derivation of the alternative measure is based on this analogy. The theoretical and conceptual analysis of the measure of education's contribution to productivity is followed by a discussion of the empirical measures implemented by various authors.

The paper proceeds as follows. In the first section we present a simple tautological two-period characterization of growth to illustrate the questions that might be asked. In the next section, we develop a stereotype of the marginal accounting framework that emphasizes the role of intermediate factors of production, like education. This model illustrates that in a one-period framework, a fully specified calculation of an intermediate factor's contribution to growth is zero if necessary conditions for efficient allocation are satisfied. We then suggest an alternative calculation that yields a positive measure of the contribution of education in a limited but well-specified sense. Finally, we use an explicit model of production to illustrate differences in the computed contributions of education that arise from differences in procedures followed in some of the better known studies.

THE SIMPLE TWO-PERIOD FRAMEWORK

At any point in time, the potential consumption of an economy can be divided into two parts: what is actually consumed and what is diverted from current consumption to increase potential consumption at a later date. Therefore, current potential consumption can be thought of as what is autonomously endowed and what stems from foregone previous consumption. If the entire past is collapsed into a single period, then current potential consumption is:

$$y_t = y_t^* + (1+r)I_{t-1}, \tag{4.1}$$

where y_t^* is autonomously available, I_{t-1} is previous investment or foregone consumption, and r represents the rate of return on the investment and is a function of the level of that investment. The contribution of foregone consumption to current potential consumption is illustrated in Figure 4-1. In this figure, the productivity of investment schedule, $(1+r(I))$, is plotted against investment, I, and the shaded area represents the income

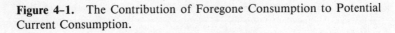

Figure 4-1. The Contribution of Foregone Consumption to Potential Current Consumption.

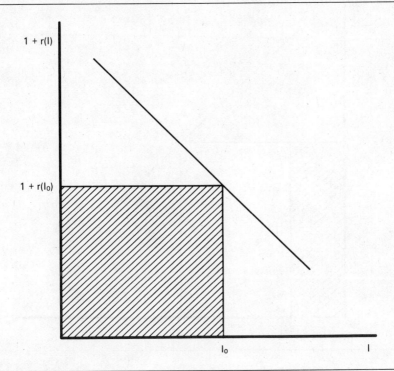

available from the investment, I, in the period after which the investment is made.

This naive characterization allows us to highlight what we consider the two fundamental questions concerning the process of growth in an economy. First, what determines the height of the schedule $(1+r(I))$? This schedule summarizes growth potential, and its determinants are critical to understanding the process by which economies can increase the return to investment. Education viewed as knowledge acquisition may be a critical determinant of the productivity of investments, but the accounting literature as we understand it does not speak to this issue.

Given the schedule $(1+r(I))$, the next question is what determines the level of investment, I? The basic issue here is the relative value of future to present consumption or the societal rate of time preference. The role of education in this determination of time preference is unexplored. If education were to reduce the rate of time preference, it would add to growth by

Figure 4-2.   Education's Contribution to Growth in Output.

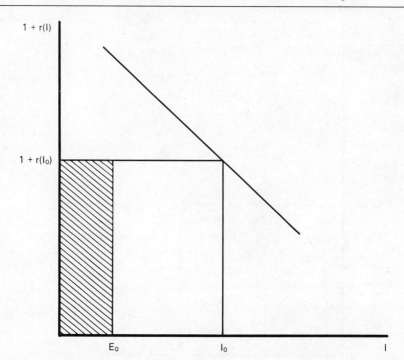

increasing investment. Again, current studies in growth accounting do not address this issue.

The studies known to us that present measures of education's contribution to growth address neither education's role in determining the productivity of investment nor the overall level of investment. Both are presumed to be given. The task undertaken is considerably less ambitious. The total investment, I, is simply divided into various components that include education among other things like physical capital. Thus in Figure 4-2, if E represented the portion of investment, I, devoted to education, the shaded area, $(1+r)E$ would be measured as education's contribution to growth in output. If education constitutes some fraction of total investment, standard growth-accounting procedures count that fraction as education's share of productivity growth.

We believe that education cannot be viewed simply as an alternative form of investment to generate future consumption. It is an important determinant of the rate at which foregone consumption can be transformed into future potential consumption, and it is an important determinant of the overall level of investment activity. These are unexplored and difficult issues that the growth-accounting literature has not addressed. Instead, growth accountants have concentrated on the division of investment activity into various sectors. Our purpose in the remainder of the paper is to look critically at the marginal growth-accounting procedures by which this dissection is made and to propose an alternative procedure that measures the contribution of education in a nonmarginal framework.

THEORETICAL APPROACHES TO MEASURING THE PRODUCTIVITY OF EDUCATION

In this section we develop a one-period prototype of the basic growth-accounting framework and analyze its usefulness in measuring the contribution of the growth in input to the growth in output. We concentrate on the characterization of education as a productive input and show that the standard procedures when applied to an intermediate input like education lead to some counterintuitive conclusions that warrant consideration of an alternative approach.

Let us consider a very simple economy that produces one output Y, as a function of two homogeneous inputs, capital, K, and labor services, N, according to the relationship:

$$Y = f(K, N).$$

The standard growth-accounting question as characterized in the previous section is a simple one. Suppose we observe growth in the amount of output produced. What part of that growth can be attributed to growth in each of the inputs? Suppose, first, that the amount of capital, K, were fixed and labor services grew exogenously. Then, ignoring any possibility for technical advance, all output growth is due to the growth in labor. If both output and labor are easily measurable quantities, then the contribution of the increase in the input is easily measured. No complex formulas need to be called into play: All growth is simply attributed to the growth in labor.

The situation becomes considerably more complicated, both conceptually and empirically, when we allow for growth in more than one input. The basic problem is that it is difficult to identify the source of the growth in output if both inputs increase exogenously. There are numerous conceptual experiments we could perform to attribute fractions of output growth to each of the growing inputs. Denote the initial endowments of capital and labor as K^0 and L^0 and initial output as Y^0. Let the superscript 1 denote quantities in period 1, and thus $K^1 > K^0$, $L^1 > L^0$, and $Y^1 > Y^0$. First we could consider a sequential process, first incrementing the capital stock and then incrementing the labor stock. Thus, the contribution of capital to the increased output is:

$$S_K = f(K^1, L^0) - f(K^0, L^0),$$

and labor's contribution is:

$$S_L = f(K^1, L^1) - f(K^1, L^0).$$

Clearly the order in which we sequence events will make a difference in such measurements. If we conceived of the incremental process as adding the $L^1 - L^0$ units of labor first, then labor's contribution would be:

$$S_L^1 = f(K^0, L^1) - f(K^0, L^0),$$

and S_K^1 would be the residual growth in output. There is no guarantee that $S_L = S_L^1$ or $S_K = S_K^1$. It depends on the algebraic form of the production function. In fact the only production function for which the measured contribution is independent of sequence is a linearly separable production function. If $f(K, L)$ is linearly separable, then each input has a marginal product independent of the level of the other inputs and thus the contribution of the exogenous growth in inputs is easily measurable. Such a functional form essentially assumes away the interesting part of the production process since it assumes all factors of production are perfect substitutes. If the production function is nonseparable (that is, there exists factor complementarity), then even conceptually we cannot attribute part of the growth in output to one input and part of the growth in output to another. The extent of output growth depends on the extent of growth in both inputs. The products of the two are inextricably entwined because there is factor complementarity. There is no logical way to distinguish which input is "responsible" for a part of output.

Since there is no theoretically clear way to establish the individual contribution to growth of various inputs, it is appropriate that a convention be chosen that will allow growth accountants to partition growth in output among its various determinants. Either one of the two conceptual experiments illustrated above could serve as such a convention, but in a multiple input framework such ordering conventions are inconvenient. Instead the growth accountants have chosen to use a first-order expansion of the production function and the mean value theorem to decompose the change in output into its various determinants. If, in fact, change in inputs were infinitesimal, this approach would be exact, but in the presence of discrete changes in inputs it is an approximation at best.

To characterize the standard growth accounting approach, let us rewrite the production function in a more general form:

$$Y = f(X, \tau),$$

where X denotes a vector of inputs and τ summarizes the part of technology that is subject to change. Implicitly Y, X, and τ carry time subscripts. Denoting $\partial z/\partial t$ by $\dot{z}$, the standard growth-accounting formula decomposes growth in output into two components—that due to growth in inputs and that that occurs because of technical advance:

$$\frac{\dot{Y}}{Y} = \sum_i S_i \frac{\dot{X}_i}{X_i} + \frac{\tau(\partial Y/\partial \tau)}{Y} \frac{\dot{\tau}}{\tau}, \tag{4.2}$$

where $S_i = X_i f_i / Y$ and $f_i = \partial Y/\partial X_i$. The production shares, S_i, are typically not observed, but assuming cost minimizing behavior and exogenous factor prices we know that:

$$S_i = SC_i, \tag{4.3}$$

where C_i is the share of the ith input in total cost, $C_i = P_i X_i / \sum P_i X_i$, and S is the scale elasticity that is simply equal to the ratio of average to marginal cost.[1] If we assume constant returns to scale, average cost equals marginal cost, and since the C_i are observed we have the following accounting definitions:

$$\text{Explained growth} = \sum_i C_i \frac{\dot{X}_i}{X_i}, \quad \text{and} \tag{4.4}$$

$$\text{Unexplained growth} = \frac{\dot{Y}}{Y} - \sum_i C_i \frac{\dot{X}_i}{X_i}. \tag{4.5}$$

The contribution of the ith factor is defined as $C_i(\dot{X}_i/X_i)$ and the residual is referred to as growth in total factor productivity.

By evaluating the contribution of a growth in an individual input by using an indirect measurement of marginal product, the economist is taking a linear approximation to the production function as his basis for attributing output growth to the various factors. The growth accountant's use of this linear approximation to decompose total growth assumes that the contribution of a discrete change in an input can be evaluated as that change multiplied by the marginal product of the input. As a convention used to measure the contribution of inputs that are growing exogenously, this decomposition seems reasonable. Granted, the marginal product of any input will decrease as additional units of that input are added to the productive process, and thus there will be some unmeasured "surplus" associated with the growth in each input. However, as we showed above, decomposition of output can be done many ways, and some convention must be established. The use of this marginal product growth-accounting framework is much more problematic when we want to consider the growth of output due to inputs, like education, that are determined endogenously. Growth in these intermediate inputs is often treated as being exogenous and thus costless. If the growth in some inputs is endogenously determined, and thus costly, we must consider what would have been produced had the basic factors of production used to fabricate the intermediate inputs been used differently.

To distinguish education as an intermediate product we rearrange the simple model proposed above. Specifically let the production technology be described by:

$$Y = g(X_1, E), \tag{4.6}$$

$$E = h(X_2), \tag{4.7}$$

and:

$$X = X_1 + X_2.$$

The subscripts on X, the vector of inputs, indicate use in primary and intermediate production. We have omitted exogenous technology, τ, for the moment.

The economic problem is to allocate X between primary and intermediate production. If we use as our allocation rule the maximization of output Y, subject to the resource constraint X, the first order efficiency conditions are:

$$g_i = h_i \frac{\partial g}{\partial E}. \tag{4.8}$$

The right-hand side (RHS) of (4.8) measures the indirect marginal product of primary factors and the left-hand side (LHS) measures the direct product. A factor is efficiently allocated when direct and indirect marginal products are equal. The RHS of (4.8) measures the value of factors diverted to production of E, while the LHS measures the opportunity cost of those factors. Suppose, now, that X grows exogenously and we want to observe the contribution of education to observed output growth. If we view education not as an intermediate input but as a basic input, using equation (4.2) we find the "contribution" of educated labor is:

$$\frac{\partial Y}{\partial E} \frac{dE}{dX} = \frac{\partial Y}{\partial E} \sum h_i \frac{dX_{i2}}{dX}. \tag{4.9}$$

This calculation ignores the cost of factors used to produce E. If we explicitly recognize opportunity costs, we find that education's contribution to growth is zero. To see this, consider the change in output associated with a change in the ith input, dX_i:

$$\frac{dY}{dX_i} dX_i = g_i \, dX_{i1} + \frac{\partial Y}{\partial E} h_i \, dX_{i2}. \tag{4.10}$$

Using equation (4.8) this implies:

$$\frac{dY}{dX_i}dX_i = g_i\,dX_{i1} + g_i\,dX_{i2}, \tag{4.11}$$

$$= g_i(dX_{i1} + dX_{i2}),$$

$$= g_i\,dX_i,$$

since, by definition:

$$dX_i = dX_{i1} + dX_{i2}.$$

Equation (4.11) demonstrates that the *net* marginal product of the factor X_{i2} diverted to the production of education is zero. By the definition of efficient production, the *marginal* contribution of education is zero. If it were not, basic resources could be rearranged to increase total output. Therefore, the use of marginal accounting to measure education's contribution to growth seems inappropriate, since at the margin the educational process makes no net contribution. Where, then, do growth accountants err in their calculations of a positive contribution of education, and how might we interpret or reconstruct their results?

Let us consider a simpler model that will help illustrate the problem with the calculations made by the growth accountants. Let Y denote per capita output, let N_1 denote the number of uneducated workers in the labor force, and let N_2 denote the number of workers who receive education. Suppose:

$$N_1 + N_2 = N.$$

Then we characterize our production relationship as:

$$Y = g(N_1, K_1, E), \tag{4.12a}$$

$$E = h(N_2, K_2), \tag{4.12b}$$

$$N_1 + N_2 = N, \tag{4.12c}$$

$$K_1 + K_2 = K, \tag{4.12d}$$

where K is the amount of a second primary input that we call capital and is allocated between primary and intermediate production, K_1 and K_2 respectively. In equations (4.12a) through (4.12d) we have depicted a production process where the education process is factor absorbing. Assume that the number of educated laborers who provide services E is N_2. That is, no person works only in the education sector. A worker is educated, and then the worker's services are used for primary production. The educational process merely embodies capital in workers. We can apply the standard technique to equations (4.12a) through (4.12d) to get:

$$\dot{Y} = g_1\dot{N}_1 + g_2\dot{K}_1 + g_3\dot{E}, \tag{4.13a}$$

$$\dot{E} = h_1\dot{N}_2 + h_2\dot{K}_2. \tag{4.13b}$$

Using the standard growth-accounting approach we would say that the contribution of education to total growth in output was $g_3 \dot{E}$ and would calculate the contribution by measuring the wage return to the N_2 educated laborers. However, we cannot ignore equation (4.13b). Substituting (4.13b) into (4.13a) we get:

$$\dot{Y} = g_1 \dot{N}_1 + g_2 \dot{K}_1 + g_3 h_1 \dot{N}_2 + g_3 h_2 \dot{K}_2. \tag{4.14}$$

Since firms are cost minimizers, the marginal product of any "unrefined" unit of labor must be the same and the marginal product of capital must be the same across sectors. Thus:

$$g_1 = g_3 h_1, \tag{4.15a}$$

$$g_2 = g_3 h_2. \tag{4.15b}$$

Substituting equations (4.15a) and (4.15b) into (4.14) we get:

$$\dot{Y} = g_1 (\dot{N}_1 + \dot{N}_2) + g_2 (\dot{K}_1 + \dot{K}_2),$$

$$\dot{Y} = g_1 \dot{N} + g_2 \dot{K}.$$

We find that all growth in output is due to growth in the total amount of primary inputs. Because factors are always allocated so that marginal productivities in different uses are equal, there is no *marginal* contribution of education to the production process.[2] The accounting error comes in treating $g_3 \dot{E}$ as the total contribution of educated laborers. In fact:

$$g_3 \dot{E} = g_3 h_1 \dot{N}_2 + g_3 h_2 \dot{K}_2.$$

The marginal productivity of the educated laborers is the same as that of unskilled laborers. Because education is an intermediate good that is factor-absorbing in its production, simply calculating the financial rewards to workers who are educated as a measure of their productivity ignores the opportunity cost of producing the education.

This brief review of the growth-accounting literature illustrates two points. First, the dissection of the growth in output into its component parts is a description task that can be done in many different ways. Growth accountants have chosen the convention of using a linear approximation to the production function and approximated the average increase in production due to an exogenous increase in basic inputs by the marginal product of that input. Again, this is nothing but a useful convention, and there are alternative decompositions. Secondly, the marginal accounting framework, applied to intermediate inputs, will result in no net contribution of those inputs, if the opportunity cost of provision of the endogenously determined input is correctly calculated. Since the purpose of this paper is to consider methods of accounting for education's input to production and education is an intermediate input, another approach is required.

AN ALTERNATIVE MEASURE OF THE CONTRIBUTION OF EDUCATION TO PRODUCTIVITY

Careful application of standard marginal growth-accounting methods would lead us to conclude that the net contribution of education to production is zero. Clearly this is not the case. If the resources are being allocated efficiently, the net contribution of the last worker educated is zero, but the inframarginal educated workers have a positive contribution to output. The correct way to evaluate the contribution of education is to measure its inframarginal contribution to production. To provide motivation for our proposed measure of education's contribution to growth, let us consider an analogy from consumer goods. Suppose we increase a consumer's income by $1,000, holding commodity prices constant, and we observe that the consumer's expenditure on food increases by $200. We might be tempted to conclude that the contribution of this additional food to his increased welfare is $200, but in doing so we would ignore the alternatives on which the $200 could have otherwise been spent. The correct measure of the contribution of food to his welfare is his utility given he can spend his $1,000 as he pleases minus his utility if he is constrained to spend the additional $1,000 on anything but food. This measurement is his increase in welfare because he can spend money on the available food. We can make two observations in this case. First, we can account for an individual's expenditures: "Out of the additional $1,000, $200 was spent on food." Second, we can calculate how much this expenditure increased the consumer's welfare: "The welfare contribution of the additional $200 in food is the excess of his utility over what he would have attained had he been unable to buy food." These are two very different statements. Both are interesting observations, but the first has only descriptive import and the second has normative import. It tells us what the option of being able to buy food is worth.

Before completing the analogy by presenting the production equivalent to this example, let us reinforce our point with another simple illustration. Suppose that food were an inferior good. Our consumer, when given the extra $1,000 income, would decrease his expenditure on food, say, by $50. We could hardly argue that food reduced the consumer's welfare! The accounting observation would show that expenditures on food had decreased. The correct welfare measurement of the contribution of food would measure the consumer's utility given his additional $1,000 spent as desired minus the consumer's utility if constrained not to change his expenditures on food. Clearly the welfare measure would show a positive value to the ability to reallocate his food expenditures.

The consumer example is fully analogous to the production case. Consider an exogenous increase in primary factors of production, such that marginal rates of substitution among factors remain constant if resources are efficiently allocated. This change is equivalent in the consumer example to increasing income holding commodity prices constant. Output will increase. The growth accountant's measure of the increase in output due to the increase in education is the opportunity cost of factors diverted toward education. It is a measure of how much of the growth in endowments is "spent" on education. To claim that this is the contribution of education to increased welfare ignores the alternative ways those basic resources could have been allocated. The correct measure of the contribution of education to output is the amount of output that actually is produced minus the output level that would have been chosen had none of the additional resources been allocated to the education sector. The pure growth-accounting approach tells us how much of our resources' growth we devoted to the education sector. Although this is interesting as a descriptive measure, a more illuminating measure of education's contribution must take into account what would have been had the education option been unavailable.

The theoretical distinction between the growth accountant's measure and the surplus measure we propose should be clear. The question now becomes how one might implement the second measure empirically. Let us consider the consumer example again. To derive the measure of increased welfare due to food we first have to trace the value of food as income changes—that is, the shadow price of food. Let Z denote quantity of food, I denote income and P denote the actual price, while $\tilde{P}$ denotes the shadow price. Then the movement of the shadow price is described by:

$$\frac{dZ}{dI} = \frac{\partial Z}{\partial I} + \frac{\partial Z}{\partial P}\frac{\partial \tilde{P}}{\partial I} = 0. \tag{4.16}$$

The first term on the RHS of (4.16) is the ordinary income effect. The second term has two parts. The first is a pure substitution effect, and the other is the induced rate of increase in food's shadow price. The induced price increase is just enough to hold the net change in Z at zero given the change in income. In other words, equation (4.16) implicitly describes the marginal value of food at the initial level of consumption of Z as income changes. To a second order approximation the consumer's surplus is:

$$\tfrac{1}{2}\Delta\tilde{P}\Delta Z, \tag{4.17}$$

where:

$$\Delta\tilde{P} = \frac{\partial \tilde{P}}{\partial I}\Delta I = \frac{-\partial Z/\partial I}{\partial Z/\partial P}\Delta I \quad \text{(from 4.16)}, \tag{4.18}$$

and:

$$\Delta Z = \frac{\partial Z}{\partial I}\Delta I. \tag{4.19}$$

Substituting (4.18) and (4.19) into (4.17) and rearranging terms we find that the measure of consumer's surplus is:

$$\frac{-C}{2} \frac{\epsilon^2}{\eta} \frac{(\Delta I)^2}{I},$$

where C is food's expenditure share, ϵ is the income elasticity of food, and η is the utility constant own price elasticity.[3] We have estimates or observations on all the components of our measure, and thus it can be empirically implemented.

The same analysis can be done for the production side of the economy. The analogous formula (see Appendix A) for education's net productivity is:

$$-\frac{S}{2} \frac{\xi^2}{\sigma_{ii}} \frac{(\Delta Y)^2}{Y}, \tag{4.20}$$

where S is the scale elasticity described in equation (4.3), ξ is the elasticity of demand for education with respect to aggregate output (holding marginal rates of factor substitution constant), σ_{ii} is the Allen–Uzawa[4] own substitution elasticity, and Y denotes the value of aggregate output.[5]

We are not familiar with estimates in the literature of any of the requisite parameters needed to evaluate the net contribution of education to productivity. If the production process were Cobb–Douglas with parameter β_i as a coefficient on education, and subject to constant returns to scale, then

$$S = \xi = 1 \quad \text{and} \quad \sigma_{ii} = \frac{-(1-\beta_i)}{\beta_i}.$$

If $\Delta Y/Y$ were equal to 1 and $\beta_i = 0.25$, then education's net contribution would be approximately one-sixth of the increase in output. If $\Delta Y/Y$ were equal to 0.1, then education would have only contributed $\frac{1}{60}$ of the growth.[6]

In the next section we examine a few of the empirical attempts to measure education's contribution to growth. None of them uses either of the concepts presented above in their extreme form, but they are usually closer to the first method than the second.

METHODS OF EMPIRICAL MEASUREMENT

Much detailed empirical work has been aimed at measuring the sources of growth in the economies of the United States and other developed countries. Clearly education must have played a role in this productivity growth, but as argued in the first section, the standard approach for measuring the extent of that role asks a very limited question: What part of investment is devoted to education? The marginal accounting framework does not enable us to ask the more interesting question of what output would have been had the resources devoted to education been allocated differently. In this section we describe several methods of measuring the contribution of education and show the difficulties with standard measures using two simple examples.

The work by Jorgenson and Griliches (1967) is exemplary of the "pure" growth-accounting approach to measuring the effect of education on productivity.[7] They begin with the basic growth-accounting equation as we have characterized it in equation (4.2):

$$\frac{\dot{Y}}{Y} = \sum_i S_i \frac{\dot{X}_i}{X_i} + \frac{\tau}{Y} \frac{\partial Y}{\partial \tau} \frac{\dot{\tau}}{\tau}.$$

One of their inputs is labor, and they construct the index of labor services as:

$$\frac{\dot{L}}{L} = \sum S_i \frac{\dot{L}_i}{L_i}, \tag{4.21}$$

where the L_i represent hours of labor input of education type i. They separate the rate of growth of labor input into three components: the rate of growth of the labor force, $\dot{N}/N$; the rate of growth of hours per man $\dot{H}/H$; and the change in the proportional distribution of labor among the educational types. Letting e_i denote the proportion of workers of education type i,

$$\frac{\dot{L}}{L} = \frac{\dot{H}}{H} + \frac{\dot{N}}{N} + \sum S_i \frac{\dot{e}_i}{e_i}. \tag{4.22}$$

The last term on the RHS is computed by summing the share weighted change in proportions. They break labor into eight educational groups and using the last term of (4.22) compute what they call the annual percentage change in labor-input per man hour. This index varies from 0.62 percent during the period from 1948 to 1952 to 1.2 percent from 1957 to 1959. The average annual rate of change from 1940 to 1965 was 0.74 percent. The Jorgenson and Griliches study of productivity is certainly a pioneering work, and it is improper to criticize it for not computing a fine enough index of change in labor input. They admit that the classification of labor should be made by age, sex, occupation, and industry, among other components, but such detailed data was not available to them. Thus their only breakdown of labor is by educational level, and the value of each additional hour of labor in any educational group i is measured at its "value of marginal product" as reflected by cost share. They treat additional education as if it had no opportunity cost or alternatively as if the determination of the education level were exogenous. Such an index is an adequate way of measuring changes in the labor force due to exogenous demographic shifts in composition but ignores the whole notion of opportunity cost of factors whose allocations are determined endogenously. The Jorgenson and Griliches study represents a descriptive decomposition of how we spent an exogenous increase in primary inputs and does not measure the opportunity costs of those inputs.

The recent analyses by Chinloy (1980), Christensen, et al. (1980), Denison (1980), and Gollop and Jorgenson (1980), are similar in nature to the Jorgenson and Griliches study, but they make some attempt to use the notion of the opportunity cost of an educated worker's time. We characterize Chinloy's work since he constructs a more complete index of labor productivity than do the other authors. The Chinloy model follows the basic growth-accounting model as introduced in the first section. Changing notation slightly, let superscripts denote time period and subscripts denote educational group. We observe N^t laborers in period t, N_1^t of them being uneducated and N_2^t of them educated. The wages paid to each uneducated laborer in period t is w_1^t, and educated laborers receive w_2^t for their services. Consider only two periods, $t = 0, 1$. Then the growth in the total labor force (Chinloy uses hours, we will use number of workers) is defined by:

$$h = \ln(N^1) - \ln(N^0), \tag{4.23}$$

$$= \ln\left(\frac{N^1}{N^0}\right).$$

Chinloy compares this growth in pure units of input to an index in the change in labor productivity derived from an assumed translog production function. Specifically, let V_1 be the average share of the total labor bill received by uneducated workers and $V_2 = 1 - V_1$ be the average share received by educated workers. Then:

$$V_1 = \frac{1}{2}\left(\frac{w_1^0 N_1^0}{w_1^0 N_1^0 + w_2^0 N_2^0} + \frac{w_1^1 N_1^1}{w_1^1 N_1^1 + w_2^1 N_2^1}\right). \tag{4.24}$$

These shares are used to compute a weighted average of indices in the growth of the size of each segment of the labor force. Specifically, let:

$$\Delta \ln h_1 = \ln\left(\frac{N_1^1}{N_1^0}\right),$$

$$\Delta \ln h_2 = \ln\left(\frac{N_2^1}{N_2^0}\right). \tag{4.25}$$

The index of the growth rate for labor productivity is:

$$d = V_1 \Delta \ln h_1 + V_2 \Delta \ln h_2.$$

The growth rate for quality change is

$$q = d - h.$$

In this setting, q represents the contribution of education to productivity growth. Chinloy's index of quality change, q, implicitly includes a measure of opportunity cost of the education process. The index, h, is a measure of what the growth in output would have been had the initial proportions of educated and uneducated labor been maintained and thus measures the opportunity cost of educating proportionately more workers. Specifically, if:

$$\frac{N^1}{N^0} = \frac{N_1^1}{N_1^0} = \frac{N_2^1}{N_2^0},$$

then:

$$d = V_1 \ln\left(\frac{N_1^1}{N_0^1}\right) + V_2 \ln\left(\frac{N_2^1}{N_0^2}\right),$$

$$= V_1 \ln\left(\frac{N^1}{N^0}\right) + (1 - V_1) \ln\left(\frac{N^1}{N^0}\right),$$

$$= \ln\left(\frac{N^1}{N^0}\right),$$

$$= h,$$

which implies

$$q = d - h,$$

$$= 0.$$

Chinloy would conclude there has been no quality change in the composition of the labor force. This conclusion is in some sense correct. The average level of education of the populace has not changed, and the proportion of output rewarded to educated workers has not changed. It seems the entire growth of output is due to population growth. It would be incorrect, however, to say that the increased level of education contributed nothing to increased output. Consider, for example, the simple production process depicted in Figure 4–3. Initially there are N^0 laborers available; N_2^0 are educated and N_1^0 are uneducated. Output is initially Y^0. Suppose the total workforce expands from N^0 to N^1, output expands from Y^0 to Y^1, and the proportion of educated workers remains constant. As shown, the Chinloy formulation would show a zero contribution to the change in the educational level of the population. However, suppose the education alternative had not been available for the $N^1 - N^0$ new workers. Clearly, output would not have increased to Y^0 but to $Y^* < Y^0$ as depicted in Figure 4–4. The contribution of education at the margin is zero, but there is an inframarginal contribution that is positive.

Denison (1974, for example) explicitly forms an index of labor services based on the norm of an eighth-grade educated worker. Using the ratio of wages of higher educated workers to eighth grade workers he forms an index that computes base productivity of labor as if all workers were eighth-grade educated (correcting for the correlation of ability and education) and attributes the excess of actual returns to labor over baseline returns to labor

Figure 4–3. Growth in Output Due to Equiproportional Changes in Labor.

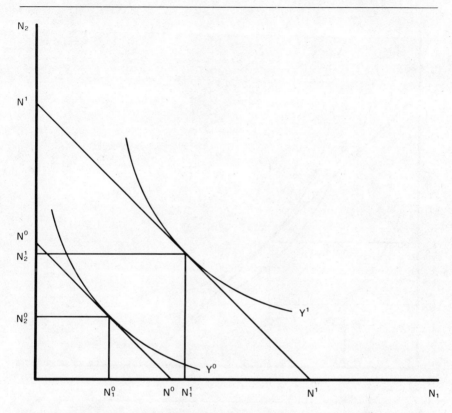

as the contribution of education to the productive process. In essence, Denison recognizes that (part of) the opportunity cost of educating a worker is his foregone productivity as an uneducated worker. However, Denison, like Chinloy, uses a marginalist approach to the productivity accounting. The "returns" to education that he measures are returns to factors used in the production of education that he does not include in his measure of opportunity cost. Referring back to the second section of this paper, Denison and Chinloy implicitly use a model like that represented in equations (4.12a) through (4.12d), but the returns they measure are returns to the capital "embodied" in the workers who are educated. The increased wages rewarded to educated workers are a return to a costly investment and at the margin the net value of that investment is zero.

The Denison and Chinloy studies are an intermediate stage between a purely descriptive characterization of the sources of growth and an evaluation

Figure 4-4.   Growth in Output Due to Growth in Type One Labor Only.

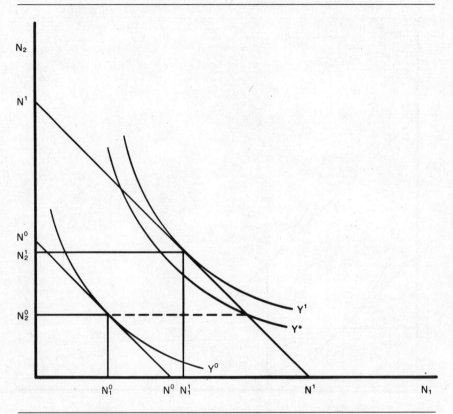

of the contribution of intermediate production processes using an opportunity cost measure. Both authors partially compute the opportunity cost of an educated laborer. Since the calculation is a marginal one, if they had calculated the cost fully, the contribution of the educational process would have been zero.

At first glance Schultz (1961) takes a completely different tack in evaluating the educational process. He explicitly recognizes that education is an intermediate good that is costly to produce. The productive value of education in the economy is the yield from a stock of education. His method is to evaluate that stock in terms of resource cost and extrapolate the contribution of education to total product by imputing a value of the flow of services from that stock. Schultz begins by evaluating the stock of education in two years. Let us denote the resource cost of that stock as V^i, $i = 0, 1$. Let Y_i continue to denote output in period i. The growth in the labor force over time is:

$$\Delta N = \frac{N^1 - N^0}{N^0}.$$

To keep the per capita value of the stock of education constant, the value of the stock in the latter period would be $(1+\Delta N)V^0$. Thus the difference between actual value and the value needed for constant per capita value is:

$$V^1 - (1+\Delta N)V^0.$$

Of course, the actual increase in the total value of the stock of education is simply $V^1 - V^0$. Assuming that education is purely an investment good and is not made for consumption purposes, then the return to a dollar of capital invested in education should be the market rate of return, r. Thus, the annual contribution of the additional stock is:

$$r(V^1 - V^0).$$

Schultz assumes that over time the proportional contribution of labor to total product is a constant, s_N. Therefore, the proportion of labor's share of income growth due to increasing the total stock of education is:

$$\frac{r(V^1 - V^0)}{s_N(Y^1 - Y^0)}.$$

The proportion of labor's share of output due to the increase in education per person is:

$$\frac{r(V^1 - (1+\Delta N)V^0)}{s_N(Y^1 - Y^0)},$$

and the contribution of the increased stock of education to the increase in *total* output is simply:

$$\frac{r(V^1 - (1+\Delta N)V^0)}{(Y^1 - Y^0)}. \tag{4.26}$$

To implement these formulas, Schultz makes some involved calculations regarding the costs of education and assumes that labor's share of output is a constant, $s_N = 0.75$. His most critical assumption is that the correct rate of return is the individual, internal rate of return to an investment in schooling, such as the rates calculated by Becker (1975). At the margin, that rate of return must be chosen so that the present value of the earnings stream of the educated individual just equals the present value of the opportunity cost of that education, otherwise more individuals will become educated until the marginal return to an education is zero. Using a market rate of return to value the return to the inframarginal units of education is wrong for the same reasons we have outlined in the second section above. At the margin the net return is zero, but for inframarginal units the net contribution is positive.

Although Schultz's method is cosmetically different from the mainstream growth accountants' techniques, in essence he is making the same measurement. The application of the internal rate of return to the value of the stock of education simply translates the contribution of education into a flow measure such as those used by the other authors. His comparison measurement of contribution represented in equation (4.26) is basically the same as that of Denison and Chinloy: rV^1 is simply the output that resulted from the actual capital outlay on education and $r(1+\Delta N)V^0$ is the output that would have been produced had the per capita "amount" of education remained constant. This does not measure what would have been produced had the $V^1-(1+\Delta N)V^0$ dollars' worth of capital been used in the next best alternative productive use. Thus, as in Chinloy and Denison, the Schultz baseline measure is the growth that would have taken place if no resources had been devoted to education in excess of those that would have kept per capita education the same (i.e., all new labor comes in as "eighth" graders). Instead, the appropriate measure is the output we would have had if the additional rsources spent on increasing the educational level of the population had been devoted to other production processes.

To illustrate the inability of the marginal accountants' approach to evaluating productivity to explain education's share in that productivity, we present two simple numerical examples. First consider the following non-CRS production function:[8]

$$Y = \frac{(N_2-4)}{(N_1-8)^2},$$

where $N_2>4$ and $N_1<8$, where N_2 represents the number of educated laborers and N_1 represents the number of uneducated laborers. Suppose that in period 0, $N_1+N_2 \leqslant 9$, and in period 1, $N_1+N_2 \leqslant 10$, that is the labor force grew by one unit. The output maximizing labor allocations and values of marginal product are:

$$N_1^0 = 2 \qquad \text{VMP}_1^0 = 0.027,$$
$$N_2^0 = 7 \qquad \text{VMP}_2^0 = 1,$$

and:

$$N_1^1 = 4 \qquad \text{VMP}_1^1 = 0.0625,$$
$$N_2^1 = 6 \qquad \text{VMP}_2^1 = 0.25.$$

In period 0, $Y^0 = 0.0833$, and later $Y^1 = 0.125$. Clearly, in this example, educated labor is an inferior good, since as total labor available increases, output increases, but the amount of educated labor decreases. Using base year weights, the basic growth-accounting formula would be:

$$\frac{y^1 - y^0}{y^0} = s_1^0 \left(\frac{N_1^1 - N_1^0}{N_1^0} \right) + s_2^0 \left(\frac{N_2^1 - N_2^0}{N_2^0} \right) + \tau,$$

$$\frac{y^1 - y^0}{y^0} = .01 \left(\frac{4-2}{2} \right) + .99 \left(\frac{6-7}{7} \right) + \tau,$$

$$= -0.13 + \tau.[9]$$

The "growth" attributed to the educated work force would be negative, and in fact, due to the non-CRS nature of the production function, most of the growth would be attributed to the residual term, which in fact reflects a change in scale. Using marginal growth accounting would lead us to conclude education contributed -13 percent to the 50 percent growth in output! The measure we proposed in equation (4.20) in the preceding section yields a different answer. Our measure demonstrates that education contributes 18 percent to the total growth in output in this simple example.[10] Clearly, education has had a positive contribution, but the fact that in this example educated workers were an inferior input shows plainly how simple application of marginal growth accounting can err.

We have presented the previous example not with realism in mind, but instead as a polar case—one in which the surplus measure of the value of education gives a reasonable answer and the growth accounting measures does not. The second example we present uses a more standard production technology and is designed to show how different measures of the contribution of education to productivity can vary in a nonpathological setting. Specifically, growth accountants will overestimate the contribution of education because they ignore the opportunity cost of the resources used.

Let the production process be characterized by a two-step process in which a certain amount of capital is "embodied" in a number of workers we will call educated and these educated workers enter and help in the production of the final product. Specifically, let K_1 denote the number of units of capital devoted to production of the final product and K_2 denote the number of units of capital devoted to the education process. Then our economy is characterized by the relationships:

$$E = g(N_2, K_2),$$

$$Y = f(N_1, K_1, E),$$

$$N_1 + N_2 \leqslant N,$$

$$K_1 + K_2 \leqslant K.$$

For illustration's sake assume g is a constant elasticity of substitution production function and f is a Cobb–Douglas production function:

Table 4-1. Production Function Example.

Values of Parameters

$\gamma_N = 0.3$
$\gamma_K = 0.7$
$\rho = 0.5$
$\beta_N = 0.1$
$\beta_K = 0.2$
$\beta_E = 0.7$
$K = 1$

Period 1 $N = 1$

$N_1 = 0.3195$	$N_2 = 0.6805$
$K_1 = 0.2911$	$K_2 = 0.7089$

$$Y = 0.5431$$
$$VMP_N = 0.1700$$
$$VMP_K = 0.3731$$
$$VMP_E = 0.5430$$

Total payments to uneducated labor = 0.05431
Total payments to capital in productive sector = 0.1086
Total payments to educated labor = 0.3801
Payment per educated worker = 0.5587

Period 2 $N = 2$

$N_1 = 0.7364$	$N_2 = 1.2636$
$K_1 = 0.2746$	$K_2 = 0.7254$

$$Y = 0.6649$$
$$VMP_N = 0.09029$$
$$VMP_K = 0.4843$$
$$VMP_E = 0.5517$$

Total payments to uneducated labor = 0.06649
Total payments to capital in productive sector = 0.1330
Total payments to educated labor = 0.4654
Payments per educated laborer = 0.3683

$$E = (\gamma_N N_2^{-\rho} + \gamma_K K_2^{-\rho})^{-1/\rho},$$
$$Y = N_1^{\beta_N} K_1^{\beta_K} E^{\beta_E},$$

where $\gamma_N + \gamma_K = 1$ and $\beta_N + \beta_K + \beta_E = 1$. For the following example we assume the production technology remains fixed over time, as does the available number of units of capital K. In Table 4-1, we present the parameter values used in the production functions and the resulting allocation of resources in each of two periods. In the first period we assume $N = 1$ and in the second period $N = 2$. As N grows, the marginal productivity of labor decreases in both educated and uneducated forms because the capital stock remains fixed. We assume that the education process is not "labor-using"—that is, that all N_2 workers are employed in producing Y and they each receive equal fractions of the total payment to educated labor.

Let us first apply the Chinloy method of computing the quality of the labor force to this example. Using the formulas presented earlier, the following indices can be computed using the information in Table 4-1:

$$V_1 = 0.125,$$

$$V_2 = 0.875,$$

$$\Delta \ln N_1 = 0.8353,$$

$$\Delta \ln N_2 = 0.6187,$$

$$d = 0.6457,$$

$$h = 0.6931,$$

$$q = -0.0474.$$

Thus, Chinloy would conclude that the quality of the labor force has decreased. We get this "decrease in quality" because we are increasing the size of the labor force holding the capital stock fixed, thus decreasing the marginal product of the labor force. One might be led to conclude from the Chinloy accounting method that had education growth "kept pace" with population growth output would be higher. In fact, this is not true, since the allocations presented for period 2 maximize output subject to the resource constraints. We will grant that the proportion of educated workers has decreased from 68.05 percent to 63.18 percent, but this does not imply increased productivity had the proportion remained constant.

As an alternative to Chinloy's approach to the quality of the labor force, we can consider the standard growth-accounting approach as used by authors such as Jorgenson and Griliches (1967). The basic accounting equation for this simple model would be:

$$\frac{\dot{Y}}{Y} = s_{K_1} \frac{\dot{K}_1}{K_1} + s_{N_1} \frac{\dot{N}_1}{N} + s_E \frac{\dot{E}}{E}.$$

In theory one would like to measure the units of education E, but these are not observed. Only the number of educated workers N_2 is observed. Using base year percentages (i.e., $\dot{Y}/Y \approx \Delta Y/Y_0$) to make the required calculations from Table 4-1, we get:

$$\dot{Y}/Y = 0.2243,$$

$$\text{explained growth} = 0.7189,$$

$$\tau = -0.4946.[11]$$

Clearly, ignoring the means by which educated labor is generated, the growth accountants would make a serious mistake in evaluating the progress of the economy. Because the education process is capital using and a growing labor force is being applied to a fixed stock of capital, the marginal product of labor decreases substantially. However, the technology of the economy has not changed at all. The constraint of a fixed resource being used as input to the fabrication of an intermediate input is being interpreted as technological "regression."

Perhaps we are being too harsh on the growth accountants. Suppose that they recognize that part of the capital stock is used in the educational process and can measure its value to the economy as a separate input. Then the growth-accounting equation would be:

$$\frac{\dot{Y}}{Y} = s_{K_1}\frac{\dot{K}_1}{K_1} + s_{N_1}\frac{\dot{N}_1}{N_1} + s_{N_2}\frac{\dot{N}_2}{N_2} + s_{K_2}\frac{\dot{K}_2}{K_2} + \tau,$$

where s_{N_2} and s_{K_2} would be the share in value of inputs of labor and capital used in the education process. Somehow, the returns to the labor input would have to be separated from the returns to the capital input. Using this last accounting identity we get:

$$\dot{Y}/Y = 0.2243,$$

$$\text{explained growth} = 0.2956,$$

$$\tau = -0.0713.$$

This accounting is clearly more reasonable, although it still misinterprets fixed resource constraints as decreased technical progress.

The Schultz formulation of the marginalist growth accounting in this simple example can also be computed. Using the figures in Table 4–1, we can compute:

$$V^0 = \text{VMP}_K^0 \times K_2^0 = (0.3731)(0.7089) = 0.2644,$$

$$V^1 = \text{VMP}_K^1 \times K_2^1 = (0.4843)(0.7254) = 0.3513.$$

Furthermore:

$$\Delta N = \frac{2-1}{1} = 1,$$

and thus the value of the stock in the latter period, had per capita education remained the same, would have been 0.5288. The difference between actual and constant per capita educational stock is −0.1775.

Since the capital stock in this example has no intertemporal nature, the return to capital is simply its valuation in the market. That is, a dollar's worth of capital returns a dollar per year, and the capital is regenerated each year, thus $r = 1$. Rather than assigning a constant share to labor output we can compute that the total rewards to labor in period zero are $0.05431 + 0.3801 = 0.4344$ and in period 1 are $0.06649 + 0.4654 = 0.5319$. Thus, the contribution of education to the rewards to labor is:

$$\frac{V^1 - V^0}{s_n^1 Y^1 - s_n^0 Y^0} = \frac{0.3513 - 0.2644}{0.5319 - 0.4344} = 0.8914.$$

The contribution of the increased stock of education to total output is:

$$\frac{V^1 - V^0}{y^1 - y^0} = \frac{0.3513 - 0.2644}{0.6649 - 0.5431} = 0.7135.$$

Schultz's method also demonstrates the proportion of growth due to the change in per capita education. Since per capita education has decreased, we are calculating the extent of growth that would have occurred had per capita education remained constant. In particular, labor's share would have grown by 182 percent more than it did ($-0.1775/(0.5319 - 0.4344)$), and total output would have grown by 145 percent more than it did ($-0.1775/(0.6649 - 0.5431)$).

Finally, we can compute the contribution of education to growth using the surplus measure in equation (4.20). Since the production function is Cobb–Douglas, this equation simplifies to:

$$\left| \frac{1}{2} \frac{\beta_E}{1 - \beta_E} \frac{\Delta Y}{Y} \right| \Delta Y,$$

which in our example is equal to:

$$(0.2616)\Delta Y.$$

(For a derivation, see the second section above and note 6). That is, the growth in education is responsible for 26 percent of the growth in total productivity. Clearly, we have at our disposal the true parameters and the true functional form from which to make our calculation. Although this is a luxury not afforded the actual investigator, it illustrates the potential variation in the two different approaches to measurement. Table 4-2 summarizes the various measures in this simple example.

CONCLUSION

The level of foregone consumption in an economy is an important determinant of future consumption possibilities. The relationship between investment and future income needs to be well understood if cogent policy towards economic growth is to be formulated. In this paper we have criticized the current attempts to measure education's role in economic growth

Table 4–2.   Summary of Measurements of Growth in Productivity Using Examples in Table 4–1.

Chinloy:	Quality of labor force decreased by -0.0474
Standard growth accounting:	Actual growth $\quad = \quad 22.43\%$ Explained growth $= \quad 71.89\%$ Residual $\qquad = -49.46\%$ Educated labor's share of explained growth $= 83.5\%$
Sophisticated growth accounting:	Actual growth $\quad = \quad 22.43\%$ Explained growth $= \quad 29.56\%$ Residual $\qquad = \quad -7.13\%$ Educated labor's share of explained growth $= 42.01\%$
Schultz:	Contribution of increased stock of education $= 71.35\%$
Plant–Welch:	Contribution of increased stock of education $= 26.2\%$

and have offered an alternative measurement technique that we feel better reflects education's contribution to growth in output. We make three basic points. We contend, first, that growth accountants have asked a very limited question in their studies. They have taken the return to investment schedule and the level of total investment as given and asked what the components of that total investment are. The two more fundamental questions—what determines the level of investment and the height of the investment return schedule—are left unanswered by the current literature. Clearly, education could play an important role in determining these more fundamental relationships. We do not address these questions directly. Second, the accounting convention used in various studies, if strictly applied, will result in a measurement of a zero contribution of education to output because at the margin resources invested in education have a zero *net* rate of return. The growth accountants err in not fully accounting for the opportunity cost of resources devoted to education. Finally, we offer a measure that does not rely on a marginal accounting framework that leaves the contribution of education, net of the opportunity costs devoted to the educational process, positive.

There are many avenues for future research. A careful empirical estimate of our alternative measure should be made. This involves considerable work in specifying and estimating the various production parameters to make the required calculation. The other important research task is to ask the more basic questions of education's role in the determination of investment possibilities and the level of investment chosen in the economy. The answer to these questions will require a fresh look at the methods used to evaluate the role of investment in a growing economy.

APPENDIX
DERIVATION OF EQUATION (4.20)

The measure of the contribution of the ith input (education) is simply:

$$\tfrac{1}{2}\Delta f_i \Delta x_i, \tag{A.1}$$

where f_i denotes $\partial f/\partial x_i$. By first-order conditions of cost minimization:

$$\Delta f_i = \frac{\Delta p_i}{\lambda}, \tag{A.2}$$

where λ is the marginal cost of production. The constraint that defines the shadow price is:

$$\frac{dx_i}{dy} = \frac{\partial x_i}{\partial y} + \frac{\partial x_i}{\partial p_i}\frac{\partial p_i}{\partial y} = 0.$$

Therefore:

$$\Delta p_i = \frac{\partial p_i}{\partial y}\Delta y = \frac{-\partial x_i/\partial y}{\partial x_i/\partial p_i}\Delta y. \tag{A.3}$$

Also:

$$\Delta x_i = \frac{\partial x_i}{\partial y}\Delta y. \tag{A.4}$$

Substituting (A.2), (A.3), and (A.4) into (A.1), we get:

$$-\frac{1}{2\lambda}\left[\frac{\partial x_i}{\partial y}\right]^2 (\Delta y)^2 \frac{\partial p_i}{\partial x_i}. \tag{A.5}$$

Rearranging terms we get:

$$\frac{-1}{2\lambda}\left[\frac{\partial x_i}{\partial y}\frac{y}{x_i}\right]^2 \left[\frac{\partial p_i}{\partial x_i}\frac{x_i}{p_i}\right]\frac{x_i^2}{y^2}\frac{p_i}{x_i}(\Delta y)^2 \tag{A.6}$$

which equals:

$$\frac{-1}{2\lambda}\frac{\xi_i^2}{\eta_{ii}}\frac{p_i x_i}{y}\frac{(\Delta y)^2}{y}.$$

But:

$$\frac{p_i}{\lambda} = f_i,$$

and:

$$\eta_{ii} = \frac{f_i x_i}{\sum f_j x_j}\sigma_{ii},$$

so:

$$\frac{-1}{2} \frac{\xi^2}{\sigma_{ii}} \frac{\sum f_j x_j}{y} \frac{(\Delta y)^2}{y}. \tag{A.7}$$

But:

$$\sum f_i x_i = \sum S_i \, y = \sum SC_i \, y \qquad \text{(see equation (4.3) in text),}$$
$$= Sy \sum C_i,$$
$$= Sy,$$

where S_i = the production shares and C_i = cost shares. So (A.7) becomes:

$$\frac{-1}{2} \frac{\xi^2}{\sigma_{ii}} S \frac{(\Delta y)^2}{y}, \tag{A.8}$$

which is the desired formula.

NOTES

1.
$$S_i = \frac{X_i f_i}{Y},$$
$$= \frac{P_i X_i}{\sum P_i X_i} \cdot \frac{f_i}{Y} \cdot \frac{\sum P_i X_i}{P_i},$$
$$= C_i \left[\frac{\sum P_i X_i}{Y} \right] \frac{f_i}{P_i},$$
$$= C_i (\text{average cost}) \left(\frac{1}{\text{marginal cost}} \right).$$

2. This model can be reformulated in per capita terms if the production function is linear homogeneous. The result is that per capita growth in output is completely explained by the per capita growth in nonlabor inputs. Letting lower-case letters denote per capita growth, the result is derived as follows:

$$\dot{y} = \dot{g}_1 \dot{n}_1 + g_2 \dot{k}_1 + g_3 \dot{e},$$
$$\dot{e} = h_1 \dot{n}_2 + h_2 \dot{k}_2,$$

and using (4.15a) and (4.15b) in the text we get:

$$\dot{y} = g_1 (\dot{n}_1 + \dot{n}_2) + g_2 (\dot{k}_1 + \dot{k}_2),$$

but:

$$\dot{n}_1 + \dot{n}_2 = 0,$$

since all units are in per capita terms. Thus:

$$\dot{y} = g_2 \dot{k}.$$

3.
$$\frac{1}{2}\Delta\tilde{P}\Delta Z = \frac{1}{2}\left|\frac{-\partial Z/\partial I}{\partial Z/\partial P}\right|\Delta I\frac{\partial Z}{\partial I}\Delta I,$$

$$= -\frac{1}{2}(\Delta I)^2\cdot\left(\frac{\partial Z}{\partial I}\right)^2\frac{\partial P}{\partial Z},$$

$$= -\frac{1}{2}\frac{(\Delta I)^2}{I}\left(\frac{\partial Z}{\partial I}\right)^2\frac{I^2}{Z^2}\left(\frac{\partial P}{\partial Z}\frac{Z}{P}\right)\left(\frac{PZ}{I}\right),$$

$$= -\frac{1}{2}\frac{(\Delta I^2)}{I}\frac{\epsilon^2}{\eta}C.$$

4. For an explanation of the Allen–Uzawa substitution elasticity see Layard and Walters (1978).

5. Note that $\eta_{ii} = C_i\sigma_{ii}$. Also $\sum S_i\xi_i = 1$ and since $S = S_iC_i$, we conclude $\sum C_i\xi_i = S^{-1}$. The derivation of (4.20) is given in the Appendix.

6. Suppose without loss of generality that:

$$Y = K^{1-\beta}E^\beta,$$

and consider the producer to be minimizing costs: $p_KK + p_EE$ subject to an output constraint.

(a) The scale elasticity is derived by introducing a scale parameter λ into the production function:

$$Y = (\lambda K)^{1-\beta}(\lambda E)^\beta,$$

$$= \lambda K^{1-\beta}E^\beta,$$

and computing:

$$S = \frac{\lambda}{Y}\frac{\partial Y}{\partial\lambda} = \frac{\lambda}{Y}(K^{1-\beta}E^\beta),$$

$$= \frac{\lambda K^{1-\beta}E^\beta}{\lambda K^{1-\beta}E^\beta},$$

$$= 1.$$

(b) The demand function for education is:

$$E = Y\left|\frac{P_E}{P_K}\left(\frac{1-\beta}{\beta}\right)\right|^{\beta-1}.$$

The elasticity of demand with respect to output holding the price ratio constant is:

$$\frac{Y}{E}\frac{\tilde{\partial}E}{\partial Y} = \frac{Y}{E}\left|\frac{P_E}{P_K}\left(\frac{1-\beta}{\beta}\right)\right|^{\beta-1},$$

$$= \left[\frac{P_E}{P_K}\left(\frac{1-\beta}{\beta}\right)\right]^{1-\beta}\left[\frac{P_E}{P_K}\left(\frac{1-\beta}{\beta}\right)\right]^{\beta-1},$$

$$= 1.$$

(c) The Allen–Uzawa own elasticity of substitution is equal to (see Layard and Walters (1978)):

$$\sigma_{ii} = \frac{\epsilon_{ii}}{\nu_i},$$

where ϵ_{ii} = output constant elasticity of demand,
ν_i = share of input i in total costs,

and for input E:

$$\epsilon_{ii} = \frac{P_E}{E} \frac{\partial E}{\partial P_E},$$

$$= -(1-\beta),$$

and:

$$\nu_i = \beta,$$

so:

$$\sigma_{ii} = \frac{-(1-\beta)}{\beta}.$$

The computations in the text then follow directly.

7. In all fairness to Jorgenson and Griliches, later work is much more sophisticated. We present their early model as a prototype and recognize that this was a seminal paper. See the references for more recent papers. These later papers are best characterized as being like Chinloy (1980).

8. This production function was found on page 199 of Ferguson (1969). We thank Michael Darby for pointing us toward this monograph.

9.

$$S_1^0 = \frac{N^0 \cdot \text{VMP}_1^0}{N_1^0 \cdot \text{VMP}_1^0 + N_2^0 \cdot \text{VMP}_2^0} = \frac{0.054}{7.054} \doteq 0.01,$$

$$S_2^0 = 1 - S_1^0 = 0.99.$$

10. For this production function:

$$S = \frac{N_2}{N_2 - 4} + \frac{2N_1}{N_1 - 8},$$

$$\xi = \frac{N_2 - 4}{N_2},$$

$$\sigma_{ii} = -\left[\frac{N_2 - 4}{N_2}\right] \cdot (\text{cost share}).$$

These formulas used with base-year values in equation (4.20) lead to a contribution of education that is 17.99 percent of the growth in output.

11.
$$\text{Explained growth} = s_{k_1} \frac{\Delta \dot{K}_1}{K_{10}} + s_{n_1} \frac{\Delta N_1}{N_{10}} + s_e \frac{\Delta N_2}{N_{20}},$$

$$= 0.2(-0.05668) + (0.1)(1.3049) + (0.7)(0.8569),$$

$$= 0.7189.$$

Note that due to the production technology the ν's are constant over time.

REFERENCES

Becker, Gary. 1975. *Human Capital.* New York: National Bureau of Economic Research.

Chinloy, Peter. 1980. "Sources of Quality Change in Labor Input." *American Economic Review* 70, no. 1 (March): 109-19.

Christensen, L.R.; D. Cummings; and D.W. Jorgenson. 1980. "Economic Growth, 1947-73; An International Comparison." In *New Developments in Productivity Measurement and Analysis,* edited by J.W. Kendrick and B.N. Vaccara, pp. 595-682. Chicago: University of Chicago Press.

Denison, Edward F. 1974. *Accounting for United States Economic Growth, 1929-1969.* Washington, D.C.: The Brookings Institution.

———. 1980. "The Contribution of Capital to Economic Growth." *American Economic Review* 70, no. 2 (May): 220-24.

Ferguson, C.E. 1969. *Neoclassical Theory of Production and Distribution.* Cambridge: Cambridge University Press.

Gollop, F.M., and D.W. Jorgenson. 1980. "U.S. Productivity Growth in Industry, 1947-1973." In *New Developments in Productivity Measurement and Analysis,* edited by J.W. Kendrick and B.N. Vaccara, pp. 17-136. Chicago: University of Chicago Press.

Jorgenson, D.W., and Z. Griliches. 1967. "The Explanation of Productivity Change." *Review of Economic Studies* 34 (July): 249-83.

Layard, P.R.G., and A.A. Walters. 1978. *Microeconomic Theory.* New York: McGraw-Hill.

Nelson, Richard R., and E.S. Phelps. 1966. "Investment in Humans, Technological Diffusion, and Economic Growth." *American Economic Review* 56, no. 2 (May): 69-75.

Schultz, T.W. 1961. "Education and Economic Growth." In *Social Forces Influencing American Education,* edited by Nelson B. Henry, pp. 46-88. Chicago: National Society for the Study of Education.

Welch, Finis. 1970. "Education in Production." *Journal of Political Economy* 78, no. 1 (January): 35-59.

Chapter 5

Comment: Alternative Views of the Quality of U.S. Education

Richard J. Murnane

My task in this chapter is to explore the relationships between the papers in this volume and the ongoing public debate concerning education policies in the United States. Let me begin by summarizing the themes of the papers by Jorgenson, Plant and Welch, and Haveman and Wolfe.

Jorgenson adopts a growth-accounting framework to estimate the contribution of education to U.S. economic growth. He finds that the contribution is large, accounting for approximately 11 percent of growth during the period 1948 to 1973. An implicit assumption underlying the work presented in the first half of the Jorgenson paper is that the contributions of education to productivity are approximated by the added earnings of the individuals who received the education.

Plant and Welch question the growth-accounting methodology used by Jorgenson by pointing out that education is an intermediate product produced by inputs of labor and capital. They argue that growth accounting calculates the contribution of education to economic growth without accounting for the fact that inputs used to produce education could be put to other uses that also could contribute to growth. This omission produces a biased estimate of the contribution of intermediate products, such as education, to growth. Plant and Welch go on to develop an alternative methodology for estimating the contribution of education to economic growth. They then compute estimates of education's contribution to growth, using

My treatment of these papers was informed by Richard R. Nelson's comments on these same papers, presented at the meetings of the American Economic Association, New York, 1982. I would like to thank Edwin Dean, Harold Howe, and Edward Pauly for helpful comments on a draft of this chapter.

their own methodology and alternative growth-accounting methodologies. Their estimates, which are based on illustrative data, indicate that education has made an important contribution to growth but a smaller one than those estimated by Jorgenson and some other writers working in the growth-accounting tradition.

Haveman and Wolfe survey the burgeoning literature dealing with the effects of education on health, child care, and a variety of other nonmarket activities and conclude that many important returns to education are not reflected in wage differentials. The magnitude of the effects that they report suggest that the Jorgenson findings should be modified to take into account the effects of education on activities not reflected in U.S. income and product accounts. (While Jorgenson does take account of education's effects on the value of leisure and other home time in the second half of his paper, these effects do not enter into the growth-accounting work of the first half.)

The specific questions addressed by Jorgenson, Plant and Welch, and Haveman and Wolfe differ, as do their methodologies. However, all of their empirical work indicates that education has made important contributions to U.S. economic growth and to the quality of the lives of the individuals who invested in education. In other words, the papers provide a relatively optimistic assessment of U.S. education.

In contrast, a number of recent studies of U.S. education have been extraordinarily critical. While the nature of the criticisms has varied, the general tone is captured by the following quotation from *A Nation At Risk,* the report of the National Commission on Excellence in Education (1983):

> [T]he educational foundations of our society are presently being eroded by a rising tide of mediocrity that threatens our very future as a Nation and a people.... If an unfriendly foreign power had attempted to impose on America the mediocre educational performance that exists today, we might well have viewed it as an act of war.

The report goes on to document its criticisms with statistics on the number of Americans who are illiterate and on the almost unbroken twenty-year decline in college-board scores.

The optimism about American education implicit in the Jorgenson and the Haveman and Wolfe papers contrasts strikingly with the dismay about U.S. education voiced in recent reports, and leads one to ask the following questions:

To what extent are the optimistic assessments of the papers in this volume and the SOS-like quality of recent reports simply two perspectives on the same educational system?

In what respects has American education changed in recent years so as to merit criticisms about declining quality made by the National Commission and other fact-finding groups?

One strategy for answering these questions is to reread the papers by Jorgenson and Haveman and Wolfe with an eye to identifying the educational institutions or policies that contributed to the success of U.S. education. If we could identify these institutions and policies, we could then investigate whether they are still in effect. Carrying out this strategy results in the surprising discovery that neither paper even mentions educational institutions or policies. They view education as a homogeneous input to production with variation only in the level of education that individuals attain. These papers do not examine whether education's contributions to economic growth and to the well-being of U.S. citizens are simply the bright side of a system that always has had a dark side or whether U.S. education has deteriorated in important ways in recent years. We must look elsewhere to explore this issue.

DIFFERENT PERSPECTIVES ON THE SAME SYSTEM

Criticisms of U.S. education are not new. Recall, for example, the distress calls concerning the quality of U.S. math and science education that followed the Soviets' launching of Sputnik in 1957. In the 1960s, distress calls were heard again. This time the focus was on the poor quality of education provided to students from low-income and minority-group families.

Is it surprising that the American educational system could be an important source of economic growth and at the same time could permit many students to leave schools without even basic skills? Perhaps not, given the structure of the U.S. educational system. Among its critical characteristics are the following:

1. Education is compulsory for all children—in most states, up to age sixteen. As a result, all children attend school, even if it is not a high quality school.
2. The governance of public schooling is extraordinarily decentralized in the United States. There are more than 15,000 public school districts in the country, and each has the power to set teacher salary scales, hire teachers, assign students to schools, and exercise considerable control over curricula. In addition, there are several thousand nonpublic schools in the United States that operate with even fewer constraints than public schools do in selecting teachers, students, and curricula. This decentralization of authority creates the potential for enormous variation in quality.
3. The number and quality of schooling choices available to a family depend on family income. Families with above-average incomes can purchase good schooling for their children—either by paying the high

housing prices or high property taxes that tend to be present in public
school districts with good schools, or by choosing a high-quality (usually expensive) private school. Lower-income families typically cannot
afford the housing prices or property taxes in public school districts
offering high-quality education, nor can they afford the tuitions charged
by most high-quality private schools.

Among the consequences of universality, decentralization, and income-
dependent choices is the large variation in the quality of education provided
by different U.S. schools. Many high-quality schools, both public and
private, offer an education as good as is available anywhere in the world.
These schools provide students with the skills they need to be productive
contributors to economic growth. Although there are many exceptions,
these high-quality schools tend to be attended primarily by students from
above-average-income families (Murnane 1983a).

Unfortunately, many American schools are not successful in helping
children acquire the skills needed to be productive workers and contribute
to economic growth. These schools, again with many exceptions, tend to be
attended by students from families that either have below-average income,
are of minority-group status, or both.

Various reform strategies have been employed over the last twenty years
in an attempt to improve the education offered to students unable to attend
high-quality schools. These strategies include compensatory education,
school finance reform, and school desegregation. Some of the programs
have been successful in helping students to improve their skills. However,
it is one of the more troubling conclusions of social policy analysis that it
is very difficult to improve the position of disadvantaged groups without
constraining the opportunities of advantaged groups. The reason is that
advantaged groups typically respond to programs aimed at equalizing opportunities by finding ways to maintain their advantages.

Policies have been conceived, in some cases even tried, that do constrain
the options of the advantaged—for example, mandatory busing programs
and caps on the spending of affluent school districts. However, the unpopu-
larity of these policies has led to primary reliance on strategies that do not
constrain the options of the advantaged and consequently are not powerful
equalizers of opportunities. As a result, the quality of education provided to
children from different backgrounds continues to vary, although the variation is probably smaller and is less well explained by family income and
racial or ethnic status than was the case in 1948, the start of the period
examined in the Jorgenson paper.

The last sentence includes the word "probably" because systematic data
on the distribution of student achievement in 1948, which would be needed
to examine this hypothesis, do not exist. In fact, one of the most striking

trends in U.S. education over the post-World War II period is the increasing quality of the documentation on the distribution of student achievement. The 1965 Equality of Educational Opportunity Survey, which collected data on the achievement of more than 500,000 American students, was without precedent in the United States or elsewhere. This survey provided the first detailed documentation of the distribution of U.S. student achievement and the gaps that existed between the average achievement of white students and minority-group students.

Other surveys followed, including the National Assessment of Educational Progress, the National Longitudinal Study of the High School Class of 1972, and High School and Beyond, a national longitudinal study of students who were in American high schools in 1980. These large-scale surveys and the extensive analyses of the data they produced—analyses that only modern computer technology permits—resulted in much new knowledge about the distribution of the cognitive skills of U.S. students. This knowledge intensifies the realization that U.S. schools have not provided a high-quality education to all U.S. students.

CHANGES IN U.S. EDUCATION

Not all of the current criticisms of U.S. education can be explained in terms of greater awareness of problems that have always existed. As many of the reports emphasize, data such as the declining trend in college board scores suggest that reductions in at least some dimensions of student skills have taken place. It has been extremely difficult to isolate the reasons for the test score declines. However, the limited evidence that exists suggests that the declines are due in part to changes in U.S. education and in part to changes in society at large.

One recent change in public education that may have contributed to the test score declines is the growing difficulty of attracting and retaining talented teachers, especially teachers of math and science. There are at least two related reasons for this difficulty. First, twenty years ago many talented women became teachers because they felt that teaching was the only profession open to them, and their choices were quite insensitive to teaching salaries. Today it is easier than it once was for talented women to succeed in other professions. Consequently, the number of talented women who choose to become teachers is much more sensitive to the competitiveness of teacher salaries than it once was (Murnane 1983b).

Second, teacher salaries in the United States were never high relative to salaries offered in other professions. During the 1950s and 1960s, salaries did improve. However, this trend was broken during the 1970s, when the salaries of U.S. public school teachers lagged behind inflation and the salaries offered in other parts of the economy to college graduates with strong training in science or mathematics (U.S. Department of Education 1980: 50).

Important changes in U.S. society at large during the 1970s have also probably influenced the cognitive skills of students. One of these concerns the changes in the demographics of U.S. families, particularly black families. In 1965, 25 percent of black families were female-headed. In 1980, 40 percent were female-headed. The comparable numbers for white families are 9 and 12 percent (Darity and Myers 1983). Since single-parent families typically have much lower income than two-parent families do, children in such families probably have fewer of the home resources, broadly defined, that contribute to the development of cognitive skills than children in two-parent families have. This kind of change in demographics may have contributed to test score declines.

The high unemployment rates, especially for minority group teenagers, that characterized much of the 1970s may also have contributed to test score declines. Although the relationship between employment opportunities and schooling decisions is not well understood, it seems a plausible hypothesis that poor employment opportunities reduced incentives for teenagers to work hard in school and to acquire the basic cognitive skills that help in jobs, had jobs been available.

EVIDENCE UNDERLYING POLICY SUGGESTIONS FOR IMPROVING U.S. EDUCATION

There is no scarcity of recommendations for improving U.S. education. A vast range of recommendations includes a longer school day, a longer school year, more homework, more discipline, higher teacher salaries, merit pay for teachers, minimum competency tests for teachers, minimum competency tests for students. Each of these recommendations has surface plausibility, but upon greater reflection, each proposal raises significant questions. For example:

How will students and teachers respond to a longer school day or a longer school year? Will effort levels be paced so that total learning increases only marginally while total costs increase significantly?

How do we get students to do more homework? What do we do to students who do not do the additional assigned homework? How do we improve discipline while still maintaining the public schools' commitment to educate all children?

Will a 10 percent increase in pay (which will increase a typical school district's current account budget by approximately 6 percent) have a significant impact on the quality of applicants for teaching positions?

Will poor teachers respond to merit pay by improving their performance or by behaving in a way that only makes them appear to be effective in the eyes of the evaluators? Will effective teachers resign because they dislike the sense of competitiveness and the undermining of morale that may accompany merit pay?

If minimum competency tests for teachers are introduced without large increases in teacher salaries, will there be enough teachers to staff the schools?

How will weak students, especially those in low-quality schools, respond to a graduation requirement that they pass minimum competency tests? Will they work harder or drop out earlier?

Proponents of various proposals typically assert that they know the answers to questions raised by their proposals and that the answers support the wisdom of their programs. However, their supporting evidence is often either nonexistent or of dubious merit. When this is pointed out, a frequent response is that the effects of the proposal are obvious.

In thinking about the extent to which outcomes of policy initiatives are obvious, consider the paper in this volume by W. Lee Hansen. Hansen's paper examines the impact of federally sponsored student aid programs on college enrollment rates of low-income students. Development of these programs assumed that enrollment rates of low-income students are extremely sensitive to the costs of education and that aid programs are a powerful way to reduce these costs. Hansen's results raise important questions about the validity of these assumptions. He found that enrollment rates of students from low-income families did not rise significantly during the 1970s despite large increases in the number and funding levels of federal student aid programs.

Hansen's results are not definitive—as he points out. Other researchers have found greater responsiveness of enrollment rates to college costs net of financial aid. Moreover, it is possible that the primary effect of the aid programs was to elicit a response that Hansen did not investigate—namely, that students who would have attended college even without aid programs chose a higher-cost institution because aid was available to defray part of the cost. At any rate, Hansen's evidence calls into question widely accepted notions about the accomplishments of student aid programs.

The critical lesson of the Hansen paper for the current debates about education policy is that no effects of significant policy change are obvious. Since education is essentially an activity involving the interaction of human beings, it is extremely difficult to predict how new policies will alter incentives or how humans will respond to changes in the incentives they face. This is particularly true in a social situation such as the school, where the range of possible responses is very large and the attractiveness of alternative responses is influenced by the responses of other students and teachers.

UNDERSTANDING THE CONFLICT AMONG
ALTERNATIVE ASSESSMENTS OF U.S. EDUCATION

What should we make of the conflict between the optimistic assessments of U.S. education presented in papers in this volume and the critical assessments presented in recent reports? Attempting to address this conflict is difficult because the approaches of the two assessments are so different. Moreover, the strengths of one approach correspond in important ways to the weaknesses of the other approach.

One strength of the papers in this volume is that the dependent variables in the analyses are clearly things that we care about, such as wages, per capita incomes, and health. Knowing how education affects these outcomes is of real interest. One weakness of the papers, at least from the perspective of thinking about education policies, is that education is characterized in an extremely abstract manner. The only variable used to characterize education in the empirical work reported in this volume is the number of years of schooling that individuals complete. There is no mention of variation in the quality of the education students receive, how quality is related to wages and other outcomes, or how quality is influenced by institutions and policies.

The recent reports criticizing U.S. education have almost the opposite strengths and weaknesses. Almost all of the reports present details about educational policies and institutions and suggest how these policies and institutions are related to educational quality. In these papers, however, educational quality tends to be measured by variables like test scores and graduation rates. We do not have very good evidence about how these variables are related to the outcomes people care about, such as incomes and health.

Perhaps the most significant link between the papers in this volume and recent reports on U.S. education is that most of their authors unconsciously assume answers to the following questions:

What does education do?
Who gets the benefits?
What forms do the benefits take?

After all, how can one investigate either education's contribution to growth or trends in educational quality without making at least implicit assumptions about the answers to these questions?

Assumptions not only facilitate the application of potentially powerful research techniques to an issue, they also limit the range of phenomena that the research considers. I suggest that unrecognized differences in assumptions play an important role in generating differing assessments of U.S. education. One important step in achieving a coherent, internally consistent understanding of the many roles that education plays in our society may be to explore systematically the assumptions implicit in different education research strategies.

REFERENCES

Darity, Jr., William, and Samuel L. Myers, Jr. 1973. "Changes in Black Family Structure: Implications for Welfare Dependency." *American Economic Review* 73, no. 2 (May): 59–64.

Murnane, Richard J. 1983a. "How Clients' Characteristics Affect Organization Performance." *Journal of Policy Analysis and Management* 2, no. 3 (Spring): 403–17.

———. 1983b. "Understanding the Sources of Teaching Competence: Choices, Skills and the Limits of Training." *Teachers College Record* 84, no. 3 (Spring): 564–69.

National Commission on Excellence in Education. 1983. *A Nation at Risk*. Washington, D.C.: NCEE.

U.S. Department of Education, National Center for Education Statistics. 1980. *The Condition of Education, 1980*. Washington, D.C.: U.S. Government Printing Office.

Chapter 6

Comment: Overeducation or Undereducation?

Jacob Mincer

Recent sessions of the American Economic Association devoted to education indicated that the intellectual pendulum has swung away from fashionable revisionist notions of the near-uselessness of education as an overly costly ability sorter and of its positively harmful role in the "great training robbery" or in the capitalist brainwashing conspiracy. Papers presented at those sessions also appear to be antidotes to the more recent appearance of a form of neo-Malthusianism that sees dire consequences in the demographic and educational expansion of recent cohorts.

Academic views of education tend to be countercyclical: At the height of the educational expansion in the late 1960s, complaints about sinister aspects of the traditional educational process were fashionable, while today its praises are beginning to be heard once again, when financial retrenchment, a slack economy, and demographic declines are reducing the demand for education. Perhaps this is mere contrariness, but to the extent that economists are involved in the analyses they may be carrying out their accustomed conservative function of mitigating the succession of wide swings in our social climate.

What follows are comments prompted by analyses of the economics of education presented at recent AEA sessions and revolving around the question of whether our school systems are producing over- or undereducation. I conclude with a plea for research informed by the distinction between schooling and education.

EDUCATION AND ECONOMIC GROWTH

Interest in the economics of education originated simultaneously and independently in two fields: (1) in the study of its role in economic growth and (2) in the study of its effects on wage structures in the labor market. It soon became apparent that the concept and analysis of investment in human capital, which is more general than school education, is common to both fields of application. Economic growth is, indeed, the focus in both applications: Just as accumulation of personal human capital is a factor in individual economic growth, so it is at the aggregate (national, and even international) level. Although there has been no shortage of warnings against a possible fallacy of composition, the proposition remains theoretically and empirically viable in the large.[1]

Educational activities (broadly construed) involve not only the transmission and embodiment in people of available knowledge but also the production of new knowledge, which is the source of innovation and technological change. The new knowledge and technical progress are diffused throughout industry and across national boundaries, creating national and worldwide economic growth. If the rates of technical change and its diffusion are complementary with education, the marginal product of education is augmented by the rate of technical progress. At the aggregate level, therefore, education is a factor of production that is both a cause and a consequence of economic growth. Such feedbacks play a large role in the long-term dynamics of the economy. Consequently, estimates of effects of education on economic growth are understated if they confine themselves to effects on the quality of labor and leave out the effects on technological change and if effects on the growth of technology are not captured in private returns of those contributing to it.

The extent to which such contributions are captured in private returns is, of course, a matter of degree. Still, the 75 percent decline in the (relative) production of engineers and the 50 percent decline in the production of scientists (at the B.S. level) in the United States over the past twenty years, as well as the decline in the volume of private and public R&D, represent a disquieting set of statistics (Mansfield 1982), whether or not the decline is a result or a partial cause of slow economic growth.

OVEREDUCATION?

The decline in productivity and economic growth in the 1970s began just about the time when large numbers of young graduates of colleges and postgraduate institutions began to enter the labor market. In a deteriorating labor market these new job entrants were bound to experience at least temporary difficulties in job finding and in the quality of jobs and careers they eventually found and settled for.

Richard Freeman (1976) dubbed the atypically large cohort of college graduates the "overeducated Americans." His evidence of overeducation was the decline in relative incomes of college graduates compared to high school graduates in the 1970s. As Smith and Welch (1978) pointed out some time ago, this decline was observed only for new entrants into the labor force and was overstated (doubled) by Freeman's procedure.[2] Smith and Welch claim that the decline in wages of new entrants relative to wages of peak earners was shared by all education groups, though these wage effects were somewhat larger at the college level. They conclude that young workers in all education groups suffered from the increased labor supply and falling aggregate demand. The baby boom of the 1950s and the market recessions of the 1970s rather than overeducation, were responsible for the plight of young workers in recent years. At any rate, Smith and Welch believe this setback to be temporary. A 10 to 15 percent reduction in starting incomes, *relative* (not absolute) to incomes of older workers in the same education groups, hardly justifies the long-term dire consequences predicted by Richard Easterlin (1978) or the more cosmic predictions of Landon Jones (1980).

Equating overeducation with a rapid increase in labor supply due largely to the past baby boom is hyperbole: Oversupply is equivalent to "underdemand," and as supply and demand fluctuate there will always be an adjustment period of shortages and surpluses during which new graduates may be called overeducated or undereducated. But even when defined solely in economic terms, what matters is the rate of return on the educational investment. Although this declined somewhat in the 1970s, the rate is not so small as to lead us to consider the volume of graduates turned out by schools to be excessive.

Indeed, there are at least two reasons to believe that the calculations of rates of return restricted to monetary payoffs understate true rates: They omit some of the labor-market returns in the form of fringes and nonpecuniary job benefits, including congenial working conditions, and they exclude a variety of nonmarket benefits.

The argument is not new; it was expressed by Ted Schultz many years ago (Schultz 1963). But the menu of omissions is now more solidly informed by the intervening research in human capital and in household production (or in the so-called new home economics).

Among the omitted returns are the following: (1) fringe benefits, which are proportionately larger for the more educated, whose higher marginal tax rates due to higher incomes induce a demand for (proportionately, not just absolutely) larger fringes; (2) education appears to increase productivity arising from other forms of human-capital formation, such as job training, household management, and health maintenance. (I say "appears to" since, in part, the relation is a correlation due to common factors, rather than cause and effect); and (3) better sorting in job and marriage markets, reduction in crime, informed migration, and citizenship, which are the other more or less well-documented benefits.

In their article in this volume, "Education, Productivity, and Well-being," Haveman and Wolfe attempt to convert to monetary values the nonwage and nonmarket contributions of education in order to correct the understatement in the usual narrowly defined estimates of returns to education. They estimate that complete returns would probably increase the usual numbers by about two-thirds. This result suggests that the overeducated American is a myth, despite the declines in the narrowly calculated rates of return in the mid-1970s.

OR UNDEREDUCATION?

At this point, it may be helpful to consider the concept of education as distinguished from schooling since the discussion thus far refers to schooling. The term "overeducated" is an unfortunate one, for more reasons than indicated above, but the terms "overschooled" or "misschooled" are not necessarily inappropriate. If we think of schooling as an input and education, in its basic cognitive sense, as the output, perhaps what we experienced in the late 1960s and early 1970s was an expansion of schooling but no improvement, and perhaps even a deterioration in education.[3] The simultaneous decline in the productivity of schooling and the much discussed decline in productivity in the market economy may be a coincidence, or it may reflect some common causes, even if there is no direct connection between them. Both may be responsible in some measure for the observed declines in the calculated rates of return to schooling, apart from the much (and I think too much) touted invasion of the labor market by the baby-boom crop of the 1950s armed with diplomas.

Suggestive evidence on the performance of our school system comes from cross-national comparisons and changes over time in scholastic achievement. Twelve volumes of studies published between 1967 and 1977 by the IEA (International Association for the Evaluation of Educational Achievement)[4] describe results of a number of (identical) achievement tests in eight subjects given to students (age ten, fourteen, and eighteen) in twenty-one countries.

The National Academy of Education reviewed the IEA studies in 1977. In one review, Alex Inkeles (1977) reached the following conclusions: (1) "The more emphasis on a subject in the curriculum and more time students spend on it, the more knowledge and skill they show in the subject''; (2) at least 80 percent of the variance in test scores remain to be explained by factors other than socioeconomic background; and (3) school qualities alone account for as much as home background, age, and sex taken together. Inkeles also concluded that despite the great value of the endeavor, the results have been left seriously underanalyzed, for reasons that he enumerates. Inkeles did not indicate the relative standing of U.S. students in the international comparisons.

In a more recent analysis of the IEA volumes, Barbara Lerner (1982) finds that the mean scores of U.S. high school seniors (age eighteen) were in the bottom half of the rank order distribution thirteen times and in the top half only six times, when four less developed countries (LDC's) were excluded. Results for younger students (fourteen and ten years of age) were somewhat better but not much. American students ranked especially low in mathematics and in some of the science tests. Yet the volume of inputs, as measured by educational expenditures per capita or fraction of GNP spent on education, was surely higher in the United States than in most of the other countries.

Herbert Walberg (1983) finds a less dismal comparative standing for ten- and fourteen-year-old U.S. students in scores of tests in scientific literacy. In the same subject, however, eighteen-year-olds were at the bottom rank among fifteen industrialized countries. This low standing Walberg attributes in part to the far higher retention (high school completion) rate in the United States than elsewhere. Walberg's general conclusion on the scientific literacy of American youth is nonetheless similar to that of Lerner and Inkeles: "Test scores (of American youth) in science and mathematics of a decade or two ago compared unfavorably with these of youth in other industrialized countries, and, since that time, have declined substantially." Moreover, referring to verbal achievements, Walberg quotes estimates that "about 20 percent of all American seventeen year olds were verbally illiterate in 1975."

Although Inkeles tends to agree with some of the IEA authors (the summary Volume 9 by Walker) and with Walberg to the effect that larger retention rates (larger proportions of the age-group enrolled) result in lower scores at the eighteen-year-old level, Lerner claims that these differences carry little weight, especially as the rankings on most tests are similar at the younger ages (ten and fourteen)—when retention rates do not differ much among the developed countries.

While these findings refer to the late 1960s, changes since then have not been salutary. The observed declines in SAT and other achievement tests, which date from that time, cannot be blamed on increasing high school retention rates, which stabilized by 1970. Similar declines have been observed in the upper grades of elementary schools, according to Lerner.

If spending and retention rates do not explain the cross-national differences and time-series changes, what does? Lerner finds four variables that are significant: amount of time spent on homework, amount of class time spent directly on relevant school work, frequency of class attendance, and textbook demand levels. Of those, the first, which she calls "hard work," appears to dominate. She also cites evidence of decline in all these factors in U.S. schools. In a similar vein Walberg ascribes the top-ranking score achieved by Japanese youth (including eighteen-year-olds, whose school retention rate is about as high as the U.S. rate) to "large amounts of diligent study and instruction."

Declines of test scores for grades five through twelve have been analyzed by several researchers, as reported by the Task Force on Education and Employment (1979) in the NAE volume *Education for Employment*. Reviewing a report by Wiley and Harnischfeger (1977) that analyzes a number of test scores and their changes over time, the task force concludes (1979: 73) that "basic reading skills are increasing, but the more advanced skills of comprehension and interpretation are on the wane." Of a variety of factors considered the task force analysts are inclined to think (1979: 73) that "changes in the amount of time spent studying and modification in the curriculum" are the most important. They note that students are taking fewer courses in traditional academic subjects such as history, foreign languages, algebra, geometry, chemistry, and physics. The task force also noted that Fine (1966) reported declining class time devoted to instruction and increasing time devoted to administrative and disciplinary activities. Others have noted the relative decline in scores of students who apply to colleges of education. On the whole, these findings are consistent with Lerner's blunter statements.

High levels of absenteeism, especially in upper high school grades, may be both a cause of and a response to the observed problems. Perhaps fixed ages of school entrance and of completion are as much out of tune with changes in personal development and in health as are fixed ages of retirement.

The effect of changes in the quality of education on measured rates of return to schooling is a matter of concern to economists. But the problem of low-quality education is of urgent concern to the U.S. society and economy. The United States' preeminence among Nobel prizewinners in the sciences does not contradict our conclusions. These achievements largely reflect the past. Current educational trends affect the present and future.

NOTES

1. For detailed analytical surveys of these issues, see Mincer (1979, 1980).

2. Specifically, Freeman compared young college graduates with high school graduates of the same age rather than with the same years of work experience. The

correct procedure puts the decline in the rate of return closer to the 1 than to the 2 percent point range. The decline halted in the late 1970s and may be on its way out. See Smith and Welch (1978).

3. In the months since these comments were voiced (at the December 1982 meetings of the AEA), several reports, including one by a commission appointed by the secretary of education and one by the Carnegie Foundation for the Advancement of Teaching, have increased public awareness about the problems of quality in the current U.S. education system, especially at the elementary and high school levels.

4. The twelve volumes are listed in Lerner (1982).

REFERENCES

Easterlin, Richard A. 1978. "What Will 1984 Be Like? Socioeconomic Implications of Recent Twists in Age Structure." *Demography* 15, no. 4 (November).

Fine, B. 1966. *Underachievers: How They Can Be Helped.* New York: Dutton.

Freeman, Richard B. 1976. *The Over-Educated American.* New York: Academic Press.

Inkeles, Alex. 1977. "The International Evaluation of Educational Achievement: A Review of International Studies in Evaluation." Proceedings of National Academy of Education, vol. 4.

Jones, Landon. 1980. *Great Expectations: America and the Baby Boom Generation.* New York: Coward & McCann.

Lerner, Barbara. 1982. "American Education: How Are We Doing?" *The Public Interest,* no. 69 (Fall).

Mansfield, Edwin. 1982. "Education, R&D, and Productivity Growth." Paper presented at the annual meetings of the American Economic Association, New York, N.Y., December.

Mincer, Jacob. 1979. "Human Capital and Earnings." In *Economic Dimensions of Education,* edited by Douglas Windham, National Academy of Education. Washington, D.C.

———. 1980. "Human Capital and Economic Growth." National Bureau of Economic Research Working Paper No. 803, Cambridge, Mass.

Schultz, Theodore W. 1963. *The Economic Value of Education.* Columbia University Press: New York.

Smith, James, and Finis Welch. 1978. "The Over-Educated American?" Proceedings of National Academy of Education, vol. 5.

Task Force on Education and Employment. 1979. *Education for Employment: Knowledge for Action.* Washington, D.C.: Acropolis Books, National Academy of Education.

Walberg, Herbert J. 1983. "Scientific Literacy and Economic Productivity in International Perspective." *Daedalus* 112, no. 2 (Spring).

Wiley, D.E., and A. Harnischfeger. 1977. "Statement to the House Committee on Education and Labor, Subcommittee on Elementary, Secondary, and Vocational Education." May 11. Unpublished.

*

Index

213

About the Editor

Edwin Dean, a supervisory economist at the Bureau of Labor Statistics in Washington, D.C., is in charge of research on comparative productivity growth in the United States, Canada, Japan, and several European countries. He was previously an assistant director of the National Institute of Education and head of NIE's Education Finance Program. At NIE, he initiated a research program on education's contribution to productivity growth. He has also been an assistant professor of economics at Columbia University and an associate professor at Queen's College, City University of New York, where he specialized in labor economics and the economies of Africa. His other publications include *Plan Implementation in Nigeria, 1962–66* (Oxford University Press, 1972) and *Supply Responses of African Farmers* (North–Holland Publishing Co., 1966). He holds a doctorate in economics from Columbia University and a bachelor's degree from Yale University.

List of Contributors

Edwin R. Dean
Economist
Office of Productivity and Technology
Bureau of Labor Statistics
Washington, DC 20210

W. Lee Hansen
Professor of Economics
Department of Economics
University of Wisconsin—Madison
Madison, WI 53706

Robert H. Haveman
Professor of Economics
Department of Economics
University of Wisconsin—Madison
Madison, WI 53706

Dale W. Jorgenson
F.E. Abbe Professor of Economics
Department of Economics
Harvard University
Cambridge, MA 02138

Jacob Mincer
Buttenwieser Professor of Economics
Department of Economics
Columbia University
New York, NY 10027

Richard J. Murnane
Associate Professor of Education
Graduate School of Education
Harvard University
Cambridge, MA 02138

Mark Plant
Assistant Professor of Economics
Department of Economics
University of California, Los Angeles
Los Angeles, CA 90024

Finis Welch
Professor of Economics, U.C.L.A
President, Unicon Research Corporation
2116 Wilshire Blvd.
Santa Monica, CA 90403

Barbara L. Wolfe
Associate Professor
Departments of Economics and Preventive Medicine
University of Wisconsin—Madison
Madison, WI 53706

Participants in Meetings on Education and Economic Productivity

Preliminary versions of the papers in this volume by Robert Haveman and Barbara Wolfe, W. Lee Hansen, Dale Jorgenson, and Mark Plant and Finis Welch were presented at a conference sponsored by the National Institute of Education in November 1982 and at the annual meetings of the American Economic Association in December 1982. In addition to these four papers, papers by Edwin Mansfield and Edward Lawler were commissioned under the NIE research program on education and productivity. All six papers were presented and discussed either at the NIE conference or the AEA meetings. Titles of the Mansfield and Lawler papers and names of some other participants in these two meetings are presented below.

I. NIE Conference on Education, Productivity, and the National Economy, Leesburg, Virginia, November 1982

John T. Dunlop, Harvard University, delivered the keynote address.
Edward E. Lawler, University of Southern California, presented a paper entitled "Education, Management Style, and Organizational Effectiveness."

Addresses

Carolyn Shaw Bell
(Discussant, Jorgenson paper)
Coman Professor of Economics
Department of Economics
Wellesley College
Wellesley, MA 02181

David Breneman
(Discussant, Hansen paper)
President
Kalamazoo College
Kalamazoo, MI 49007

John T. Dunlop
(Keynote address)
Lamont University Professor
Harvard University
Cambridge, MA 02138

F. Thomas Juster
(Discussant, Haveman and Wolfe paper)
Professor of Economics
University of Michigan
Director
Institute for Social Research
Ann Arbor, MI 48106

Edward E. Lawler
(Author of paper)
Director
Center for Effective Organizations
Graduate School of Business Administration
University of Southern California
Los Angeles, CA 90089

Henry M. Levin
(Discussant, Plant and Welch paper)
Director
Institute for Research on
   Educational Finance and Governance
Stanford University
Stanford, CA 94305

Richard J. Murnane
(Discussant, Lawler paper)
Associate Professor of Education
Graduate School of Education
Harvard University
Cambridge, MA 02138

II. Two sessions of the American Economic Association annual meetings, New York, December 1982

Edwin Mansfield presented a paper entitled "Education, R & D, and Productivity Growth."

Addresses

Edwin Mansfield
(Author of paper)
Professor of Economics
Department of Economics
University of Pennsylvania
Philadelphia, PA 19104

Jacob Mincer
(Discussant, Mansfield and
   Haveman and Wolfe papers)
Buttenwieser Professor of Economics
Department of Economics
Columbia University
New York, NY 10027

Richard R. Nelson
(Discussant, Hansen, Jorgenson, and
   Plant and Welch papers)
Stout Professor of Social Science and Economics
Department of Economics
Yale University
New Haven, CT 06520

Theodore W. Schultz
(Discussant, Mansfield and
   Haveman and Wolfe papers)
Professor Emeritus of Economics
Department of Economics
University of Chicago
Chicago, IL 60637